*T*ransformational
Regional Bodies

by
Roy M. Oswald
& Claire S. Burkat

"Few leaders of the church have worked with as many dioceses, districts, presbyteries conferences and regions as Oswald and Burkat. The enduring question they have brought to that work has been this - **How can such regional bodies support creative growth in their congregations?** In this book, Oswald and Burkat share what they have learned. It is **worth reading and pondering.**"

Loren Mead
Founder & President Emeritus, The Alban Institute

"Most of the transformational literature has focused on the local church. Regional judicatories are often viewed as more of a hindrance than a help to congregations. This book portrays a **key positive role for regional church bodies**. A must-read for regional church leaders."

Ed White
Former General Presbyter,
National Capital Presbytery
Former Alban Institute Senior Consultant

Detail of *Papilio Zalmoxis*, the second largest butterfly in Africa.
Papilio Zalmoxis soars very high in the rainforest and appears as
patches of blue sky falling through the trees.

The simple caterpillar has no concept of the reason he builds his
cocoon. But because of his determination an important transformation
can take place, resulting in the creature realizing his true potential.

As long as we believe that dramatic improvement like this is possible,
we must believe, put simply, *change is good.*

We must focus on realizing our full potential. As long as there is a
potential to improve, *change is good.*
Cover design by Stevie Cater

TRANSFORMATIONAL REGIONAL BODY

CONTENTS

PREFACE

PROLOGUE... 1 – 14

CHAPTER 1
Reconnecting with our Roots... 15 – 29

CHAPTER 2
The Urgency of Goal Setting for Regional Bodies.................... 30 – 40

CHAPTER 3
Structuring Time for Redevelopment Work – Delegating
the Majority of Crisis Intervention Tasks....................... 41 – 65

CHAPTER 4
Redeveloping Congregations... 66 – 81

CHAPTER 5
Locating and Nurturing Redevelopment Pastors.................... 82 – 86

CHAPTER 6
Establishing New Missions.. 87 – 95

CHAPTER 7
Developing Separate Strategies for Each Size of
Congregation.. 96 – 110

CHAPTER 8
Recruiting Transformational Leaders for Tomorrow's Church.... 111 – 136

CHAPTER 9 Redeveloping Congregations
--- An Alternative Approach.................................. 137 – 142

CHAPTER 10
The Revolution Taking Place in Texas............................... 143 – 148

CHAPTER 11
Insights From the Corporate World on How to Become a
Transformational Regional Body...................................... 149 – 153

APPENDIX 1.. 154 – 168

APPENDIX 2.. 169 – 179

APPENDIX 3.. 180 – 196

BIBLIOGRAPHY.. 197 – 199

TRANSFORMATIONAL REGIONAL BODIES

PREFACE

For the past five years, the two of us, Roy and Claire, have been conducting workshops for Regional Body Bishops and Executive under various titles. At first we titled our seminars, "Re-inventing the Middle Judicatory." We ran into some difficulty with that title as we had some Bishops/Executives coming to the event to find out new ways to structure their regional body. We then moved to the title of "Middle Judicatories and Congregations." That title stuck for awhile. When we began writing this book, we got some feedback from some people, mainly Roman Catholics, that the term "Middle Judicatory" was not one that was familiar to them. The term "Regional Body," made more sense to them. We have concluded that there is no title that will suit everyone so we went with the term, "Regional Bodies." Most, not all, denominations have some type of regional or middle entity or entities, which have both authority and resources for working directly with congregations. Some have two or three such entities, but one of the three clearly has more authority and resources than the other two. It is to that body that we direct this work.

RECOMMENDATION: READ APPENDIX 3 BEFORE GETTING INTO THE MATERIAL IN THIS BOOK.

We had almost completed this work when Hartford Seminary, which mainly conducts research in congregational systems, asked Loren Mead to write a paper, bringing his vast experience within church systems, to the subject of regional bodies or middle judicatories. After reading it, we concluded that it made a fine contribution to the main body of our message in this book. In very practical, down to earth terms, Loren spells out both the challenges and the opportunities for there to be a stronger connection between a congregation and its regional body. In many ways, it is an excellent prelude to our book. For persons new to regional body work, it is an excellent introduction as to how to improve upon the connection between their regional bodies and congregations. It is for this reason that we recommend that you consider reading his paper before digging into our vision for moving a regional body from maintenance to mission. It can be found in appendix 3 at the back of the book.

For us, it feels like Loren's work here completes the LEADER---MANAGER polarity in this book. All regional bodies need to be managed well. They also need leadership, which deals mainly with casting an exciting vision for the regional body and working at aligning clergy and congregation with that vision. Yet, before clergy and congregations respond to an exciting vision they need to know that the regional body is first managed well. When they are confident about this, they can then get on board with an exciting vision.

Loren's paper will give you some wonderful guidelines for managing your regional body well by improving the connection between congregations and your regional body. When trust is nurtured and developed between congregations and regional bodies, both will be more willing to take some risks with a new vision for the system.

The challenge here will be to learn from Loren's paper on how better to manage your regional body without getting stuck there. The opposite pole to effective management is effective leadership. The whole point of our book is to assist regional bodies move out from merely maintaining a system to also moving it into mission. Both are a challenge. Yet, no matter how well one of these poles is managed, the ultimate critique of any regional body system is how well it did on managing both of these poles well. Our prayers and blessings go with you as you take on this challenge.

Roy M. Oswald   Claire S. Burkat

ON BECOMING A TRANSFORMATIONAL REGIONAL BODY

PROLOGUE
A TALE OF TWO REGIONAL BODIES

Once upon a time there were two Regional Bodies (Middle Judicatories). The two were very similar. Both belonged to the same denomination. Each had 100 congregations under its care. Each had three full-time professionals on its Regional staff, all ordained, plus a variety of support staff, varying from bookkeeping to administration to secretarial. Of the three staff professionals, one was the elected Bishop/Executive with the other two being both field representatives and specialists within their own field. One carried the title Director of Mission and Outreach, and the other carried the title Director of Congregational Life. All three worked together to respond to congregational crises as they arose, as well as managing the Regional Body and offering its members a variety of supportive programs.

The 100 congregations committed to their care could be categorized as follows:
   7 Corporate Sized Congregations serving a total of 3930 members.
   16 Program Sized Congregations serving a total of 3843 members
   33 Pastoral Sized Congregations serving a total of 3960 members, and
   44 Family Sized Congregations serving a total of 1980 members.
The total number of members served in each of these Regional Bodies was 13,713. These two Regional Bodies had similar statistics in August of the year 2001. Both were located in the Northwest section in the USA.

The two differed in major ways. One Regional Body (Wise Virgins Regional Body) was committed to becoming a transformational Regional Body, exercising substantive leadership in starting new missions and re-developing congregations that were on a slow decline when their demographics suggested that they should be growing. Wise Virgins (Transformational) Regional Body had worked for several years with its Executive Council and some key lay and clergy leaders within their Regional Body to develop a strategic plan which would transform it from being a "caretaker" Regional Body to one that pro-actively fostered growth and development among the congregations committed to its care.

The Bishop/Executive of Wise Virgins Regional Body realized that business as usual was no longer working. After several years of merely responding to crisis, she asked that a Strategic Planning Task Force be formed to design a way they could focus more of its energy on assisting congregations to thrive and grow, as well as do more preventive maintenance over against being consumed by the many crisis situation that always seemed to overwhelm the staff. Following a year of study, this Strategic Planning Task Force, headed by the Bishop/Executive, asked that a special convention be called to explore the goals recommended by this Task Force, and vote up or down their proposal for a new way of being a Regional Body. After three days of presentations, small group discussions, and plenary sessions, this Regional Body in Assembly accepted the following goals on a ten-year trial basis.

1

WISE VIRGINS REGIONAL BODY COMMITS ITSELF TO GROWTH AND REVITALIZATION IN THE FOLLOWING WAYS:

- Deployment of its current staff to give primary attention to the training and development of clergy/lay teams that will be the main responders to the variety of crisis situations, to free the staff to focus more energy on revitalization.
- Re-development of four declining congregations per year.
- Developing two new missions each year for the next ten years
- Provide training and coaching for clergy and congregations that are committed to growth and development.
- Focus major energy on the recruitment of transformational leaders for the future with special emphasis on the recruitment of racial/ethnic minority candidates.
- Conduct a Capital Funds Campaign for the sole purpose of supporting the goals defined above.

Foolish Virgins (Caretaker) Regional Body had no explicit goals that were held in common by the Regional Body. Their unwritten goals seemed to be as follows:

- Respond to whatever crisis occurs in the life of congregations or in the life of clergy.
- Staff the various committees of the Regional Body.
- Focus on clergy placement and congregational transitions.
- Provide services and resources for congregations as needed.
- Prepare for and conduct an annual convention for their Regional Body.

The Bishop/Executive plus his/her two staff members all appeared to have too much to do, often spending between 55 and 65 hours per week at their various roles. They tended to treat all congregations alike, responding to those congregations that demanded the most from them, which usually were small, dying congregations. In one particular year they had two clergy sexual malfeasance cases to deal with. In trying to manage this by themselves, their time spent at work often exceeded 70 hours per week. They naturally concluded they must be doing good work, since all three were exhausted most of the time. From the point of view of some of their healthy, growing congregations, little of significance was taking place in their Regional Body that assisted them in any positive way.

In utilizing the concept of Jesus' parable of the 10 wise virgins and the 10 foolish virgins, we believe we are being true to Jesus' admonition in that parable. He is really talking about the difference between those who are ready to capture the moment over against those who are unprepared for that moment. Jesus was consistently talking about the Kingdom of God as being within you, or near you. The Kingdom of God is at hand; are you ready to capture the moment and celebrate it? It is as though there is a certain "kairos" moment, which if not captured in that time, passes by and the opportunity is lost.

Jesus' parable of the unjust steward has a similar message. This individual realized his boss was going to fire him. He captures the moment and pulls off some shady deals with his boss's debtors. And the master commends this unjust steward for his voracity.

In a similar fashion, there is a "kairos" moment that Regional Bodies need to capture if they are to have an impact on the congregation under their care. When this moment is squandered, it becomes lost, and all members of that Regional Body suffer as a consequence. Hence the reason for our giving these Regional Bodies these titles.

Each of these two Regional Bodies continued to function in these two differing ways over the course of ten years. We will now visit each of these Regional Bodies ten years later in the year 2011. The following results could be observed.

WISE VIRGINS REGIONAL BODY TEN YEARS LATER

Of the seven Corporate Congregations:
- Two had declined yet changed their identity to become minority congregations
    (One became an Afro-American congregation worshipping 210 per Sunday, while the second became a Hispanic congregation worshipping 250 per Sunday.)
- Four remained stable and grew slightly.
- One became a mega-church worshipping 2450 per Sunday.
- Two new missions which were started grew to corporate size in eight years,
    (One worshipping 385 per Sunday, the other 412 per Sunday.)
- One congregation targeted for re-development reversed its decline and grew
    from worshipping 80 per Sunday to worshipping 420.

The number of members these ten Corporate Congregations served grew from 3930 in 2001 to 6185 in the year 2011.

Of the sixteen Program Sized Congregations:
- Three declined to Pastoral size.
- Seven held their own. Two did so by inviting in a minority group to develop a ministry to their own people within their congregation, one Hispanic, the second
- Korean.
- Five grew in size.
- One grew to mega-church size, which worshipped 1823 per week.
- Four mission congregations started by the Synod grew to 250, 185, 210, and 280, with two serving Anglo congregations, one an Afro-American congregation, and one a Hispanic congregation.
- Eight of the congregations targeted for re-development reversed their decline and became Program Sized congregations, worshipping 185 ,215, 287,165, 192, 210, 267 and 310.

The number of members served by these Program Sized Congregations rose from 3843 in the year 2001 to 7819 in the year 2011.

Of the thirty-three Pastoral Sized Congregations:
- Five declined badly and eventually closed their doors and sold their buildings.
- Twelve declined to family size and were served by part-time clergy.
- Sixteen congregations targeted for re-development grew to Program Size, four by becoming Hispanic congregations.
- Four new missions started in this Regional Body had developed to Pastoral Size. (One mission was developed to serve Hmong congregants, another mission served only Cantonese members and a third served only Mandarin people. The remaining two served Anglo members.)

The number of members served by these Pastoral Sized Congregations grew from 3960 in 2001 to 4320 in the year 2011.

Of the forty-four Family Sized Congregations:
- Thirty closed their doors and sold their buildings.
- Ten remained open, six being served by Bi-Vocational clergy, and four becoming yoked and serviced by one ordained clergyperson and two Bi-Vocational clergy.
- Two grew to Pastoral Size.
- Two inner city congregations closed and then re-opened, one to become a Hmong congregation serving 120, and the second to become a Hispanic congregation, serving 90 people.

The number of members served by these Family Sized Congregations dropped from 1980 in 2001 to 730 in the year 2011.

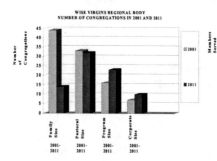

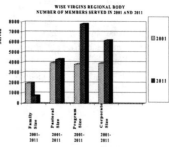

When Wise Virgins Regional Body pulled together its statistics in the year 2011 they discovered they had dropped from 100 congregations to 82 congregations, yet the total number of members served grew from 13,310 in 2000 to 19,644 in 2011. They also observed that they went from having 100 Anglo congregations to serve in 2001 to having 82 congregations to serve in 2011, yet of those 82, only 67 were Anglo congregations, the remaining 15 were serving minority congregations, 8 Hispanic, 2 Afro-American, 1 Korean, 2 Hmong, and 1 Cantonese.

The reason for this extraordinary turnaround had to do with the visionary leadership of the Bishop/Executive. When she was elected she went about her task in a traditional fashion. She soon realized that minimal was being done to assist congregations to grow to greater health and vitality. Her strategy of putting together a blue ribbon Strategic Planning Task Force and presenting their results to the entire Regional Body in convention had paid off.

She was also curious about the phenomena of mega-churches growing in various parts of the country. She built into her study leave the visitation to a variety of these mega-churches and concluded that she had at least two congregations that had that potential. These were congregations who had the potential for growth and development, but were clearly not living up to their potential. These congregations had the right location with the demographics indicating significant growth likely in that area. They had sufficient property, which would allow them to expand their facilities considerably. And they had the right type of charismatic clergy leadership to accomplish this. She visited these two congregations to present their senior pastors and their councils with this challenge. Once the congregation and their leaders had thought it over and had accepted this challenge, she recommended that each congregation offer its Senior Pastor a three month sabbatical to study intensively how these various mega-churches in the country actually attained that status. After the study, the Regional Body offered to support the congregation's hiring additional staff to help start such a plan.

When the Regional Body chose other congregations, which were ripe for re-development, it utilized the concept of triage. This may sound brutal. However, in times of war this made sense in winning a battle against an enemy. It also made sense in the immense struggle that mainline congregations were having within this culture. The concept, which was laid out for medics in time of battle, determined the order in which the wounded would get treatment. The first to get treatment were those who were wounded slightly and who, with some attention, could be sent back into battle. The next attended to were those whose life could be saved with treatment. The people who got the tail end of a medic's attention were those who were going to die no matter what the medic did.

Using this concept with congregations, they decided to limit attention on the small-membership congregations who would not grow regardless of what they were offered. Instead they would focus attention on key congregations which were in demographically growing areas, with reasonably adequate facilities and a good location, but which were declining in membership in spite of all this. The strategy developed by the planning task force was to wait until the current pastor within these key congregations decided to move.

When this happened, Regional Body leadership visited these congregations and challenged them to develop their potential. They were offered the opportunity to enter into a special relationship whereby the Regional Body would appoint their new pastor for a period of three years, guaranteeing the congregation that they would find a pastor who had transformational abilities. If at the end of three years, they liked this pastor, they could then extend this person a permanent call. The task force planned on re-developing a minimum of four congregations a year in this way.

With the help of their national church, this Regional Body received training in how to select transformational clergy through an extensive interview process. They then searched the country for such transformational clergy.

The Regional Body also committed to starting two new missions each year for the next ten years in their territory. They knew a significant amount of money would need to be raised to realize such an ambitious vision. They began immediately to put into place a major capital fund campaign drive. Contributors were promised that every penny of these funds would go to four undertakings:
- The starting of new mission congregations.
- The re-development of congregations with strong potential.
- Evangelization training for all congregations in the Regional Body.
- The recruitment of transformational leaders, especially racial/ethnic minority candidates for the ordained ministry.

When people with financial means, who also had a deep commitment to Christ, caught the vision of this strategic plan, their wallets and purses opened and $2,000,000 was raised over a two-year period.

The planning task force also realized that such an ambitious plan would not come to pass unless it was adequately staffed to pull it off. It adopted an Alban Institute plan of identifying cadres of clergy and lay teams to receive training over the course of several years and then be assigned to manage the majority of crises that were currently eating up all the Regional staff's time and energy. The staff could then devote at least 30% of their time to the execution of the re-vitalization vision. For two years this staff located the best trainers in the country to teach clergy and lay teams in how to assist a congregation in resolving internal conflict; how to advise a search/call committee; how to make an intervention into a situation in which a pastor was accused of sexual malfeasance; and how to assist clergy making a transition into a new congregation by closing well with the congregation they were leaving and starting up strongly in the new congregation. Different teams developed different specialties. The job of the Regional Body staff was to make an initial visit to a congregation that was troubled in some way, make an assessment, and then recommend that one of the clergy/lay teams work with them for a period of time to resolve their difficulty.

This was a hard sell for the Regional Body in that the planning task force concluded the only way they would be able to retain quality clergy/lay teams to stay with a specialty and continue to offer time for this outside work was to pay them. Many within the Regional Body objected to this idea since they felt their benevolence dollars were meant to pay for these services performed by the staff. People needed to be convinced that the role of staff was that of selecting, training, delegating, supervising, supporting, and evaluating these clergy/lay teams to conduct this ministry to clergy and congregations. People eventually came to see that this policy, in the long run, would strengthen their entire Regional Body. Besides, it gave talented clergy and lay leaders the opportunity to receive training in a consultation specialty and develop the skill necessary to do a professional job within congregations in addition to their own.

Lastly, this planning task force realized that if there was going to be an impact upon the unchurched within their territory, they were going to have to recruit qualified minority candidates for ministry who would assist them in reaching out to the changing demographic culture that was emerging in their territory. In observing the demographic changes taking place on this continent, they realized that White Euro-American would soon be a minority. Since all mainline denominations would continue to compete for these Euro-Americans, all would decline, as this percentage of the population continued to decrease. A special task force was appointed with the sole purpose of attracting motivated clergy who could develop a ministry to the growing numbers of Hispanic, Afro-American, and Asian people within the Regional Body.

It is with this basic framework that Wise Virgins Regional Body launched into an exciting transformational adventure. Now, ten years later, they decided to evaluate how well this plan had served them.

Upon evaluating their strategic plan over the past ten years they concluded that they had attained some of their goals and missed on others. They had committed themselves in the year 2001 to establish two new missions a year for the next ten years. They had stayed on course with that difficult goal. They were pleased that they had become a much more multicultural by adding fifteen minority congregations to their rolls. They felt they could have done better at encouraging congregations to consider becoming mega-churches as they had two other congregations where all the pieces were in place. They had the right locations and enough land to expand significantly. Yet each congregation struggled with pastoral leadership and floundered. They also felt they could have begun at least four more minority congregations, but they could not find competent minority clergy to head up those re-development efforts. Lastly, they had nothing but praise for the cadres of clergy and lay consultants they had developed over these years which continued to offer valuable consultative help to congregations. The current staff had done a good job in continuing to recruit, train, and utilize these consultants whose availability freed them to devote the necessary attention to the transformational work, which was adopted as its goal.

FOOLISH VIRGINS REGIONAL BODY TEN YEARS LATER

Of the seven Corporate Sized Congregations in their care:
- Two experienced modest growth.
- Three had slight growth.
- One declined to program size.
- One was hit with a clergy scandal and dropped to pastoral size.

Total number of member served dropped from 3930 in 2001 to 2910 in the year 2011.

Of the seventeen Program Sized Congregation in their care:
- Five declined to Pastoral Size.
- Eight held their own.
- Three grew to Corporate Size.
- One new mission grew to 280 per Sunday.

Total number of members served dropped from 3843 in 2001 to 3670 in the year 2011.

Of the Thirty-three Pastoral Sized Congregations in their care:
- Thirteen closed their doors and sold their buildings.
- Thirteen declined to Family Size, with five clergy serving ten congregations and three bi-Vocational clergy serving the remaining three.
- Six congregations held their own.
- One congregation grew to Program Size.

Total number of members served by their Pastoral Sized Congregations dropped from 3960 in 2001 to 1430 in the year 2011.

Of the forty-four Family Sized Congregations in their care:
- Thirty-six closed their doors and sold their buildings.
- Eight congregations remained Family Size, currently being served by three full time and one part-time clergyperson.

Total number of members served dropped from 1980 in 2001 to 320 in the year 2011.

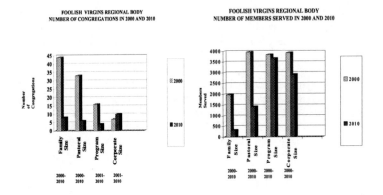

FOOLISH VIRGINS REGIONAL BODY
NUMBER OF CONGREGATIONS IN 2000 AND 2010

FOOLISH VIRGINS REGIONAL BODY
NUMBER OF MEMBERS SERVED IN 2000 AND 2010

In the year 2011 the statistician for the Regional Body reported that numbers had dropped from serving 13,713 in the year 2001 to serving 8,330 in the current year. The number of congregations being served had dropped from 100 in the year 2001 to 53 in the current year. A motion was made at that year's convention that, since they were only serving half as many congregations as ten years ago, that one staff member be terminated immediately and consideration be made for the second staff member be dropped to part time.

For whatever reasons, Foolish Virgins Regional Body continued to function the way they had functioned in previous years. They continued to do the same things, but expected different results. However, the results never changed. Each year they saw that congregations that were no longer viable needed to be closed. The number of members that were served continued to decline. Rather than venture out to learn how they might approach their work differently, they decided to try harder at their given roles. The number of hours this staff put in on a weekly basis increased from 60 hours per week to 65 hours per week. It never occurred to them to work smarter rather than harder.

Foolish Virgins Regional Body conducted no evaluation session covering the last ten years. Staff was too busy responding to congregational and clergy crises to set up an evaluation. The newly elected Bishop of Foolish Virgins Regional Body in his opening presentation at the convention recommended that a task force be set up to study the plan adopted by Wise Virgins Regional Body to see if it would merit consideration.

Now the tale of these two Regional Bodies makes some trembling assumptions. It assumes that the Christian Church is going to continue to be exempt from property taxes on this continent. It has not taken into consideration what the handwriting on the wall seems to indicate, namely that we are moving into a cultural environment in which religious institutions are tolerated at best, and ignored, laughed at, and humiliated at worst.

For those people who have not taken seriously the writings of Loren Mead on this subject (The Once and Future Church and The Financial Meltdown of Mainline Denominations), may be the ones that are caught most off guard by a major shift within Western civilization. They really will be the foolish virgins who are not at all prepared when different times spring upon us. The following scenario is likely to be much more realistic as we look at the next ten years.

WORST CASE SCENARIO

These two Regional Bodies began to move in separate directions in the year 2001. In the year 2004 in the USA the State of Montana passed a referendum that made it possible for localities to tax all non-profits in their state. Within the next 24 months, eight other states adopted similar referendums. The states that refused to pass such a resolution were in the mid-West and the South. Almost all the states on the West Coast passed such a referendum and a handful of states on the East Coast did the same. Each of these was directly impacted by this referendum.

In order to give non-profits a break, the localities in the states involved began to tax non-profits, including churches, at only 40% of what would normally be paid if they were required to pay taxes on their entire property. Each year after that, this figure would rise by 10%.

The smaller congregations were hit the hardest. All Family Sized Congregations and most Pastoral Sized Congregations were unable to pay property taxes on top of ongoing expenses.

In his book "The Financial Meltdown of Mainline Denominations," Loren Mead calculates many churches within these denominations have a budget of $100,000.00 or less. This ranges from the denominations, which have the fewest congregations with total budget figures, this size, namely Episcopal (59%) and Lutheran (61%) to denominations which have the most congregations of this size or less, namely United Methodist (79%) and American Baptist (79%). This is probably the percentage of congregations, which would need to close down and join another congregation or to begin working with a Bi-Vocational pastor. Possibly most of us Christians in the country would come to realize that our denominational differences are really a luxury we could afford only if we continue to go tax-free, exempting our churches from paying taxes. even for police and fire protection.

As you might guess, Foolish Virgins Regional Body fared much worse than Wise Virgins Regional Body. The staff of Foolish Virgins was caught completely by surprise when this referendum passed. They could not comprehend this taking place. When it did pass, they continued in their normal fashion of responding to congregational calls for help one at a time. The Bishop/Executive and the program staff were now logging 70 hours per week, responding to each congregation's request for assistance. This did not last very long, however. The first thing that congregations usually cut out of their budget when money is not available, is their benevolence giving. Most of the congregations, during the first year of paying taxes on their church property, cut their benevolence giving by 60%. By the end of the year, the Bishop/Executive had to lay off all the program staff, and reduce many of the support staff to part-time status. By the end of the following year, congregations cut their benevolence giving even further, and the Bishop/Executive had to begin working on a part-time salary as well. He began looking for a congregation that he could serve as part-time pastor and run the Regional Body part time.

Among the things cut out of the Regional Body budget was its contribution to the National Church. The staff of the National Church had to be cut by 50% in 2006, and it continued to shrink to 15% of its current size by the year 2011.

By the year 2011, only the seven corporate size congregations and five of the program size congregations still had full time pastors. The program staffs of these congregations had to be terminated. The congregations that thrived in this environment were the ones who had trained lay leaders who were already doing most of the pastoral care work. The remaining congregations survived with part-time clergy and lay volunteers.

Since the Bishop and staff were so unprepared for this turn of events, they had no plan of action to recommend to their congregations. As a result they left the congregations under their care to fend for themselves to survive in this type of political environment. As a result, close to 40% of the congregations with a budget of $100,000.00 or less simply decided to close their doors and recommended that their members seek membership in neighboring congregations. There is a saying, that "IF YOU UNBUNDLE PEOPLE, YOU LOSE THEM." One would assume that these faithful Christians would in fact seek membership in other congregations in their area. Unfortunately, history has shown that when a congregation disbands, a high percentage of their former members simply stop going to church altogether. They may give a neighboring church a visit or two, but when it doesn't feel right, and they do not see all those old familiar faces when going to church, they simply find the transition too difficult, and stop going. Families that had grown up having the Christian rituals meaningful to them conducted in church rather than at home had no home rituals to fall back on to continue to ground them in a Christian identity. As a result many became nominal Christians and only watched religious services on television occasionally.

When the remaining congregations in Foolish Virgins Regional Body realized they could no longer pay property taxes on their church property and have a full time pastor, they began to make overtures to neighboring congregations. They had to do this on their own, without much assistance or guidance from the Regional Body staff. Some actually did try to merge with a nearby congregation of their same denomination, but few of these succeeded. Four out of five church mergers do not work. Yes, two congregations do follow through on becoming a new single congregation, but the fallout of members is heart breaking. As Lyle Schaller observed years ago, when a congregation of 80 members merges with another congregation of 80 members, the end result after a number of years is a new congregation of about 80 members.

Wise Virgins Regional Body was not caught by surprise by the passage of this referendum. They had already begun to set up ecumenical teams, which were made up of representatives of differing denominations. Long before the referendum to tax non-profits came to a vote, they were out among congregations exploring some options with them should such a referendum pass.

In conjunction with other denominations, they began to develop strategies, which would move two or three congregations of differing denominations into one building, thereby cutting down on the tax bill each would have to pay. All participating denominations in this region began studying the Alban Institute material on Ecumenical Shared Ministries.* In these ministries, two congregations, usually of differing denominations, come together to share one facility while maintaining some autonomy and denominational identity.

The following options come under this heading of Ecumenical Shared Ministries:
- Two congregations share the same building, each maintaining complete autonomy with its own worship services, programs, and staff.
- Two congregations share one pastor and hold worship services and programming in common. The combined congregation maintains loyalty to two denominations (sending apportionments to two denominations and representatives to two denominational conventions).
- Two congregations actually merge, but are served by a clergyperson from one denomination during one tenure, and then calling a clergyperson from the other denomination on the next round.

Ecumenical Shared Ministries was only one among many other options that these ecumenical teams began to explore with their congregations. Some congregations could, for example, become satellites to larger congregations, with one decision- making body, but shared staff. Going the route of having a bi-vocational clergyperson was another option.

The Bishop/Executive began approaching Jewish Synagogues who were facing the same financial difficulties. The advantage here was having two congregations share one facility, since the sanctuary of Jewish Synagogues is not used on Sundays. A Christian congregation would then be able to retain its own clergyperson who would work in colleagueship with the Rabbi or other clergy but work with them out of one property.

When the Regional Body's budget was cut dramatically, Wise Virgins Regional Body was also prepared. They had approached several of their key contributors to their capital funds campaign and asked if they would endow the Bishop/Executive's salary. Once this budget item was taken care of, they had some resources to sustain the salary of another staff person who continued to recruit, train, supervise and evaluate clergy/lay consultant teams who were able to respond to clergy and congregational crisis.

By the year 2005 when the taxation of church property took effect, Wise Virgins Regional Body had already established five new missions, two of which had moved to Program Size and were able to sustain a viable ministry. Two mission congregations that had not yet begun building programs began to experiment with ways they might remain viable congregations without having to build a building. One mission congregation had just started a building program and needed further support from the Regional Body's endowment funds to remain viable.

Wise Virgins Regional Body had also re-developed twelve of its congregations by the year 2005; eight of them had gained in strength and were able to pay taxes on their church building plus retain a full time pastor.

The two congregations who had each been challenged to become a mega-church had succeeded to the point where they were able to sustain a thriving congregation in spite of this dramatic change within the culture.

This Regional Body had also been successful in recruiting minority candidates for ministry and by this time had been able to establish four Hispanic congregations, two Korean congregations, two Afro-American congregations, and one Hmong congregation. These congregations had established enough loyalty to their ethnic pastors that they were not about to let them go. Four of the nine new ethnic pastors were able to find part-time employment in their neighborhoods, which took some of the financial burden off their congregations.

Because Wise Virgins Regional Body had conducted a successful capital funds campaign for re-development, new missions, and evangelization training, they still had three quarters of a million dollars to help their strongest congregations adjust to this new paradigm shift. The advantage of having an endowment of some order is that it allows you time and space to figure out how you will adjust to a major paradigm shift. This Regional Body continued to begin new missions in its territory, exploring ways to begin new congregations without thinking in terms of their need for their own buildings.

By the year 2011, Wise Virgins Regional Body was every bit as strong as it was when the referendum to tax church property passed. As a whole, they seemed energized by the challenge that this shift thrust upon them. They certainly had been drawn in closer to each other. Many expressed the sentiment that they now felt like first-century Christians, who were able to have their faith thrive in the face of obstacles and persecution. Their commitment to Christ had certainly been challenged and many felt they were stronger for it.

Thus ends the tale of two Regional Church Bodies. It will give you some idea of where we are headed with this document. Unlike the tale we have just spun, the recommendations we will be making to you are by no means fiction. What we are recommending in this book are ideas that have come out of three Regional Bodies that have successfully put such plans into effect. This work also grows out of seminars conducted by Claire and Roy on this subject for Alban Institute for over five years now. Development of this book is our way of pulling together what we have learned from working with Middle Judicatories or Regional Bodies over this period of time.

Chapter 1

Reconnecting with out Roots
A Church Deeply Into Mission

We, the authors, are making a trembling assumption in our offering of a parable of two Regional Bodies. This assumption is that mainline denominations really do want to be about the business of transforming human lives. The early church was unhesitatingly clear about this missional emphasis. It is here that we need to reconnect with our roots and once again be about the business of bringing people into a primary, surrendered relationship with the God that is revealed in Jesus Christ. Such human transformation will, most often, take place at a congregational level, yet we are assuming that the main function of any Regional Body will be that of initiating, supporting, training, equipping clergy and congregations in this missional task. It is assuming that the basic task of any Christian congregation is that of making disciples out of its members, and through these transformed members, making disciples out of the millions of spiritually hungry people who are not yet associated with any congregation. We are talking here about people being healed and lives being changed.

There is no question about the spiritual hunger that is rampant in our post-modern society. Books on spirituality continue to make it to the New York Times best seller's list. Several years ago, the book "The Celestine Prophesy" was number one on the Times best seller list for months. Then came "Care of the Soul," by Robert Moore, followed by "Chicken Soup for the Soul" and half a dozen "Chicken Soup" follow up books. If anything should convince us about the spiritual hunger of our culture, it should be the phenomenal success of the "Chicken Soup" series that keeps making it to the bestseller list. This is religious "lite" material. It is like offering a teaspoon of water to a person dying of thirst in a desert. "Conversations with God," by Donald Neal Walsh hit the times bestseller list as well, and remained there for months. In the musical world, the record "Chant" sold over a million copies, which is little more than a group of monks singing some basic Christian chants. As we try to read what is happening in our North American culture, we see that spirituality is "in" but organized religion is "out." Possibly it is the nature of Baby Boomers, or the Gen X generation to distrust institutions, yet many will still seek out congregations that can address the spiritual cavity they experience within. These people may try a variety of "do it yourself," "new age religion" stuff, but when a crisis hits, these "new age" experiences usually do not hold up. They are not rooted solidly in any religious tradition and thus do not have the depth that is called for in any sort of tragedy. It is at such a point that they may give organized religion another try. It has been our experience that any Christian Church, if it is well situated and reasonably attractive, will have visitors walking in its doors every Sunday. These are not people who simply did not have anything better to do that Sunday morning. These are busy people who know they need something more to assist them deal with the lack of meaning in their lives, and their innate hunger for an experience of the Transcendent. Whether they will return for another visit really depends upon their sense that the church they are visiting really can and will address the spiritual hunger they have, which never seems to go away.

For whatever reason, many mainline congregations have turned their backs on these questing souls. The ministry of these congregations has turned inward, focusing all of their time and energy on serving existing members. It is the main reason for our continual decline as mainline denominations. This turn of events has sent these questing souls to our more Fundamentalist, Evangelical or Charismatic congregations who continue to have a passion for reaching out to those still not in a primary relationship with Jesus Christ. It is one of the main reasons why these congregations now regularly have at Sunday worship as many people as attend all mainline congregations combined. Fifty percent of those worshipping on Sunday do so at congregations other than mainline churches. What will it take to once again re-orient our ministries so that we spend as much time and energy reaching out to these searching souls as we do in ministering to our own members?

Jesus said, "Come unto me all you who labor and are heavy laden, and I will give you rest." Can we once again see how this applies to the millions of people who are not yet acquainted with this Jesus and the healing balm he offer to the over-burdened people in our society? These are people who are yearning for God. They are searching for a relationship that is real, reliable, and lasting. They want to be transformed in such a way that their relationship with themselves and others is also dramatically changed. They are searching for a peace that this world cannot give. They may be surrounded by more possessions than they ever could have dreamed of, yet their lives are not filled full as they expected when they put most of their effort into accumulating these things. Instead, the emptiness within has increased and they must contend daily with thoughts of how meaningless their lives have become. What they thought would bring them an enriched life has turned out to be, for the most part, empty and hollow.

There is no question that the Holy Spirit is alive and active in the lives of the millions who have not surrendered to a relationship that is able to transform their lives. We are not in this work alone. We have this powerful ally that is consistently throwing people off balance that brings about an awareness of how lost and broken they really are. It is this Spirit that has these people visiting our congregations in search of something that has eluded them here-to-fore. When the congregations they visit are totally absorbed in only serving their members, these visitors soon conclude that their needs are not of much concern to the people who are members here, and they realize, with disappointment, that they must search elsewhere.

This imbalance on congregational focus can be viewed more clearly when seen through the lens of a polarity map. Polarities are those unavoidable but unresolveable issues we confront regularly. For the most part, we are taught to think in "either/or" terms. Our whole school system is based on "either/or thinking. To most questions there is one right answer. If you have that right answer, everyone else who has a different answer is wrong. There are some issues however that cannot be deal with through either/or thinking but must embrace "both/and" thinking. Polarities are two truths that are inter-locking, and the complete picture involves two right answers. An example might help. At the top of the polarity map is the higher purpose that will result if this polarity is managed well.   At the very bottom of the map is our worst fear of what will happen when this polarity is managed poorly. As you can see, each polarity has two positive poles and two negative poles. A well-managed polarity has us living within the two (upper) positive poles. A poorly managed polarity has us spending too much of our time in the lower one or two (negative) poles. What follows is a personal polarity that every human being alive today needs to manage in some way or other. If any human being can say there is a one-time solution to this problem, then it isn't a polarity.

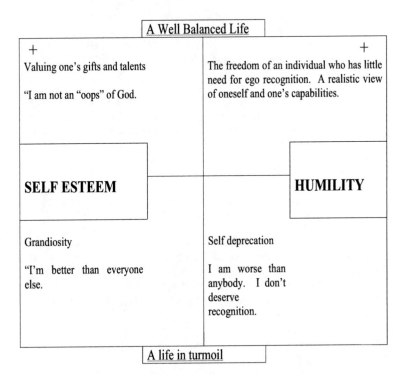

A Well Balanced Life	
+	**+**
Valuing one's gifts and talents	The freedom of an individual who has little need for ego recognition. A realistic view of oneself and one's capabilities.
"I am not an "oops" of God.	
SELF ESTEEM	**HUMILITY**
Grandiosity	Self deprecation
"I'm better than everyone else.	I am worse than anybody. I don't deserve recognition.
A life in turmoil	

As indicated before, a polarity is unavoidable and unsolvable. There is no one right answer to this polarity. Our only choice is to manage this polarity well or to manage it poorly. People who manage this polarity well spend most of their time in the upper two quadrants of this polarity map. They do value themselves. However, when they find themselves thinking more highly of themselves than the data indicates, they move over into the "HUMILITY" side of this polarity and take a more humble approach to their achievements. A poorly managed polarity is spending most of your life in the bottom two quadrants of the polarity map. What is more likely the case of managing this polarity poorly is spending huge chunks of time in the down side of one of these poles. Many of us have friends/relatives who spend much of their time in the downside of "HUMILITY," and we are constantly encouraging them to value themselves more.

When we have friends/relatives who hang out most of the time on the downside of "SELF ESTEEM", we usually find ourselves having to listen to their proclaiming how great and wonderful they are. As Barry Johnson, the author of the book, "*Polarity Management*," has discovered, the longer one hangs out on one particular pole in a polarity, the more one is going to experience the downside of that pole. Hence the reason why some people with high self esteem will often sink into feelings of grandiosity and self- aggrandizement.

Are you getting the hang of how polarities work? Only a small fraction of the life issues we deal with are polarities that require both/and thinking. When we try to treat a polarity as a problem to be solved, we will look for one right answer. There is no one right answer to the polarity listed above. Both self-esteem and humility are positive characteristics that live side by side, and throughout our life we will find ourselves oscillating between these two poles.

Lets now look at a polarity that relates to the subject matter of this chapter, namely promoting healthy congregations that have as much concern for the unchurched as they do for their own members. We are talking here about congregations that take seriously the Great Commission and the Great Commandment.

The Great Commission: (Matthew 28:18-29) "All authority in heaven and on earth have been given to me. Go therefore and make disciples of all nations, baptizing them in the name of the Father and of the Son and of the Holy Spirit, teaching them to observe all that I have commanded you; and lo, I am with you always, to the close of the age."

The Great Commandment: (Matthew 22: 35 – 40) "And one of them, a lawyer, asked him a question to test him. 'Teacher, which is the great commandment in the law?' And Jesus said to him, 'You shall love the Lord you God with all your heart, and with all your soul, and with all your mind. This is the great and first commandment. And a second is like it, You shall love your neighbor as yourself. On these two commandments depend all the law and the prophets'."

A Church Centered in Love and Mission	
+	**+**
Spiritual feeding of members. Quality worship and educational opportunities. Service opportunities Building community Pastoral care	Living the Great Commission. Inviting non-churched people to receive spiritual nurture. Seeker friendly worship. Serving hungry, homeless, marginalized people
INREACH MISSION TO SERVE CHURCH MEMBERS	**OUTREACH MISSION TO SERVE THE UNCHURCHED**
Creates Co-dependence. The church is here to serve me. Membership decline and death Insular congregation. Stagnation Denial of the Great Commission.	Burnout Member's spiritual needs being neglected. Quality of ministry to members suffers Lack of pastoral care of members Members strung out and over-burdened.

Congregational in ill-health and decline

Within mainline denominations we are all too familiar with congregations who spend most of their time, energy and resources on the left side of this polarity. As we have learned from polarity management theory, when we spend most of our time on one pole, we then experience much more of the downside of that pole. Mainline congregations have been in decline for the last 25 years. The United Methodists, for example, are losing 40,000 members per year for the last 30 years. They have shrunk from 11.1 million to 8.5 million within this time span. Other mainline denominations are shrinking at about the same rate.

What is the role of the Regional Body in the face of such decline? Is it to simply manage a system that is slowing dying? We are not questioning here whether a Regional Body is managed poorly. Many declining Regional Bodies are well managed. What is lacking is leadership. Can a Regional Body create initiatives to assist congregations to manage the above polarity better? We believe they can. What is required is vision and risk through leadership.

Throughout this document you will hear us hammer away at three basic initiatives that Transformational Regional Bodies need to take seriously:

- Training in Evangelization
- Redeveloping Congregations
- Starting new missions.

Managing the above polarity well involves a Regional Body consistently encouraging its constituents, both clergy and lay leaders, to participate in seminars that deal with Evangelism, church growth, new member assimilation, spiritual formation and becoming an inviting church.

We may need to begin with how little we know about human transformation (conversion) within mainline denominations. This may come as a surprise to our lay readers, but we as clergy are not taught a whole lot about conversion at our seminaries. Of course, we always have the theological cop-out by saying and believing that it is not we who bring people into a faith relationship with God: it is the Holy Spirit who does that. To that we can only say, "right on". Does that mean we are to remain passive and simply leave everything up to the Holy Spirit? Is there not some role we can play in this? Does not the Holy Spirit use us as catalysts, which are the occasion for someone surrendering their life to Christ? If in fact there is a role for us in this, what could it be? What are the ways in which we can prepare ourselves for being used by the Holy Spirit in this task? Only a small minority of us has had a mid-life conversion experience. Close to 95% of people attending our congregations have been raise in a Christian home since birth, and have been Christians since birth. Roy would like to share four stories of how little we, within mainline denominations, know about conversion.

Story One

During one of the clergy seminars I was leading, a clergywoman approached me during a break time to share an experience she just had the previous week. On Sunday morning a college student approached her and said, "For most of my life I have had no experience with Christianity. My parents weren't Christian, so I was not brought to church or Sunday school. I have not had anyone really explain to me what it means to be a Christian. At this point in my life I think I want to become a Christian. Where do I start, and what should I do?" The clergywoman, who was relating this incident to me said, "You know, I didn't have the foggiest notion of what to say to this young man." In hearing this clergywoman share this incident with me, I wondered to myself. "How is it possible for someone to go through a mainline seminary for three years and not have a clue as to what to say to someone who claimed they wanted to become a Christian?"

I then asked her, "Would you be willing to ask him to begin reading one of the gospels; reading at least one chapter a day?" She thought she could do that. "Would you also be willing to ask him to begin praying daily, after you introduced him to a simple way to bring his concerns and his thanksgiving to God?" She thought she could do that as well. I then asked her, "Do you think you could find three people in your congregation who would be welling to meet with this college student weekly to be in dialogue with him about what he was discovering about God in scripture and in his prayer life?" She thought she could find three people who would be willing to do that. "And would you be able to meet with him once a month for a one on one sessions to inquire how he was progressing in his discovery of Christianity, dealing with his questions and doubt, and possibly recommending some additional reading he might do on his own?" She said she would be willing to do this as well. As I reflected upon this conversation, I began to wonder why this ordained clergyperson was not challenged during her training as a minister to be prepared for such a request.

Story Two

Some eight years ago I went to members of Alban's Education Department and asked if they would be willing to sponsor a seminar that I would conduct entitled, "Transformational Spirituality." They agreed to give it a try. I did not claim to know a whole lot more about this that my fellow clergy within mainline denominations, but I realized if we did not learn to do this, we would continue to decline as denominations. I put together a simple design and each year I taught the course I invited someone whom I thought knew something about this subject to co-lead the seminar with me. At the first of such seminars, I invited a Southern Baptist minister I had come to know and trust to share his perspectives on conversion.

After three years of conducting this seminar with other leaders, about mid-week in the fourth of such seminars, I decided to set aside the design for the afternoon and simply have us gather in a circle and tell stories of persons we thought we have brought into a surrendered relationship with Christ. There were 18 in the seminar that year. We were meeting in Techy Towers in Chicago. Once in the circle I asked if anyone had a story of somebody they felt they had brought into a faith relationship with God. Deep silence! Out of 18 clergy, not a single one of them could relate a single incident in which they thought they had been a catalyst in someone's spiritual transformation.

Finally one clergyperson spoke up and said, "This isn't a story of how I brought someone to faith, but it is an incident that just recently happened to me that I would like to share. A non-member of my congregation asked if I would perform her wedding in our church. Reluctantly, I agree to do it. A week later I received a phone call that the father of the bride had just had a heart attack and was in intensive care in the hospital. They wondered it I would go to visit with him." The clergywoman relating this story agreed that she would. As she sat with this man in the hospital bed, for whatever reasons, he opened up and spilled out his life story. The Board of Directors of a sizeable corporation had just terminated him. He felt his career, as a CEO was finished. He and his wife were not on the best of terms. He thought she was having an affair with another man. He asked her if she wanted a divorce, but she declined. He then told the clergyperson that he and his oldest daughter were on such bad terms that all they could do was shout at each other. And now he had this physical setback in this massive heart attack.

"Goodness," I said to her "this was a wonderful opening for you to share with him the fact that his life would take on a whole new meaning if he was willing to surrender his life to God. You could have said to him, 'When you turn your life over to God, this relationship will reframe the way to view all of these problems. You might even conclude that all the things that have just happened are a blessing in disguise. If you are willing to do this, I would offer to pray with you as you turn your life over to God'." "Well, I certainly wouldn't know how to do that." the clergyperson replied emphatically.

It was then that the rest of the group began to explore with this ordained clergyperson what other options might have been tried with this desperate man. "Maybe, you could get with he and his wife," replied one other participant "and see if you could get them into some marital counseling. If you got his marriage back on track, it might do a lot for him." The rest of the group began to support this idea. I was absolutely stunned that a group of 18 clergy from various mainline denominations immediately turned to a psychological solution to this man's problems, when the man was at a desperate low point in his life and seemed to be crying out for some sort of spiritual answer to his life. The group completely missed how ripe this person was for a spiritual transformation.

Story Three
One Sunday morning as I was attending my local Lutheran church in Maryland. I was surprised to find Connie, a middle aged woman who lived at the top of our lane out in the country. She came from a poor mountain family in which two families were living in a small house that still did not have running water, a shower, or a flush toilet. They still drew their water from a mountain stream that was on our property. This particular Sunday morning, Connie was looking desperate. I knew that years ago she had killed her young 3-year-old son. At the time, she was living in a shack down the road, also without running water. Her son kept walking up the road to see his grandfather, inspite of the fact she had told him not to leave the yard. When he did it once too often, she took a hammer a whooped him on the head. The child never recovered. No charges were pressed as everyone supported the story that the child had fallen and hit his head. I also knew that her marriage was in serious trouble. She was working for an hourly wage cleaning houses.

I tried, as best I was able to make Connie feel welcome at our church and told her how good it was to see her there. I knew, however, that our Lutheran liturgy made little sense to her. Deep down I knew that our church was in no way prepared to have a small group of people begin to meet with Connie weekly to introduce her to the basics of the Christian faith. Yes, we had some adult classes, but Connie would clearly have felt out of place in anyone of them. Our congregation was much too absorbed in itself to make room for someone as desperate as Connie to fit in. We had never ever given any consideration as to what we might do if someone like Connie would walk through our doors. We were and are a congregation that lives totally on the left side of the above polarity. I was not surprised when Connie never returned.

Story Four
Often at the front end of a clergy seminar I am conducting, I engage the group in Open Space Technology. It is a way of building community at the front end of an event. For at least an hour I continue to ask them questions about their lives, and they need to walk to differing parts of the room depending on how they answer the questions. For example, "Those born as the oldest child in the family, move against one wall. People born as middle children, stand in the middle. Those born youngest in the family against the

opposite wall. In five seconds we see where the whole community stands on a question about their family of origin.

As we move through some simple factual data on the group I begin to move to more complex questions. I will often ask, "Those of you who have been Christian since birth, move against that wall. Those of you having become Christian through an adult conversion experience, move against the opposite wall. In most clergy groups 98% have been Christian since birth. I then say, those of you that had a course on conversion in seminary, mover against that wall. Those who had no training in seminar on conversion, move to the opposite wall. There is usually a snicker that goes through the crowd when I ask this question. Once again, about 99% of these clergy have had no course in seminary on conversion. There may be one or two who walk to the opposite side of the room. I ask them which seminary they attended. It is usually seminaries such as Gordon Conwell, Fuller, or one of several Southern Baptist seminaries.

Then I ask this group of clergy, "How many of you believe that it is your job as a church to transform human lives?" Inevitably, all hands go up. I then point out the dilemma. We all know our job is to transform human lives, yet none of us have had any training as to how to do this in seminary. We also haven't had the personal experience of coming to Christ through an adult conversion experience ourselves. However, we know that our job is that of human transformation.

In my own personal experience, I attended a Lutheran Seminary for four years (three in class plus a year of internship). Not once during all those four years did anyone ask me if a prayed, how I prayed, whether I had a rule of life or observed a personal spiritual ritual, whether I even believed in Christ. It was kinda like, "what do you want to do with that kind of stuff. We have systematic theology, biblical exegesis and form criticism and daily chapel. What else do you need?" When I entered seminary I thought I would be entering some type of monastic life, with people consulting with me about my spiritual path, coaching me on a wide variety of prayer forms. Instead, seminary was simply post-graduate studies in bible, pastoral care, and systematic theology. Between these studies and daily chapel, I was to develop into a spiritual giant. It was no wonder I hit spiritual despair during my first four years as a parish pastor. No one had taught me a thing about how to sustain an active spiritual life once I was isolated in a parish setting. Like all of my classmates, I was taught how to take a congregation full of believers and keep them on a spiritual path. There was no training what so ever in taking someone who had no experience as a Christian and turn them into people who lived and acted on faith.

There is another polarity, which relates to our difficulty as mainline congregations in inviting our non-Christian friends and relatives into a faith relationship. It is a theological polarity. It is a polarity, which points out a key difference between mainline denominations and our more fundamentalist brothers and sisters. As seen on a polarity map it looks like this:

The Redeemed Life

+	+
This is a story of great news. We come together in worship to celebrate this great thing God has done for us all. The Eucharist is more a ritual of celebration than a sacrament of penance. Affirms God's overarching love for all people. Includes entire human family in God's eternal future. Promotes acceptance/understanding of other denominations/religions.	"If I really believe that all my non-believing friends and relatives are going to spend eternity in hell, because they haven't accepted Christ, I am going to be much more motivated to tell them about Jesus." Reaching out to the non-churched becomes a central activity in our tradition. Inspires strong commitment in Jesus Christ Increases zeal for mission. Increases commitment/participation in Church.

UNIVERSALISM		FUNDAMENTALISM
What Christ did on the cross applies to everyone, even those who don't believe it, or have not been told about it.	_____	Only those who have accepted Jesus Christ as their personal Savior are redeemed. All the rest will spend eternity in hell.

Waters down the uniqueness of Christianity and Jesus Christ. Can promote indifference and religious apathy. Lose track of our religious heritage. Lose zeal for Jesus Christ and his mission. Loss of specific, spiritual grounding. Little motivation for church members to tell others about Jesus, because all are redeemed anyway. Since there is truth in all world religions, we should not be forcing our personal beliefs onto others.	This is religion that is based on fear. "We/They" mentality (I'm in and you're out) Distance/animosity between individuals and religious groups/denominations/world religions. Can promote feelings of superiority, self-righteousness. The Spanish Inquisition, Crusades, Salem Witch Trials Can promote vengeance. Our personal hostility projected upon a scapegoat—the heathen.

A Faithless Generation

We are not saying, in this polarity, that all mainline Christians are Universalists. Many are not. However, when it comes to reaching out and inviting others into the faith, they become functional Universalists. They buy into the concept that it is uncouth and arrogant to try to push your religious beliefs onto others.

In one sense this is not a true polarity in that when an individual or denomination decides on one particular interpretation of the Bible on the question of salvation, the problem for them is solved. The reason we put it into the form of a polarity, is that it points up the incredible challenge we have of motivating members of mainline denominations to invite their friends and relatives to church. Once again, any well-managed polarity has people oscillating between the two upper quadrants of the polarity. It is here that we invite you the reader to struggle with us on the question of "What is the message/theology we give to our members that is so compelling that they will be motivated to invite their friends to church? What do we have, that is so important to us, which the unchurched don't have?" We don't necessarily have to buy into the theology of fundamentalism, but we do need to isolate the clear advantages and rewards of becoming a Christian. We, the authors, believe there is a great deal that is absent in people's lives that are not in a committed relationship with God through Jesus Christ. Each denomination, each congregation, and each individual needs to become clearer about what they have that the unchurched do not have, that is very special and unique to their faith.

Both of these polarities raise the question as to whose responsibility it is to challenge clergy and lay leaders to confront the issues raised in these two polarities and bring them to some reasonable resolution. From our perspective, if the Regional Body does not take on this challenge, other organisms within a denomination will not address it. Training in Evangelization is the responsibility of the Regional Body, if it is to become a Transformational Regional Body. A "Caretaker" Regional Body will consistently dodge these issues and assume other agencies of the Church are going to handle these issues.

A Regional Body could enter into a working relationship with a nearby denominational seminary to assist them in this task. Some might like to place the entire burden of these two polarities upon their denominational seminaries. This is unlikely to change until the Regional Body makes a firm case for the urgency of this task being accomplished in conjunction with a nearby seminary. Denominational seminaries are really not that flexible. They have a permanent building and they have somewhat permanent faculty. These two items control the major portion of any seminary's budget. A seminary cannot simply go to faculty members, say one that has a Ph.D. in the New Testament, and tell them they must now head up a course on conversion, or on prayer, or on leadership. What background would this faculty member need to have in order to produce a semester course on this subject? In retaliation, the seminary could quite easily say, "You send us transformed seminarians, and we will prepare them to be a transformational pastors. If you don't send us people who have surrendered their lives to Christ, don't expect us to convert them while they attend classes here!"

What is called for here is a collaborate relationship, whereby seminary faculty and Regional Body executives meet together to confront these issues together. A course of action could then be developed whereby the seminary will promise to do what they can to turnout transformational leaders and evangelists, and the Regional Body will agree to continue this developmental process once people are ordained and placed into congregational ministries. Once again, a Transformational Regional Body will continue to offer seminars, workshops, and individual consultations on Evangelism to clergy and lay leaders. Without this persistent effort, Regional Bodies and the congregations committed to their care will continue to decline and eventually die. Should a congregation persistently refuse to take part in such learning activities, possibly they should die as they have clearly turned their backs on the Great Commission and the Great

Commandment. How they continue to define themselves, as a Christian congregation, will be a struggle.

None of the above, however, will take place without a vision. A Regional Body without a vision will inevitably revert to a maintenance model. Regional Bodies with a vision for living the Great Commission and the Great Commandment, that has broad acceptance among clergy and congregations, will find a way of moving from stagnation and decline to vitality and growth. What is required is leadership coming from Regional Body staff. A Regional Body needs to be managed well, but it also needs visionary leadership. We are talking here about another polarity to manage well. Let's review it on a polarity map.

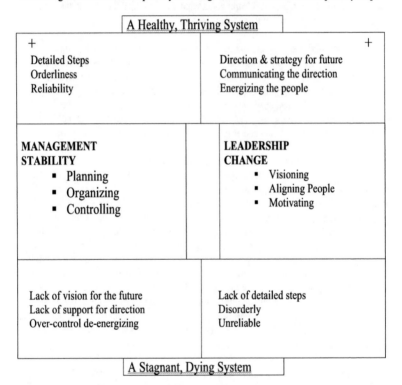

What polarity theory tells us about managing this polarity well is that Regional Bodies need both management and leadership capacities. Our experience of Regional Bodies with which we have worked, is that they are managed well, but there is a lack of leadership which involves creating an exciting vision for the system, aligning people with that vision, and moving out in risk to make the vision happen. The opposite is true of Regional Bodies that do have a vision. According to Bishop Ron Warren of Southeastern Synod, ELCA, it is an incredible experience to watch clergy and lay people grasp hold of a vision that invokes the sayings of Jesus and begin to make that vision work within their congregations.

The Diocese of Texas and its Bishop, Claude Payne, have such a vision as well. (Refer to book *Reclaiming the Great Commission* by Bishop Claude E. Payne & Hamilton Beazley). You will hear us refer frequently to this Diocese, as it is another clear example of a Transformational Regional Body. The purpose statement of this Diocese is as follows:

> *"The Diocese of Texas has a vision of being One Church, under the leadership of Jesus Christ as a 'Community of Miraculous Expectations.' It is a missionary Diocese, whose bishop is the Chief Missioner, localized in missionary outposts and missionary institutions, utilizing the historic catholic structures of classic Anglicanism, and whose purpose under the Great Commandment to love is focused on the unchurched with a goal of growing to 200,000 by the year 2005. (This diocese is currently less than half this number) This is growth beyond mere numbers toward discipleship and seeks to include all sorts and conditions of people, bringing joy to those who are reaching out and to those who are reached."*

We are struck by the notion of a Regional Body as a single missionary entity, with congregations being missionary outposts of this one body. The diocese envisions itself as a wagon wheel, with the diocesan staff and lay decision makers at the center of the wheel, providing support and resources through the spokes to the congregations that are the missionary outposts of this single entity. The entire diocese works hard at ensuring that all decisions and all support programs are centered in the Great Commission and the Great Commandment. Here is a vision that is grounded in scripture and which seeks to have all its mission outposts (congregations) manage the Inreach-----Outreach polarity well. They see themselves as a diocese that has moved from maintenance to mission. It is similar to our emphasis in this document in challenging middle judicatories to move from being a "Caretaker Regional Body" to being a "Transformational Regional Body."

For a moment, go with us on a short fantasy trip. Imagine you are part of a fast-food chain with restaurants all over a region. Rather that being a fast-food chain that is trying to make money feeding wonderfully tasting unhealthy food to people, it is a chain dedicated to providing food for the poor, possibly homeless people, or people living on the margins of society. The main menu is beans and rice, which together provide people with a whole protein diet. Add a tomato sauce which contains lots of vitamin C and you have a complete diet. The chain would serve many other combinations of food. A complete meal would cost no more than 75 cents. For that price, people could eat as much as they wanted. No child's meal would cost more than 50 cents. A family of four could eat their fill for less than $3.00 compared to paying $16.00 to $20.00 at MacDonalds or Wendy, etc. The chain would rent space in areas of low income housing, rather than purchase land and building.

The board of directors of this chain has just elected a new Chief Executive Officer. As a store manager, what would be your greatest hope for how this new CEO would begin to lead and manage this missionary effort?

Here are some ideas that occurred to us.

- The CEO would first of all make contact with all 50 store managers, listening to their ideas about how the system could be run more effectively, to provide more resources to feed more homeless and hungry people.

- As a result of this round of listening, s/he would put in place ways store managers and employees could attend seminars where they could learn from one another how to better manage their individual stores.

- Realizing that there were far more hungry people out there who could use the services of this fast food chain, the CEO put together a blue ribbon committee to work with him/her to shape a vision for how the services offered by this chain could increase by 10% each year the number of nutritious meals that would be served to poor and homeless people. After nine months of planning, all store managers and their assistants were brought together to hear and see the proposals being made, and be offered an opportunity to speak about their concerns about the plan. As a result of the dialogue that took place related to this plan, someone moved that the plan be revised to increase the output of food by 15% each year, resulting in the chain reaching an additional 75% of hungry people over a five year period. Even though this might mean establishing new stores near existing ones, store managers, rather than be threatened by a new outlet being established nearby, would celebrate the fact that so many more people in his/her area were being fed. The CEO expressed confidence in the plan and gratitude for the commitment of those representing the chain's stores.

- Whenever a certain store was having difficulty, the CEO, rather than managing these crisis situations by him/herself, had certain store managers trained as troubleshooters. They would be sent to assist the store having difficulty. In this way, the CEO was not diverted from his/her efforts to continue to establish new stores to reach hungry people in other areas of the country, plus engage funding sources to underwrite their strategic vision financially.

- As it came to the attention of this CEO that a growing number of hungry people were either legal or illegal immigrants from other countries, s/he set in motion a search for potential store managers who came from these various racial/ethnic backgrounds. Soon there were store managers who came from the same racial/ethnic background as the people being served.

- As a result of seeing how store managers were working themselves to the point of exhaustion and neglecting their families, this CEO initiated a proposal which would have all store managers have four days off each quarter, which was not counted as vacation time. In addition, s/he initiated a program for all store managers to have a three-month sabbatical every four years. One month of the leave time was to be free to visit other stores in the chain to see how they managed certain difficulties. The remaining two months were to be taken as rest and rejuvenation. Store assistants would be offered the same opportunity following the return of the store manager. This policy resulted in this chain being able to retain for longer periods of service capable, caring people.

Compare this CEO with the one that had previously managed this chain. That CEO was a good manager but had little vision for how the chain could reach out to more hungry people. This CEO was very hard working, responding personally to every crisis that occurred within certain stores. Even though the number of people being served was shrinking, no one in the system was consulted about how this trend could be reversed. Occasionally, this CEO would indirectly berate store managers for not raising the amount of revenue they were sending into the central office. Most employees at a local store level felt unappreciated, and each knew that the CEO had no idea of the local conditions under which they had to function.

If you had a choice, which of the two systems would you prefer to be a part of? The difference between the two is a simple yet profound thing called leadership. The analogies between this chain and a Regional Church Body are not that different. In a Regional Body we are about the business of feeding people who are starving spiritually. Within each Regional Church Body, there are always more spiritually hungry persons that can be reached than currently are. In addition, what might be lacking are not only an exciting vision, but also the capacity to manage a vision into reality. This is a Bishop/Executive who knows the people to whom s/he might delegate this management function so that the vision unfolds in an orderly rather than a chaotic way. Lastly, it is a Bishop/Executive who is consistently empowering other people to take hold of parts of the system and assist them to move towards greater effectiveness.

What we learn from CEOs of large, thriving corporations in North America today, is that they readily accept the challenge of moving their corporation through troubling times, and meet the challenge by inventive, creative, and courageous choices. It is this kind of leadership that needs to be at the helm of Regional Church bodies today. It is our hope that this book can offer you a blueprint of how to traverse the shoals of troubled waters and emerge stronger and healthier in the future because you demanded as much from yourself and your staff as you expect from your most committed clergy and congregational leaders.

CHAPTER 2

THE URGENCY OF GOAL SETTING FOR REGIONAL BODIES

MOVING BEYOND CRISIS MANAGEMENT

Steven Covey, in his book "Seven Habits of Highly Effective People," has a wonderful schema of how an effective manager will utilize his/her time. He diagrams this in the form of a window with four quadrants. The following is the model:

	URGENT	NON-URGENT
IMPORTANT	Being caught in the tyranny of the Urgent-Important issues of the system. Obviously, some time will need to be spent in this quadrant. However, if 100% of a leader/managers time is consumed in all the urgent and important issues, few things of lasting significance will occur.	Unless a leader/manager spends at least 20% to 30% of the time in the Important Non-Urgent issues of the system, the system will remain frozen in status quo existence. e.g. Long Range Planning -Leadership Development. -Communicating the vision -Fund Raising -Addressing destructive norms within the system
NOT **IMPORTANT**	Sometime in the frenzy of dealing with important and urgent things, a leader/manager will also get caught up in urgent but not important issues. e.g. Opening third class mail. –Attending non-essential meetings. -Getting involved in office gossip.	Hopefully, no leader/ manager will get involved in non-urgent, not important issues. -Surfing the web for no special reason.

He makes the assertion that the ineffective managers/leaders spend most of their time in the URGENT—IMPORTANT quadrant. They sometimes get compulsive and spend the rest of their time in the URGENT—NOT IMPORTANT. All managers will, of course, need to spend a significant amount of time in the URGENT---IMPORTANT quadrant. Effective managers/leaders, however, will be spending at least 20% to 30% of their time in the IMPORTANT—NOT URGENT quadrant. This has to do with such things as planning, preparation, personnel development, building team cohesion, research, strategic thinking with other staff members, leadership training, delegation, etc. When the IMPORTANT—NOT URGENT tasks are ignored, we have a type of frenzy that envelops the whole system as it responds to one crisis after another.

This same challenge is there for parish clergy. Those who, in addition to preparing and conducting worship, spend most of their time responding to crises among congregants can end up completely exhausted and ineffective. From the perspective of concerned lay leaders, little of significance is happening within the congregation. Many are completely unaware of all the urgent, important things their pastor is doing. This is due to the fact that 90% of what clergy do is invisible to 90% of lay members, 90% of the time. The clergyperson, on the other hand, feels like they must be doing a good job, else why do they find themselves so exhausted most of the time. Little effort or foresight is given to training some lay leaders to take on some of the more urgent needs of the congregation. Little effort is put into exploring ways the congregation could reach out to the unchurched within their area. In fact, the pastor is so overwhelmed managing all the crises of congregants that s/he does not have room or energy to take on additional members.

In a similar fashion, congregations and clergy within a Regional Body feel that little of significance is taking place within the regional entity, as most crisis intervention activity on the part of Regional Body staff is invisible to 90% of them 90% of the time.

What then would it take to move beyond simply managing the system and putting out fires? It really needs to begin with the development of a strategic vision which has crisis situations managed by a variety of skilled individuals, not just the regional staff, allowing the regional staff time to address more of the important, non-urgent needs of the system. The following is an example of a Middle Judicatory strategic vision that would move a Regional Body from being merely a "caretaker" entity to becoming a "transformational" one.

REGIONAL BODY STRATEGIC PLAN
POSSIBLE ISSUES TO ADDRESS

1. Committing to seek out, engage, and recruit the kind of transformational leaders needed for the 21st century church. Special attention needs to be given to recruitment of racial/ethnic minorities if the Regional Body is serious about becoming a multicultural church in a heterogeneous society.

2. To establish (three) new missions every year for the next ten years. All denominations have congregations that are in decline. The growing denominations simply are planting more new churches than others.

3. To contract to redevelop (six?) declining congregations each year by entering into a contract with the congregation at the time of a pastoral transition, promising to place a redevelopment pastor in their congregation for the next five years.

4. To work with (six?) congregations with an established pastor to turn them from decline to outreach and growth by providing the pastor and key lay leaders training seminars with follow-up coaching for a year following this training.

5. For those congregations experiencing growth in worship attendance and financial giving, to highlight, support, and celebrate their achievements and to enlist their aid in offering evangelization consultations and workshops for other congregations within the Region..

6. To develop a separate strategy for each of the four sizes of congregations within the regional body, assisting each to remain strong and vital.
   a. Commitment to family sized congregation to find them long-term pastoral care.
   b. Commitment to pastoral sized congregations to promote their growth in strength and vitality, and if possible train, support, and assist congregational leaders address the daunting task of moving them from pastoral size to program size.
   c. Commitment to program sized congregations to assist them in finding adequate staff and to establish a team ministry. To assist these clergy to focus on programs of excellence and not fall back into a pastoral way of functioning.
   d. Commitment to remain in contact with corporate sized congregations to ascertain mutually supportive ways of relating. To provide yearly Multiple Staff workshops for staff teams.

7. To engage in a superior fund-raising effort to undergird all of the above financially.

8. If a denominational seminary is located within the region, to challenge it to become relevant to the changing needs of both clergy and congregations. This may involve encouraging them to begin offering training programs for all the non-Master of Divinity personnel needed to assist the Regional Body to thrive. e.g. Begin training programs for bi-vocational clergy; development of biblical, theological and pastoral care courses that lay leaders, working full time, can enroll and complete; In developing programs for individuals to receive training online from their home computer.

9. For the Regional Body to become a prudent but skillful agency that effectively serves clergy and congregations but keeps overhead low.

ORGANIZING FOR TRANSFORMATIONAL WORK

It is the firm belief of the authors that to become a transformational regional body the personnel of that regional body, including the Executive/Bishop, will need to be spending approximately 20% to 30% of their time on transformational work. It will require a re-prioritization of where the time and resources of the regional body is spent. Later in this document we will offer you a model as to where you will find the time to do this without adding hours to your already overloaded schedule.

Given 100% of the time, energy, and resources staff currently have available to them in their Regional Body, the following is our sense of how all of that can be divided in order for you to become a transformational Regional Body.

MANAGEMENT

Approximately 30% of your personnel resources will need to go into managing the system. This will include making sure the constitution and the by-laws of your Regional Body are enforced. It will also include managing the finances of the system, maintaining a central office, finding a suitable way of relating your national body to other entities within your system, and coordinating the various committees that function within your system. Included in this category is the planning and preparation of any type of annual gathering of clergy and congregational representatives.

A function we are placing under this category is that of recruitment of effective personnel for the system. This needs to go beyond recruiting personnel for your central office. We are talking here about recruiting the best, yet most diverse group of people who will receive training at a seminary and eventually provide the kind of transformational leadership required to assist a congregation grow and thrive. We have set aside an entire chapter in this document to outline our sense of the challenge involved in this. For the most part we observe most main line denominations being passive with regards to the recruitment for ordained service within the church. We are coming out of an era of a clergy surplus, where we merely had to screen in those we felt had potential pastoral effectiveness. For whatever reasons, we are having difficulty changing this passivity and moving to aggressively asking persons with great potential to consider the ordained ministry.

PASTORAL CARE

This involves pastoral oversight of the clergy and congregations under your jurisdiction as a Regional Body. We believe approximately 15% of your staff's time and resources needs to fit under this heading.

Of primary importance in this category will be your capacity to respond to any crisis that takes place within your Regional Body. Your clergy are going to need some time and attention as they are involved in increasingly complex ministries and run into problems for which they are not equipped. In addition, some of your clergy are going to get wounded, or get themselves into some type of trouble. We should be astounded at our basic assumptions about the health and vitality of clergy. For the most part we expect that each one of them will go from being ordained through to retirement without getting sick or wounded in any way. We say we make these assumptions because there are so few resources available to clergy who become casualties of some sort. No army in the world sends people into battle without having clear plans about how the wounded are going to be managed. We as a church, however, will send men and women into battle against the principalities and powers of darkness within any congregation, and expect that none of them to get wounded, seriously demoralized, stressed beyond their capacity to cope, experience family breakup, tempted beyond their capacity to resist, or be rendered mentally and emotionally unstable. When any of them do, we treat it as a crisis, rather than having resources and personnel ready to come to their aid.

The following are the results of a confidential survey administered to clergy by Fuller Institute of Church Growth, as reported by Dr. Arch Hart of Fuller Seminary at the Care Givers Forum, held at the Glen Eyrie Conference Center, Colorado Springs, November 7-10, 1991:

- 90% of pastors work more than 46 hours per week.
- 80% believe that pastoral ministry is affecting their families negatively.
- 33% say, "Being in ministry is clearly a hazard to my family."
- 75% have reported a significant crisis due to stress at least once in their ministry.
- 50% felt unable to meet the needs of the job.
- 90% felt they were not adequately trained to cope with the ministry demands placed upon them.
- 40% report a serious conflict with a parishioner at least once a month.
- 70% of pastors do not have someone they would consider a close friend.
- 37% have been involved in inappropriate sexual behavior with someone in their church.
- 70% have a lower self-image after they've pastored than when they started.

Is it any wonder that pastors are burning out at a faster rate than ever?

There is no question your clergy are going to need some pastoral care from your Regional Body. We have some ideas of how to provide this care in such as way that a huge chunk of your staff is not consumed by these crises. Included in these ideas are seminars and workshops for church professionals that will continually challenge them theologically, biblically, strategically, and personally. Less that 40% of clergy engage in any type of continuing education involving at least a one-week seminar per year, unless their Regional Body sponsors it. When your Regional Body sponsors seminars, a much higher percentage of clergy will attend, if for no other reason than to get away from the demands of congregational ministry for a short time to be with their clergy colleagues.

Your congregations are going to need pastoral care as well. As indicated at the beginning of this document, one key reason why Regional Bodies need to remain healthy and relevant has to do with having somewhere congregations can turn when confronting a crisis of any sort. We have thousands of dysfunctional congregations within our judicatories, many of which are that way because they were severely abused or exploited by some clergy. A congregation that has been wounded by a clergyperson or two, will naturally distrust other clergy coming to serve them. Even when they succeed in calling a caring, competent clergyperson, they tend to micromanage that person, shackling them with much busywork and irrelevant activity, simply because they believe clergy cannot be trusted and need to be watched at every turn. As a result even effective ordained leaders are not given a chance to bring a congregation to greater health and growth, simply because the power people don't trust them enough to allow them to lead. It is here that the role of the Regional Body is very important. The Regional Body needs to intervene when a pastor is abusing or exploiting a congregation, as well as vice versa.

There will be times when other crises within congregations will need attention. The stress of pastoral transition will hit the top of your list followed by serious internal conflict and possibly sexual malfeasance on the part of clergy. Your Regional Body staff could become totally consumed by these three congregational difficulties alone. It is for this reason that our next section will need to have high priority in your system

TRAINING AND DELEGATION

In order for your Regional Body to have time and personnel for effect transformational work, much of what that staff is currently doing needs to be delegated to capable clergy/lay teams. We believe every Regional Body needs to be spending at least 20% of its time and energy on this task. Many of the tasks to be delegated would come under the previous category of pastoral care. Just as a congregational pastor within a growing congregation needs to delegate much of the pastoral care of members to other trained volunteers, so Regional Body Executives/Bishops need to delegate much of the crisis work with clergy and congregations to other clergy/lay teams. To ensure that everyone is confident that these teams are capable of handling these ministries, the choice of these people plus their training must have the active involvement and confidence of the Bishop/Executive.

What this involves is having your Regional Body claim as one of its primary tasks that of choosing and training capable individuals and teams to do specific tasks within the region. People can be enabled and empowered to address these clergy/congregational issues. When a Regional Body employs this approach to dealing with pastoral care issues, the entire system becomes stronger and more capable. If, for example, your Regional Body trains a cadre of conflict specialists, the clergy and lay people involved in this ministry take everything they learn and experience back to their own congregations to employ these skills and insights there. These people will gain a perspective on congregational life that they would never gain in any other way. In this way the whole system is enriched.

In the next chapter we will be spelling out a variety of consultative skills that can be developed by capable clergy and lay leaders within your Regional Body. There is no need to be overwhelmed by the variety of skill options outlined in that chapter. Even if your Regional Body has only one or two types of intervention consultants at its disposal that will at least be more than if you had none. The idea is to begin with one intervention specialty, train a cadre of skilled clergy and lay leaders in that specialty, and then begin using them on a regular basis. A common mistake we make within church systems is to train people to do a task and then never ask them to do it. When that happens, either one or two things are at play. Either the Regional Body asked the wrong people to receive the training and then fails to trust them with the task, or the staff members of the Regional Body have control needs and will not relinquish those tasks to others. It is important right up front to ask the question, "If we train the right people to consult with congregations in a crisis, will we utilize them on a regular basis?" If the answer is NO, then DO NOT TRAIN THEM IN THE FIRST PLACE! Sometimes Regional Body staff will not delegate congregational difficulties to other trained leaders in the system simply because they need to be needed. Their whole identity is tied up being the one that rides out on a white horse to confront the demons. Additionally, some simply want to be in on the juiciest problems of the system so they can have first-hand information on any scandal.

Delegating much of the crisis ministry stuff to trained people within the Regional Body will be less of a challenge when it is clear that the skills and energies of the regional staff needs to be about much more important work, namely, the revitalization of the system. It is becoming clear that Regional Bodies need to move from maintenance to mission. Little redevelopment work, or new mission work, or congregational revitalization is going to take place when the regional staff is totally consumed with putting out fires. It is no different from a pastor thinking that s/he will revitalize a congregation by allowing all of his/her time to be consumed by the needs and wants of every congregant. The polarity that needs to be managed well here is the NURTURE----TRANSFORMATION polarity. When we are spending all of our time on the nurture side of this polarity, we will inevitably sink more and more into the down-side of that pole, namely, creating co-dependent people who feel it is your job to take care of them. Few lives are changed when we spend most of our time hanging out on the nurture pole of this polarity.

To be sure, this will require changing the mindset of many people within the Regional Body who feel it is the job of regional staff to respond to their needs. Regional Bodies need to signal this change up front with all constituents. When it is part of a larger strategic vision that is shared with clergy and lay members of the Regional Body, this will be less of a problem. Members will then at least know why regional staff will not be as available as before. You can assure them that there will be an effective response to their cries for help, but it may not be coming from the regional body staff. The role of the regional staff is to recruit some of the best leaders, both clergy and lay, from within the Regional Body. These people will be receiving some of the best training available in the country. The role of the regional staff now is to train, delegate, support, and evaluate the work of these intervention specialists. Members need to come to learn that their apportionment dollars now go to pay for someone at the regional level who oversees this ministry and sees that competent help is being offered to clergy and congregations. Someone is going to need to pull together these trained specialists from time to time to have them share experiences, do case studies, and receive additional training. Someone will also have to be on the phone to follow up on these interventions to ascertain the quality of service a congregation is receiving from a trained specialist.

This in no way implies that a regional staff person will no longer consult with congregations. Some of that, of necessity, will need to continue. In fact, the first visit to a congregation that calls for assistance in some type of crisis will likely be a regional staff person. On this initial visit an assessment is made as to the type of follow-up that might prove to be most helpful. It is here that the regional staff person recommends that the congregation employ the services of a specialist in the field, whether that person be a conflict resolution specialist, a transition consultant (in the case of a pastor resigning), a sexual malfeasance team, a person with special skills in strategic planning, etc. After the congregation has worked with such a specialist for six months or more, the regional staff person may make a return visit and inquire as to what progress has been made on the issue at hand.

In the case of a serious congregational conflict, it becomes even more important for the regional staff person not to get involved in any type of resolution work. The regional staff person needs to remain as the court of last appeal. When the staff person has recommended the use of a conflict resolution specialist to work with the congregation for six months or more and that resolution work fails, the regional staff person needs to then visit the congregation again to explore other options. Possibly this time s/he needs to recommend that a judicial committee be formed to conduct interviews within the congregation and make a recommendation to the Bishop/Executive regarding the removal of a pastor or the resignation of all Vestry/Church Council members, etc. As you can see, the regional staff person continues to have oversight over that congregational dilemma, always trying to provide congregations with the resources it needs to get beyond its difficulty----all without doing the direct, hands-on work him/herself.

REGIONAL BODY AS EMBODIMENT OF THE TRADITION

This function has to do with the symbolic representation someone on your Regional Body staff needs to fulfill—at least minimally. Usually congregations and agencies want the Executive/Bishop to be present to dedicate a new wing on a building, or to acknowledge a congregation's 100th anniversary, or to install a new pastor. We would encourage you to keep this to no more than 5% of your staff's time and energy. Some Executives claim they would do little else but this if they allowed it. We encourage you to find ways to delegate this type of activity to others within the system. Here the Deans of the smaller units within your system can be effective. Generally, we don't know what to do with these people, what authority to invest in them, what function they can play beyond caring for the small group of clergy/congregations within their deanery/conference/convocation. Let them "show the flag."

We will need to place ecumenical representation within this category as well. Someone on your staff will need to speak on your behalf at certain ecumenical functions. Once again, you need to discern which of these are going to have any long-term payoff down the line. From one perspective, we are going to find ourselves needing to cooperate with other denominations to a far greater extent in the future. This will be especially true if we find ourselves more and more within a hostile environment trying to promote the work of Christ. We might avoid much duplication of ministries if we did cooperate more effectively with other denominations.

Yet sometimes these ecumenical meetings are clear time wasters. They are ill conceived and do not address anything of substance. Don't spend time with time wasters. Pick and choose the ones that will have the greatest payoff for the Reign of God here on earth.

TRANSFORMATIONAL MINISTRIES

Should you be able to keep the above-mentioned function of any regional body to the recommended percentages of time and energy, you will then have 30% of your time and resources left for transformational work. The remainder of this book is going to spell much of this out for you in greater detail. Some of the functions we see coming under this rubric are as follows:

- Engaging the key shakers and movers of your system in some strategic planning that is aimed at increasing the vitality and effectiveness of the congregations committed to your care.
- Acting as a catalyst for change in implementing this strategic vision.
- Utilizing the concept of "triage," choosing the congregations within your Regional Body that you are going to target for redevelopment. You cannot redevelop them all. Only those who have the capabilities for such change strategy are going to get your time, energy and resources. You cannot succeed if a congregation doesn't want to redevelop. Remember Jesus admonition about, "shaking the dust from your feet".
- Identifying the places where you can plant a new church. You should be thinking in terms of innovative ways to start new missions.
- Engaging in a capital funds drive which promises potential givers that every penny that is raised will go to either redeveloping existing congregations or developing new church starts, or to do evangelization training with existing clergy and congregations.
- Challenging professional church workers to embrace change and to develop those skills that will make them into transformational leaders. Invest funds in their training.

As stated earlier, the concept of TRIAGE is often frightening to church leaders. It is here that tough-minded leadership is needed. Some of your congregations are simply not going to survive over the next ten years. They should not be the ones to which we should be giving large amounts of energy. We should, first of all, identify those congregations that are strategically located, which still have financial capacity to manage a turn around, but which have been on a slow decline over the last ten years, even though they are in demographically growing areas of the region. We need to be struggling with ways we can offer them the best kind of clergy leadership in their next pastoral transition, leadership that has been proven through past experience and past records. We will spend much more time on ways you might do this in later chapters.

A kind of urgency about ministry needs to be felt in this regard. You do not have the luxury of giving everyone who asks for help whatever time you have available. Some tough decisions need to be made as to where your Regional Body is going to invest time, energy, and resources. Thinking in terms of TRIAGE is a most responsible thing to do at the present time. Congregations that will die within the next ten years should receive the least amount of time and attention. They should receive time that assists them to die with celebration and dignity. Offer these congregations a "caretaker" pastor who would give them quality palliative care until they decide to close their doors. It is this kind of tough-minded leadership that will be needed at the helm if your organization is to become a Transformational Regional Body.

QUICK SUMMARY
In short, we conceive of each Regional Body having key responsibilities in five major areas. The following is a quick summary of the function we are considering under these five headings. We state our bias up front as to how much personnel time needs to be allotted to each of these five functions if a Regional Body is to move in the direction of being a transformational entity within its denomination.

I. Management
This would involve--Recruiting effective Personnel, Finances, Conventions, Liaison with National Church, Staff Meetings, Telephone Time, Answering Mail, Congregational Meetings, Ecumenical Meetings, Enforcement of Constitution, Standards, and Out Placement.
Amount of Time Spent on this Function – 30%

II. Pastoral Care (Clergy and Congregations)
This would involve--Nurture in time of Crisis, Crisis Management, Assisting with Transitions, and Oversight of the Regional Body.
Amount of time Spent on this Function – 15%

III. Trainer/Delegater/Supporter
This would involve--Equipping and empowering clergy and lay individuals and teams to manage most of the crisis situations occurring within the Regional Body and Leadership Development.
Amount of time Spent on this Function – 20%

IV. Embodiment of the Tradition

This would involve--Symbolic Representation, Preaching/Public Speaking and Ecumenical Relations.

Amount of time Spent on this Function – 5%

V. Transformational Leadership

This would involve--Visioning and Strategic Planning for the Regional Body, Redevelopment of Congregations, Mission Starts, Challenging Clergy and Congregational Leaders and Fund Raising.

Amount of time Spent on this Function – 30%

CHAPTER 3

STRUCTURING TIME FOR REDEVELOPMENT WORK DELEGATING THE MAJORITY OF CRISIS INTERVENTION TASKS

The chart before you is a comprehensive model of the various consultative specialties that a Regional Body might offer its clergy and congregations. We call it a Cadillac model in that it contains more ministry specialties than most Regional Bodies can support. Because of this we hope you do not become overwhelmed with all the clergy/lay teams you will need to train and supervise. We firmly believe, however, that if you did train and utilize all the specialties listed here you would have significantly raised the competence of your entire Regional Body, and in addition saved yourself a huge chunk of time to engage in mission and redevelopment work within your system.

POSSIBLE INTERVENTION STRATEGIES
CREATING HEALTHIER CLERGY AND CONGREGATIONS
FOLLOWING CLERGY CAREERS
FROM RECRUITMENT TO RETIREMENT

CLERGY/LAY RESOURCE PEOPLE TRAINING PROGRAMS TO SPONSOR

RESOURCE SPECIALISTS AVAILABLE TO PERFORM A TASK ON BEHALF OF YOUR REGIONAL BODY.	TRAINING EVENTS AND COMMITTEES TO SERVE YOUR REGIONAL BODY
Silent Recruiters in Congregations----------- (Recruiting men and women for the ordained ministry)	-----------------------Recruitment Task Force
	--------------------------Screening Committee
Mentors to facilitate meetings for newly ordained clergy--------------------------------	
	---------------------------Transition Seminars Ending Well—Starting Strong, for clergy changing congregations.
Intentional Interim Pastors--------------------	
	-----------------------On-going training for Interim Pastors
Transition Companions-----------------------	
	-------------------------On-going training for Transition Companions

Call/Search Committee Consultants--------	
	--------------------------On-going training for Call/Search Consultants
Conflict Consultants---------------------------	
	----------------On-going training for Conflict Consultants
Clergy Sexual Malfeasance Teams----------	
	-----------------On-going training for Sexual Malfeasance Teams
Congregational Strategic Planning Specialists---------------------------------------	
	---------------On-going training for Strategic Planning Specialists
Out-placement Task Force-------------------- (Assisting incompetent clergy to leave ordained ministry)	--------------------Clergy Self Care Seminars
	--------------------------Sabbatical Policy for Church Professionals
Anonymous, inexpensive Therapists-------- (Clergy and their families can seek out therapeutic support without the specific knowledge of their Regional Body)	----------------------------New Visions for the Long Pastorate Seminars
	-----------Leadership Development Training Events
Clergy Wives Support Group----------------- (For Clergy Wives experiencing a Divorce)	
	----------------------Pre-retirement Seminars (Leaving ministry at the top of your game Your last years are your best years)

The chart above moves from top to bottom, with the top representing the beginning process of clergy entering this calling and the bottom represents clergy at the tail end of their active ministry. In between are most of the crisis/intervention points that can effect positive change within the lives of these clergy. What we are outlining here is two-fold:

- Consultative expertise we encourage you to develop within your Regional Body (left column).
- Training seminars that should occur periodically within your Regional Body which develop expertise within your clergy ranks, plus groups that address specific situations that your clergy and congregations will inevitably be facing (right column).

What follows is our choice of the kinds of resource persons that, with training and supervision, can relieve you of many of the pastoral needs in your Regional Body. We are talking here about the many crisis points in the lives of clergy and congregations that will inevitably land in your lap as a Regional Body staff. The process will involve one member of the staff making an initial visit to the congregation in question, listening to its problem, making an assessment of what would lead to a viable solution, and then recommending the names of one or two resource persons you have trained in that particular specialty to work with this congregation. This staff person can then monitor how things are proceeding with the resource person(s) and the congregation by an occasional telephone call. Should the congregation be helped by the use of such a consultant/resource person, you have saved one of your staff members a lot of time, which, hopefully, can be utilized in other important redevelopment work. Should things not work out well with the arrangement, the staff member will need to return for a second visit and move to a second option. Having debriefed the consultant/resource person involved, the staff member will have a much better idea as to what needs to happen next.

Here are some of our recommendations:

MENTORS FOR NEWLY ORDAINED CLERGY

Within Alban Institute's research regarding the training and development of competent clergy we discovered a real gap between seminary training and the first parish experience of ordained clergy. We have concluded that individuals do not learn how to be a parish pastor within a seminary setting. There are some very important and essential things individuals can learn in a seminary, but the role of religious authority within a congregational system involves much more than academic learning. Yes, fieldwork and clinical pastoral education, and even a yearlong internship are very helpful. However, these experiences do not completely get at what it means to assume the role of spiritual leader within a congregation. You cannot teach people how to swim by the lecture method. You can teach them some important information about swimming, but the real learning takes place when you ask people to get into the water, to put their face in it and blow air out through their nose and mouth. Learning to swim takes on a new challenge when you get some water up your nose and you start to cough, and the instructor tells you to try it again. It is only then that you confront your fears about water and how uncomfortable you feel when asked to perform certain activities in water.

In a similar fashion, we really learn how to be a pastor when we are in the role; and when people begin projecting all their stuff onto us, then we learn what this role is all about. There is this misconception that we "learn from experience." Usually this is not the case. We only learn from experiences that we reflect upon in disciplined ways.

Alban Institute has a book entitled "*Beyond the Boundary*" in which we explore the variety of approaches different denominations have taken to assist newly ordained clergy gain competence in their new role. We have concluded that there is a significant role for the Regional Body to play in the development of competent clergy. We need to stop playing the game of "kick the seminary" when we discover people coming out of it lacking in certain skills. Seminaries are doing the best they can with the resources they possess, and with the people we send to them in the first place. As the saying goes, "you can't make a silk purse out of a sow's ear." The people coming out of seminary will by and large reflect the type of people we are sending to the seminary in the first place. But that is another matter that will be addressed in another part of this document.

Our program of choice in our research on newly ordained clergy provides them with seasoned mentors who will work with them in the opening years of ordained ministry. These mentors may work with these newly ordained people individually, or clustered together with three to six other newly ordained people within a certain geographic area. The mentor facilitates their meeting bi-weekly or monthly to offer them space to share how they are experiencing this new role and explore alternative ways of approaching this role. In the process they will gain perspective on this new role by both sharing and hearing how others are experiencing it. In this case the mentor is not necessarily an answer person. S/he is there to facilitate the discussion and allow those participating to benefit from a discussion of what they seem to be experiencing. This is a fairly significant investment of time on the part of these seasoned mentors. In our research on this approach, we have discovered that some seasoned clergy, nearing the end of their career in ministry, feel a sense of call to mentor those entering the ministry. In many cases this mentoring role gives deep meaning to their lives. We should, however, be thinking in terms of the kind of preventive maintenance we are doing when we focus some energy on these newly ordained people. We will be able to shape the kind of approach they take to this new role. It may save us from a ton of problems down the line because we put into place a structure that can significantly raise the competence of these people. Once again, rather than going crazy putting out fires within your Regional Body, you are doing something to stop those fires being set in the first place.

TRANSITION COMPANIONS

The term, "TRANSITION COMPANION," may be new to you. That is because it has just been developed; growing out of some research Roy Oswald was able to do with six Episcopal Dioceses and five Lutheran Synods (ELCA) on the eastern seaboard. This research, plus the field-testing that accompanied it, is just coming to completion in 2001. A comprehensive manual directed at congregational transition teams, plus transition companions, is currently being written and should be in print in early 2002. The three-year research projected included two years of field-testing this new class of consultants. (In the middle of our process we began using the word "Companion," rather than "Consultant," as it more closely described the role of these training resource people to clergy and congregations in transition.)

Some twenty-five years ago, Roy began his ministry with Alban Institute doing research on clergy transitions. Out of this research came printed resources and seminars for training clergy how to more effectively leave one congregation and start up well in a new congregation. Those printed resources and training seminars have been a major contribution to available resources for clergy and Regional Bodies. It wasn't until two people, the Rev. Bud Holland, Deployment Officer for the Diocese of Pennsylvania and the Rev. Jim Ransom, Deployment Offices for the Diocese of Maryland, asked Roy to develop a manual for assisting clergy and congregations to begin ministry together at the front end of a new ministry, that this unique approach was developed. What they sensed was missing was the congregational component to these clergy transitions. As we needed money to complete the research on this new specialty, we enlisted three Lutheran Synods and three additional Dioceses. In order to engage congregations more deeply in this transition process, we encouraged the use of a "Transition Task Force," made up of members of the congregation appointed by their Vestries/Councils. These Transition Task Forces are to oversee the whole transition a congregation goes through when they lose their Pastor, right through to the end of the first year of new pastorates. We then trained "Transition Companions" (consultants) who would work with these Transition Task Forces over the course of approximately three years. We have just now completed our second year of field-testing the use of such Transition Companions who have been working with one congregation's Transition Task Force. The comprehensive resource manual containing a great variety of resource pieces for Transition Task Forces and Transition Companions is entitled, *"Beginning Ministry Together...A Resource for Congregations Experiencing a Pastoral Transition."* Rather than focusing attention only on the wiener (new pastor) we now place attention to the whole hot dog (new pastor and congregation) coming together and beginning ministry on the same page.

As we see it, these teams assist congregations effectively traverse the variety of transitions a congregation goes through from the resignation of a former pastor to the establishment of an effective new pastor. There are a number of stages that need to be handled well. These can be summed up in this following chart:

CLERGY/CONGREGATION TRANSITION STAGES

Call to a new congregation or retirement----	---------Announcement to the Congregation
Appointment of a Transition Task Force----	-----------Transition Companion meets with Transition Task Force
Exit interview of resigned Pastor-------------	
	-----------Coaching resigned Pastor as to how to close well
Assisting congregation to do its closure work with this Pastor----------------------	
	-----------Mini self study to ascertain issues to be dealt with by Interim Pastor
Three way contract with the called/appointed Interim Pastor--------------- (Governing Board, the Regional Body and the Interim Pastor)	--Appointment of a Search/Call Committee

Congregational Self Study completed-------	
	---Congregational Profile checked with listening groups or entire congregation
Job Profile developed from Self Study------	
	-----Initial screening of possible candidates
Interview training followed by interviews with potential candidates---------------------	
	-----On site visits to congregational finalists
Finalist(s) introduced to the governing board---	
Interim Pastor closes with congregation----	
	-----------------------Welcome of new Pastor
New Pastor begins serving-------------------- (Start-Up dynamics begin)	
	----Quarterly evaluations on how the transition is unfolding
First major conflict-----------------------------	
	-----------------------Honeymoon period ends
First and biggest change made by new Pastor---	
	-------------First year anniversary celebrated
Transition Task Force terminated------------	

Given this general overview of a Pastoral Transition supported and guided by a Transition Task Force and a Transition Companion, we have discovered several key areas where a transition may flounder.

- The Pastor and Congregation not closing well with each other. This will leave one or both with unresolved feelings that can poison a new start-up.

- There is no firm contract with the called Interim Pastor. This usually results in the Interim Pastor doing his/her thing. Usually there are some important tasks that an Interim Pastor needs to do to prepare the way for a newly called Pastor. When these things are not done, it seriously jeopardizes the ministry of the new in-coming Pastor, if s/he has to do those things. For example, if the congregation has a member who has been employed by the congregation such as a secretary, musician, children's worker, etc and this person is ineffective at their work; it is clearly hazardous for a new in-coming Pastor to terminate this person. He/she would be starting out this new ministry with a big stain on his/her garments. Much better to have this be accomplished by the Interim Pastor who does not need to leave the congregation as a popular person.

Sometimes it is not clear what important things need to take place to make way for an effective new pastorate, hence the need for a "Mini-Self Study," to determine the agenda for the Interim Pastor's Contract. If the Regional Body is not that familiar with the congregation, and the Council/Vestry does not want to touch controversy with a ten foot pole, it is usually the Interim Pastor who comes in and is given three months to determine what are the three to five key things that need to happen in this congregation if the new Pastor is to have a chance at starting well. Following this mini-study, the Council/Vestry---the Regional Body Executive---and the Interim Pastor agree on the specifics of what the Interim Pastor is to facilitate in his/her tenure. The work of this Interim is periodically evaluated to see if, in fact, these things are being accomplished.

The Transition Committee of the congregation is to give oversight to the development of such a contract, plus see to it that quarterly evaluations are conducted on this ministry. This is an important dimension of this transition time. The Governing Board may not even think it important, or that such tasks ought to be done by the new pastor. The Transition Committee should not buy this and should press the Governing Board, the Interim Minister, and the Regional Body to get on with this task.

- The Chief Decision Making Body does a poor job at appointing the right kind of Search/Call Committee. This group needs to be a good cross section of the congregation, representing various age groups and the various political entities within the congregation. This is a tough assignment when we also recommend that the Search/Call Committee not be too large----six persons being a recommended number.

- The Search/Call Committee does not have enough consultative help to assist it tackle a complex task. These are usually people who have never done this job before and will likely never do it again, yet they are to make the most important decision this congregation is going to make in ten years.

It is our recommendation that an outside consultant meet with this group every time it meets. What are needed sometimes on such a committee are process skills. People representing various political factions within a congregation can end up being quite dysfunctional without a skilled process person constantly calling them to reflect on how they are working together, and getting them to evaluate regularly on their process.

If the congregation has hired a Transition Companion that has time for this type of consultative work, so much the better. Should the Transition Companion feel s/he does not have the time to meet regularly with this group, s/he should recommend that the Council/Vestry hire such a person to work with the Search/Call Committee. Once again, unless these people are paid, your most qualified people will not continue long in offering this service. Some congregations will say they can't afford such a consultant. In one sense, they really can't afford not to hire such a person. Should they end up recommending the wrong person be called to Pastor this congregation, the congregation will pay dearly in the many years ahead as they struggle with a misfit as their Pastor.

- The newly called Pastor does not enter well and shoots him/herself in the foot several times within the first 12 months of this new Pastorate. Our early research at Alban on this subject indicates that the first 12 months of a new Pastorate is going to determine the entire ministry of this person in that congregation. In capsule form, our recommendations are that the new pastor restricts him/herself to being a Lover and a Historian for the first nine to twelve months of this new pastorate. They should refrain from using up their "poker chips" on cosmetic or peripheral issues. It is important for them to take the first nine to twelve months in this new pastorate to get to know the key players in a congregation, develop a solid relationship with them, and use this time to determine what is the most important change that needs to take place in this congregation if it is to move strongly in the direction of greater health.

It is our conviction that the above mentioned five land mines will be avoided most effectively when there is a Transition Companion working with a Transition Committee within the congregation.

Should your Regional Body not want to move in this direction, we would recommend that you develop a cadre of skilled people, each with a differing specialty to manage the above mention booby traps.

- **Closure Consultants.** These are specialists who only deal with assisting clergy and congregations to do a better job of terminating their relationship well.

- **Search/Call Committee Consultants.** Their specialty would be in working solely with the Search/Call Committee. They will have skills in assisting a congregation to do a quality self study and in helping the committee turn this into an accurate job profile. They will assist in training committee members in interview techniques and in recording their evaluations of each interviewed candidate in a disciplined fashion. Most importantly, they will be an effective process observer with skills in assisting this committee reflect frequently on the way they are working together.

- **Pastoral Start-Up Coaches.** These are seasoned clergy who know only too clearly how easy it is to get off on the wrong foot with a new congregation. Mentors/Coaches meet frequently with the new Pastor in the first 12 months of this new Pastorate so this individual begins to slowly build a solid foundation upon which to build an effective long pastorate.

Some research has been completed which details what can happen when there is a mismatch, that is, the search/call committee recommended the wrong person to the congregation, and the congregation or governing board ended up hiring them. The cost to both the congregation and to these clergy is devastating. Some of these clergy end up leaving the ordained ministry after such an experience, even though they have had successful pastorates prior to this call. It is worth your while to read through the following study and its cost to the church.

INEFFECTIVE TRANSITIONS
AND THE COST TO CLERGY, CONGREGATIONS, AND THE LARGER CHURCH.

In a recent Lilly Endowment Funded study conducted for the Divinity School at Duke University under the title of the Pastoral Leadership Project, data was collected on clergy who were forced out of their congregations. Of particular interest to Dr. Allen Klaas, President of Mission Growth Ministries, were clergy who not only were forced out of their congregations, but they ended up leaving the ordained ministry as well. As Dr. Klaas researched this phenomenon within the Lutheran Church Missouri Synod, he found that:

"Half of the issues that caused the departures from parish ministry were a mismatch of pastor and congregation before the new pastor arrived. We found that in 35% of the cases, the congregation was conflicted before the pastor arrived, and 25% of the time the congregation had a small group of people who demanded getting their way. In only 25% of the departures was personal misconduct the issue.

We had the impression that a large portion of the misconduct had roots in the mismatch issue. In only 17% of the cases had the pastor changed to a doctrinal position so different from the denomination that the pastor felt compelled to withdraw.

A significant observation about the reasons for leaving was that in at least 75% of the cases the issues that appeared to cause the loss of a parish pastor from ministry could have been prevented.

The dwindling supply of parish pastors is an issue for most denominations. Interviews were conducted with judicatory officials in eight other large denominations. In addition to the LCMS, clergy shortages were reported in the Episcopal Church, Presbyterian Church/USA, Roman Catholic, and portions of the United Methodist Church. The Evangelical Lutheran Church in America and the United Church of Christ judicatory leaders expect a clergy shortage in the coming 10 – 15 years.

A preventable loss of parish pastors is a significant financial stewardship issue for all mainline Protestant denominations and the Roman Catholic Church. In the LCMS, replacing a pastor who leaves ministry with a new seminary graduate costs the denomination approximately $50,000 (including both capital costs and operating expenses). In the LCMS, it will cost over $85,000,000 to replace the 1,775 parish pastors who retired prematurely between 1987 and 1997

More importantly, the lives of men and women, and their children are being destroyed. Interviews of former pastors and spouses revealed heartbreaking story after story of disillusion, despair, and destruction. If ways can be found to reduce the number of such instances by even as little as 25% to 50%, the savings in human and financial resources would be substantial. Most important is the possibility of reducing the amount of heartache inflicted on the lives of pastors and their families."

This research delved into the lives of 60 clergy and congregations where a forced termination also resulted in the pastor leaving the ordained ministry. The number of congregations and their denominations were as follows:

6   Assemblies of God
1   Disciples of Christ
5   Episcopal
4   Lutheran Church Missouri Synod
3   Nazarene
19 Presbyterian
2   Reformed Church in America
14 United Church of Christ

Those doing research in this study asked Regional Body executives if they thought they had given these fired pastors and these congregations less than normal attention during the search process. These judicatory representatives indicated that in 96% of these cases, the standard process used by the denomination was used. In only 2% of the cases did they indicate that the process was hurried, rushed, or very fast. The remaining 2% indicated that this was a breakaway congregation involving one of the pastors. Virtually none of these forced out situations can be attributed to not following the call process used in the denomination. Based on our own research in the "Beginning Ministry Together," research, we have concluded that congregations need more assistance during the call process that they are currently receiving from their Regional Body. It is one of the key reasons we are recommending the use of Transition Companions when a congregation enters a pastoral transition. If we desire more effective transitions we cannot keep doing things the same way yet expect different results.

The study indicates that a significant number of these pastoral terminations were the result of a poor match between pastor and congregation. When asked the question, "How long before the difficulty started, 39% cited immediately or within a few months. 35% cited a year or two. When asked for the principle reasons for leaving, 32% cited a mismatch from the beginning.

To quote the study, "almost all of the pastors and lay leaders indicated something to the effect that "in hindsight the real problem was a different understanding of being a pastor/congregation. Almost none of these differences were caused by theological or doctrinal differences. Virtually all of them were one of three differences in style. Often these style differences meant "differences from the beloved pastor" in the congregation's history.

1. Different personal style.   Some examples are outgoing versus introverted, administrative versus personal, and enthused versus reserved.
2. Different ministry style. Some examples involve frequency and content of visiting members, approach to content of preaching, or methods of conducting worship.
3. Different ministry focus. These are issues of style of ministry related to the difference between Great Commission focus and maintenance of the memory of the past.

Those who wrote up the findings of this study had this to say about the immediate onset of problems: "We were surprised, indeed shocked, to discover that large minorities of the problems that directly let to the pastor being forced out started immediately upon arrival. Indeed, some were well in place before the pastor's first day of work in the congregation. Sometimes that meant a few powerful people were opposed to the pastor being called in the first place and were dedicated to seeing the pastor forced out. At other times the style of ministry or the personality type of the new pastor were substantially different from what the members had experienced in the past and were expecting in the future.

All of this above continue to point to the Regional Body offering more consultative assistance to search/call committees as they assess their congregation's needs and the type of clergy who will do well in their congregation. This is consultative assistance that needs to come from other sources than the Regional Body staff. In most Regional Bodies, the number of congregations seeking pastors is so large that, at best, the Regional Body staff is able to make a few initial visit to the congregation, and then hand off to a TRANSITION COMPANION the major job of working with the congregation and the search/call committee so that the match between called pastor and congregation is a good one. In the case of severely troubled situations, it could be the Transition Companion who guides the congregation into a contract with an Intentional Interim Pastor that directly addresses the dysfunction of the congregation. It is then the role of the Transition Companion, working with the Transition Task Force, which conducts quarterly reviews with the Interim Pastor to ensure that the Interim is in fact addressing the issues stated in his/her working contract.

One hypothesis for these clergy being forced out of these congregations is that they were incompetent clergy to begin with. The study indicates that this was not the case. When asked, "how long ago was the pastor ordained?" the following answers ensued:

    5% five years or less
    21% Six to fifteen years ago
    38% Sixteen to twenty-five years ago
    36% Twenty-six or more years ago.

According to those conducting this research, they were amazed to observe that the concentration of these problem instances involved experienced pastors. Most of these clergy came from healthy ministries and floundered in the new location almost immediately. This is a critical finding about the call process that the methods of the search effort would result in immediate failure. As a result, pastors with an extensive history of long-term and successful pastorates came to conflicted congregations and had their ministry career brutalized and destroyed.

When the question was asked, "What role did the judicatory play in the call process?" the following answers ensued:

16% Assigned or strongly recommended the pastor to the church

30% Interviewed the pastor

40% Processed church and clergy forms and trained or guided in procedures

14% Not involved at all.

This would seem to indicate that these congregations were offer minimal guidance in their search/call process. From our perspective, Regional Bodies do not have the time to devote more energy to search/call committees. All the indicators in this study seem to point to offering congregations trained facilitators who can devote significant amounts of time to these congregations in search of a new pastor. "Time and time again, the clergy involved, identified aspects of their predicament that were known, but not disclosed to them before accepting the call." In such situations, we really do need to raise the question of the ethics of allowing a pastor to step into such a deadly trap.

This study raises some important questions regarding the use of Interim Pastors. As in our research, this research project also had a mixed review for the functioning of Interim Pastors. Question 48 asked, "If the immediate predecessor was an "interim," how did it go?

33% Yes, and it went well

67% Yes, and problems were not addressed

This re-enforces what we say in other parts of this book, namely that Regional Bodies need to do a much better job of searching out competent Interim pastors who have the capacity to address the tough issues in a troubled congregation. Too many Interim pastors do not possess either the skill or the stomach to address the conflict issues in congregations such as these. Often Interim clergy choose this role because of convenience (e.g. their spouse is located nearby and will not or can not move) or because they can't get a call elsewhere, or at least a call to their liking. For a good majority of Interims, this pastoral role is merely a stopgap role with little commitment to doing the tough work needed from Intentional Interim Clergy. To quote this study, "Sometimes the congregation experienced an unskilled interim who achieved none of the steps the new pastor assumed happened because the term "interim" was used. Some troubled churches did not realize that the best efforts of a competent, skilled "interim" had not been effective. In those situations, the new pastor was about to become the "unintentional interim."

In no way are we implying that Interim Pastors should not be used with congregations experiencing a pastoral transition. Instead, we would put the onus on the Regional Body and the governing board of the congregation to clearly identify what important tasks needed to be addressed by the hired Interim. We then recommend that either the Transition Task Force or the governing board of the congregation do quarterly evaluations to see to it that the Interim is in fact working on the issues stated in their contract.

Another issue related to the search/call process of congregations seeking a new pastor has to do with the internal focus of these "troubled" congregations. They may have given lip service to wanting to grow numerically, but are not at all committed to making the necessary changes within their congregation's life that would encourage growth. "Virtually all of the congregations in this data who forced their pastor out had a ministry focused almost exclusively on taking care of themselves. Almost none were deeply engaged in achieving the Great Commission on their local mission field.

Some of these congregations professed to be seeking a pastor who would grow the church. However, when the pastor they called to achieve that purpose began to introduce methods and activities needed, the members also discovered that they:

1. Did not actually want more people in the church
2. Did not want people who were not identical to themselves
3. Did not want to give up control, as they became the minority contingent in a growing church.
4. Did not want to add the new things needed in current times to reach new people.

Other churches had call committees made up of members who truly were committed to the Great Commission and eager for clergy leadership to help the church move in that direction. After the pastor started to implement the things they asked for, it was discovered that:

1. The call committee did not represent the opinion of a few powerful members.
2. The few powerful members were not interested in the Great Commission.
3. The congregation would continue to allow itself to be dominated by a few strong-willed people."

When a Regional Body, as it works through Transition Companions, hears that a congregation is interested in outreach in its search profile, yet that congregation has not, in any way, engaged in outreach activities prior to this search, a red flag should immediately appear. This systemic issue is more of an alert to everyone, including the congregation, that churches with no record or even attempts at outreach probably do not understand what comes with outreach. Pastors and judicatory personnel should not simply accept the word of the congregation description document or search committee that they are interested in numerical growth.

Outreach as a new direction should be accompanied by frank discussion that attracting new people means new forms of ministry and control within the congregation. Should new members begin becoming active in such a congregation, they will inevitably change the nature of that congregation. Who of us would want to join a congregation and not have congregation be open to our creative energies? This means having this frank discussion with the "power people" of a congregation. These may not be in a leadership role at the present, but most members know that if the few power people are not for an idea, it will never fly within the congregation. In realistic terms, the implications of outreach needs to be spelled out to these people, and their support of those changes within the congregation's life needs to be solicited. Once again, this type of discussion could be facilitated by a congregational Transition Task Force, which has the on-going support of a paid Transition Companion.

Our thanks to Alan Klaas and the Divinity School at Duke University for the work and insights provided in the study, *"When Pastors Are Forced Out"*. Major thanks should also go to the Lilly Endowment for funding this study. The research confirms our notion that Regional Bodies could be much more pro-active in preventing some of these pastoral disasters from taking place. It affirms the need for a cadre of skilled clergy and lay leaders within a Regional Body to become a resource to clergy and congregation's in transition. It is a sharp reminder of how things can go bad when congregations do not have the resources available to them so they can make wise choices in selecting new pastoral leadership.

INTERIM PASTORS

We wish that every regional body would have on hand a cadre of competent intentional Interim Pastors. We have come to see the significant contribution people with this talent and mission can make in moving congregations towards greater health. There are some things an Interim Pastor can do within an interim period that will pave the way for a smooth entry of the incoming pastor. We are talking here about the need to make tough decisions, which will inevitably upset some congregants. The advantage of being an Interim Pastor is that he/she can do some unpopular things. Much better that congregants be mad at the Interim Pastor than being mad at the new pastor. It is for this reason that we recommend that Regional Bodies employ tough minded, intentional Interim Pastors to intervene in their most important congregations.

We make a clear distinction between what we call "caretaker" Interims and Intentional Interim Specialists.

Not every congregation needs an Intentional Interim Specialist during the period between called pastors. In fact, we would identify clearly those situations that call for such an Intentional Interim. All the rest can have a loving, caretaking Interim who simply keeps the place humming until the newly called pastor arrives. The following are some of the situations we think call for an Intentional Interim:
- Following a pastoral impropriety, sexual misconduct being the most severe.
- When a major conflict has polarized a congregation
- Following a long pastorate (10 years or more)

- When a congregations need to maintain momentum while on a search
- When a congregation needs to be brought up to its potential
- When the environment around the congregation is shifting radically
- When a congregation needs to confront some serious issues before calling another pastor, for example, whether to merge with another congregation, or to relocate and take on mission status, or consider closing its door and disbanding.

There are some things an Intentional Interim can do which would be suicide for a newly called pastor to do. For example, introducing a new prayer book or hymnal that the former pastor failed to do or having a dysfunctional lay leader dominate the Governing Board. Sometimes the Interim needs to shake the congregation into doing a significant stewardship campaign to get giving up to par, or to get involved in some significant renovation work because the place really looks run down and they have become complacent about it. Caretaker-type Interims will not touch these issues with a ten-foot pole. They just want to come in to do their thing and be liked by everyone.

This is where we recommend that a specific contract be drawn up as to what is to take place during this interim period. A representative of the Regional Body needs to be in on that contract formation. It is from the perspective of the middle judiciary that a congregation can be challenged to do some significant but tough tasks during the interim period. The Intentional Interim is called to execute those specific tasks called for in the contract. A middle judiciary person then should meet with the Interim and the governing body to evaluate the extent to which those things were actually being accomplished.

We have discovered that most middle judicatories have Interim Pastors available to them, but they are not always comfortable with those who have self-selected themselves to take on this role. In some cases a pastor decides to become an Interim Pastor because s/he could not get a call elsewhere. Many of the clergy wanting to do interim work are already retired and don't want to work full time, or work that hard. Some would call themselves Intentional Interim Specialist because they have taken the training, but Executives/Bishops are not that confident of their skills.

It is best to identify those clergy who would really be good at this type of work and challenge them to consider this shift in call. This would entail the regional body assuring them that there would be some safety net available should they be without a call for any length of time. We know of some middle judicatories that have called clergy to this role and placed them on their staff. They usually find that these people pretty much support themselves financially as there are always more congregations that need an Intentional Interim Specialist than the specialists that are available.

For clergy who specialize in Interim work we recommend that they buy a house that is central to the region, or is within a major metropolitan area and then commute to congregations within approximately a 100-mile radius from their home. In the cases where a congregation is much further out making a commute difficult, then an arrangement can be made to have the Interim Specialist stay in an apartment supplied by the congregation, spending four or five days on site, with at least two days at home with family. Over time, it is simply too stressful moving to a new congregation every 12 to 18 months. Single clergy may be able to manage this, but clergy with a family will, over time, find this simply too disruptive of family life to be moving that often.

In short, there are some things a Regional Body can do to affirm the work of Interim Specialists and particularly support those they want to see in this work. This may mean having a cadre of Interim Specialists who meet regularly with a staff person from the region, who do case studies to improve the quality of their work. Once again, as a Regional Body, you will save yourself a bundle of problems down the line when quality Interim work takes place between called pastors.

CONFLICT RESOLUTION CONSULTANTS

It is our prediction that we are going to encounter more and more congregational conflict the further we move into the 21st century. It is clear that the stress levels of individuals within our culture are steadily rising with more and more pressure being placed on people within the corporate world. These people are going to bring their stress to their church and create more stress for their clergy. In addition, as congregations become more and more fractionalized over ways to remain relevant to the changing needs of each new generation, we will witness more church fights over whose needs this church is going to meet over the long haul.

Congregational fights can be mean and ugly. The conflicts that ensue when people feel their cause is righteous and that God is on their side, can be far worse than those in the corporate world. Often the pastor is caught in the middle, but eventually, will be drawn into the conflict whether s/he wants to or not. Having a competent, outside consultant who comes in to hear everyone's story, and to make an assessment with some recommendations is a gift, especially when the congregation buys into the recommendations and has the consultant stay around long enough to help make them work. It is a classic Alban approach, and there are far too many church fights for Alban Institute plus all other para-church organizations to manage.

We recommend that you locate some people, both clergy and lay, who feel called to this type of ministry, and who have the strength for it. Offer them some of the best training you can find. Speed Leas, senior consultant at the Alban Institute, is the best in the world at this type of training. Speed has managed more church fights that anyone else in the world. Have him train your cadre of potential consultants over the course of several sessions. Then begin referring them to the congregations that come knocking at your door for help because they are embroiled in a church fight.

This group of Conflict Consultants will need to meet together regularly and offer one another support and further development. Experienced conflict consultants claim they learn more about their craft when they are able to do case studies with other consultants doing similar work. Someone from the staff will want to sit in on those meetings to offer support and further training. They will also want to be updated as to what is transpiring within certain congregations regarding their current conflicts.

SEXUAL MALFEASANCE TEAMS

When word comes to your Regional Body that Rev. so-and-so has been accused of acting out sexually with a congregant, you should be so lucky as to have in place a SEXUAL MALFEASANCE TEAM. These teams are usually made up of six people who work in pairs—two going to visit the victim immediately, two going to minister to the accused pastor and his/her family, and two beginning work with members of the congregation. The team members need to stay in close communication with one another and keep each other informed about what is transpiring in their area of this work.

One of the reasons victims sue their clergy, their church, and their denomination is to try to get someone to hear their side of the story when they are being ignored or avoided. They are avoided because no one knows what to do with them. Often they are doubly victimized because it is generally very lovable pastors who find themselves engaged in inappropriate sexual behavior, and the remaining members are just furious with the victim because they are having their beloved pastor thrown out of the church.

Some specialized training for these teams is available. These days most middle judicatories have been put through the wringer on such sexual malfeasance situations. It is something that can tie up a staff for months if not years. It is best to have SEXUAL MALFEASANCE TEAMS trained and ready to move in when the first word of accusation surfaces. When a potential victim is willing to sign a paper outlining his/her accusations, the team moves into action. The pastor is placed on temporary leave of absence until this accusation can be investigated. There have been cases where the pastor has been vindicated in such a process, the accusations being false or inaccurate, and the proposed victim having some type of grudge against the pastor, which took this form of punitive action. In short order, a competent team will be able to report to your regional body Executive/Bishop with recommendations.

OUTPLACEMENT TASK FORCE

There are times when it is appropriate to tell certain clergy that they are not well suited for the ordained ministry. They have been failures in the last three congregations they tried to pastor. They have been unhappy throughout most of their ministries. In these cases it is best to take the surgeon's knife, and cut deep and fast.

Any regional body is going to have mixed feelings about asking someone to withdraw from the ordained ministry. The Executive/Bishop would feel much better about making such a recommendation, if s/he knew that there was a group of people who would stay with this person through their transition out of parish ministry into some other line of work. This OUTPLACEMENT TASK FORCE is not a group of people who would substitute for the assessment by a Career Center. Rather, it will guide this individual into the kind of assistance that is both helpful and affordable. This Task Force will also stay with this person throughout this transition until he/she is gainfully employed in another field.

Most often this task force assists the individual to work through some of their theological and psychological difficulties about withdrawing from the ordained ministry. Some may have entered the ordained ministry for all the wrong reasons, such as wanting to please a parent, etc. Someone or some group needs to hear this person out and help them feel good about themselves and good about the choice to leave the ordained ministry. Persons to whom the church offers this kind of assistance as they are leaving the ministry, often find these people becoming active lay leaders in some other congregation. On the other hand, when we simply drop these people over the cliff and tell them to cope as best they can, we end up with bitter people who do a lot of bad mouthing of the Church. We don't need that kind of negative publicity.

SILENT RECRUITERS

We will have much more to say about this role when we talk about going after the brightest and best people to challenge them to think about a vocation in the ordained ministry. These SILENT RECRUITERS are lay people who have been identified within certain congregations, who have their eyes constantly scanning the horizon for individuals, mostly young people, who would make great transformational leaders within the ordained ministry. They are called SILENT RECRUITERS in that no one knows that they have been assigned this task. They simply talk to people informally, challenging them to consider the ordained ministry. With young people, they will write them the occasional letter when they go off to college, simply asking them to pray for clarity about this potential vocation.

We are going to be in desperate shape over the next decade unless we begin now to do a better job at recruiting competent leaders for the ordained ministry. This effort is worth pulling together these SILENT RECRUITERS occasionally, commending them for their work, and asking them to be people of prayer for this aspect of the Church's life.

NATURAL CHURCH GROWTH CONSULTANTS

Most recently we have been impressed with some training that is available in Chicago (St. Charles, Illinois) that has some great possibilities for assisting congregations to raise their level of vitality and their ability to grow numerically. It is based on the research of Dr. Christian Schwartz who began his research in Germany and has research data backing his findings involving 4700 congregations in a dozen countries, the USA being one of them. Schwartz asserts that there are natural forces within a congregation that propel it to change and grow. These need to be unleashed by some intentional work on the part of congregational leaders. Having put forward this assertion, he then goes on to identify eight characteristics that need to be strong in a congregation if it is to thrive and grow. He has developed a questionnaire that, if taken by 30 members of a congregation, will test a congregation's health in each of these eight areas.

Once a congregation has taken the survey, the results will indicate which of these eight areas scores the lowest. His research backs the fact that if a congregation puts forth some effort to improve just one area of congregational life, they will be taking a significant step towards health and growth. The term, "Natural Church Growth" refers to the fact that a congregation already is strong in some of these eight characteristics, and with the improvement in just one of these areas will naturally lead to greater vitality and growth.

The eight characteristics are:

- EMPOWERING LEADERSHIP
- PASSIONATE SPIRITUALITY
- GIFT ORIENTED MINISTRY
- FINANCIAL STRUCTURE
- INSPIRING WORSHIP
- HOLISTIC SMALL GROUPS
- NEED ORIENTED EVANGELISM
- LOVING RELATIONSHIPS

The training to become a consultant using this material is not cheap, but the material in terms of books, audiotapes, videos, computer PowerPoint presentations, and computer programs make it well worth the price. The two days of training costs $750.00 plus room and meals. Three Alban Senior Consultants now utilize this material in their consulting practice, Alice Mann, Ed White, and Roy Oswald. It is a resource on church growth that easily fits the theology and practice of mainline denominations.

Your Regional Body would do well to have, among other consultative resources for congregations, a few who specialize in this material. It has the potential of focusing the energy of a congregation on improving just one dimension of its life and feels the impact this is having on their congregation as they improve on just one of these eight characteristics. Natural Church Growth uses the analogy of staves on a barrel. If one can raise the lowest stave on a barrel, that barrel will have the capacity to hold more water.

PERCEPT OR VISIONS/DECISIONS SPECIALISTS (Demographic Analysis Specialists)

Assisting a congregation to come to terms with its environment can be one of the more important interventions that can assist a congregation to seize an opportunity that is waiting for them in their immediate neighborhood. The above two mentioned companies

(Percept and Visions/Decisions) specialize in giving congregations information about its changing environment that, more than likely, has not caught their awareness.

There is almost no substitute for the rich information that can come to a congregation when it subscribes to one of these companies, asking for a demographic analysis on any segment of their neighborhood that it considers its field of ministry. The congregation can either use zip codes to identify the neighborhood it wished to understand more deeply, or it can specify, for example, information on a five-mile radius around its building. In either case, it will gain data on who is moving into their neighborhood, the number of people in various age groups, the racial/ethnic minorities by group, the income levels of these people, their spending patterns, what they are looking for in terms of spiritual guidance, their most favorable way of being contacted, etc. There is no question in our minds that a congregation will be in for a surprise when they receive such a demographic report.

What is often helpful is having someone who has worked with such a report from another congregation to guide them as to how to make the best use of such information. There should be no strategic plan developed within a congregation that does not first consult this body of data.

Several mainline denominations have bought into either one of these two companies, and may have this data available for its Regional Bodies. With some denominations, this information is supplied free of charge to congregations within a Regional Body. With others, congregations or Regional Bodies are able to obtain this data at a reduced cost. Should your Regional Body be one that takes initiative in planting new missions, this data is a must. There is no secular retail chain that does not have similar information available to it as it plants new stores or outlets. Percept or Visions/Decisions simply translates this information for use by religious entities, mainly congregations and Regional Bodies. To contact either one of the organizations their telephone numbers are:
Percept: 1- 800- 442- 6277   Visions/Decisions: 1- 800- 524- 1445

STRATEGIC PLANNING SPECIALISTS

"Without a vision, the people perish," The Book of Ecclesiastes states that simply and plainly in Chapter 29. Many congregations do not know how to develop a strategic vision without some outside assistance. The kind of strategic plan that is most helpful is one, which engages the entire congregation in its development, and involves key leaders in its final choices of options.

In the book, "Discerning Your Congregation's Future," authors Roy M. Oswald and Robert E. Friedrich, Jr. outline a six month process which will guarantee a specific, measurable, attainable set of strategic goals which can be used to focus a congregation's energy over the course of four or five years. The book is written in such a way that a congregation can choose to go through this planning process on its own, or it can utilize the resources of an outside consultant. The advantage of using an outside consultant is that the consultant is the catalyst for ensuring that specific events take place within the congregation that leads to formulating the best options for movement towards congregational health and vitality. The consultant then leads a congregation through a discernment process that involves the entire congregation in prayer and discernment. Following at least a month of prayer and discernment, the consultant then involves all the key leaders within the congregation in a dynamic, dialogical decision making process which results in a congregation having six to eight key priorities to focus energy and resources for the next four to five years.

Both the authors do a considerable amount of such consulting, yet their fees may be too high for some congregations. It would be much more feasible financially if your Regional Body were able to offer consultants trained in this process, to lead your congregations through such a planning/discernment process.

SUMMARY AND RECOMMENDATONS

Once again, we do not want to overwhelm you with the notion that you need to train and deploy all of the above mentioned congregational resource persons. Begin with just one or two resource areas and test their use within your Regional Body. Even having back up for one or two areas of your work will give you more breathing room to focus on transformational work within your Regional Body.

Just recently, Roy was conferring with one Regional Body Executive who bought into the process of training Transitional Companions to be deployed in his region. When it came time to send some people to the training seminar, he had no one to recommend. He claimed to be so busy he did not have time to think about people whom he would trust with such work, and actually ask them to attend the two-day training events. It became clear to us that he was functioning under the old paradigm that required him to be responsive to every congregational demand, leaving him no time to do redevelopment work. If he had simply asked two people to receive training as Transition Companions, these two people would probably have saved him at least one day a month that he could have devoted to some strategic visioning and transformational work.

We do not, however, want you to naively assume that training a bunch of congregational specialists within your Regional Body is going to be easy. Over the years we have watched ways in which clergy and lay consultant specialists have diminished in size with many going out of existence. One obvious pitfall to the use of such congregational specialists is the lack of corporate memory we have witnessed within Regional Bodies. What may have been given high priority by one Bishop/Executive, only received nominal support by a newly elected Bishop/Executive. As a result, the people trained with special skills to assist congregations soon found the new Regional Body staff was no longer utilizing them, and they simply faded into the woodwork. Some of these people discovered they enjoyed this type of work and were good at it, and eventually went ecumenical to work as a church consultant full time, to the loss of that particular Regional Body.

What follows is our sense of some of the building blocks that need to be in place for this type of referral work to have sustained positive effect on your Regional Body.

First, let's deal with the consultative teams we encourage you to develop. What is required here is that you choose well those persons within your system who have the potential to develop special consultative skills, which will be available to congregations. We have a bias about paying these people for their services. We believe the congregations that use their services should pay them. When these people are not paid for their services, you will find you are continually in the process of training new consultants, with none of them staying with the field long enough to become really competent in it. If you expect these people to donate their time free of charge to other congregations, they will gladly do so in the beginning in exchange for learning a new skill. However, consultant work can be time-consuming and demanding. When these people have other roles to fulfil in their lives, sooner or later they are going to tell you they just cannot afford the time to do it any longer. A lot of time and energy you spent equipping someone within your system to do a competent job for you is then lost. It is important to find a way to pay them for services rendered. Money in our culture signifies that somebody values what you do. Even when people don't really need the money, they need the recognition that comes from being paid to provide a service for another congregation.

Some Regional Bodies have communicated pretty clearly over a long period of time that the Regional Body staff is there to offer any services a congregation needs. These are offered in return for whatever apportionment is paid by the congregation to the Regional Body. It is our conviction that congregations need to be weaned away from expecting everything coming from their Regional Body to be free. What their apportionment pays for is the personnel who recruit, train, supervise, and do follow-up evaluation on qualified consultants who can offer their services to congregations.

In certain circumstances where a congregation needs the services of one or two of your consultants but cannot afford them, you can offer a scholarship to that congregation. Generally we would encourage you not to pay the entire amount. We are all aware of how seriously we take free advice. We tend to listen to the expertise of others when we have committed ourselves to paying for services rendered. We would encourage you to see if they can afford to match funds with you in order to secure the services of these consultants. In all cases, however, congregations need to know that these consultants are good enough to be paid, and that someone has to cover the costs. If you as a Regional Body need to cover most of the costs, they need to know that you are doing this out of concern for them, and that you are convinced they need this kind of expertise at this juncture in their lives.

With regards to the consultants themselves, we would encourage you to enter into a contract with them, in which you would agree to pay for their initial training. In return, they would agree to provide your Regional Body with an agreed amount of free hours of consultation. This would give them some field training as they increased their expertise in one field of consultative help. However, once they have consulted with one or two congregations pro bono, they need to be assured that they will be paid for future contracts. Once again, we cannot argue strongly enough how much we feel this will enhance the competence of your entire Regional Body. Every time you train an individual within your system, whether clergy or lay, that individual, when used properly, will continue to gain in competence in that field, and will be able to offer that competence to the congregation to which he/she belongs.

We would further add that should the Christendom model within this continent collapse significantly within the next few years and states decide to assess churches for property tax; you will have to significantly reduce the number of staff persons serving your Regional Body. In the worst case scenario, we can see your Regional Body's Executive/Bishop having to be someone who serves a congregation three-quarter time, with only one quarter time being available to lead and manage your Regional Body. All other staff persons on your staff would have to be terminated. This would mean that when congregations need the services of the Regional Body, you would have clergy and lay teams with expertise under their belt that would be able to offer services to clergy and congregations needing assistance. We hope this scenario does not occur. If it is to occur we hope it is a long way off. This would give us a larger window of opportunity to develop the expertise needed to intervene in the lives of troubled clergy and congregations should they occur.

Even if this should never take place, we still feel this is the route to go, as you cannot possible hire staff that will possess all the skills required to minister effectively to congregations experiencing difficulty. Neither will they have the time. If, for example, you had three congregations within your Regional Body, each experiencing a severe conflict and each needed outside expertise to assist them resolve their conflict, any assistant/associate you might have on your regional body staff could not possibly do justice to all three congregations plus carry whatever portfolios they were hired to fulfill. Much better to have this assistant/associate make an initial visit to all three congregations, gain an overview of their issues, and give them some choice as to possible consultants that might work with them over the next six months. At the end of that time, should the conflict consultants not be able to attain resolution within that congregation, the assistant/associate would then return, ascertain where they were in their conflict, and then make another recommendation. Should the conflict consultant significantly reduce the tension within that congregation, you have saved your staff member a multitude of hours that could be spent on redevelopment work within your Regional Body.

Here are some precautions when you go this route.
- People, who are trained for specific tasks within a system and then are not called upon to utilize their skills, can create a morale problem for your system. Don't train people to perform a certain task within your system and then not use them.

    One reason some people are not utilized, even after they have received some training, is that the person within your system who is to recommend their services does not trust them personally, or feels they are not competent to handle certain delicate situations. This problem needs to be addressed right up front.

Do not ask people to receive training in a certain field if you do not feel comfortable with them in the first place. This means that the people who will be doing the referring will need to approve the list of people who are to receive the training. Inevitably, you will have people who will volunteer to receive training in a certain field, who are not trusted by the people who are to refer them. Please screen these people out of the program right from the beginning. This will not be an easy thing to do as most of us church folk do not like to disappoint others. We begin thinking in terms of, "Well, why not allow them to receive the training. Maybe they will mature in the process." No! Do not go that route. Only ask people to receive training when you have basic respect and confidence in them as persons from the beginning. If you don't, you will have incompetent people pestering you to give them troubled situations to manage.

A second reason trained people are not used, even when they are respected, is that the people on your staff do not want to relinquish some of their tasks to these skilled specialists. These staff persons may need to gain some satisfaction from supervising your trained specialists, and debriefing these specialists after they have completed a task on behalf of your system.

This brings up the second issue that needs to be dealt with before you embark on training cadres of consultants within your system.

- Volunteer consultants within your Regional Body will need coaching, supervision, and time together to meet to deepen their expertise. This will mean that someone on your staff will need to give time and energy to this task. This will likely entail meeting separately with each cadre of consultants that specialize in a certain field of congregational work. For example, you will need to meet regularly with your Conflict Consultants, Transition Companions, Interim Pastors, Sexual Malfeasance Teams, plus those in every other specialty you decide you need within your system. Doing case study work with your Conflict Consultants is going to bore the daylights out of your Transition Companions. They will need to review cases within their own field of expertise.

  In addition, someone on the staff will need to be available as a shadow consultant who is available to any consultants who feel they are in over their head and need someone to coach them through the next few steps of their consultation. Do not send consultants out to do complex work and then abandon them when they run into difficulties. The same would be true if you had an assistant/associate on your staff that ran into something he/she felt unable to handle. The difference between the two is that your assistant/associate would have a staff meeting to go to where s/he can raise the difficulty and then have the rest of your staff try to help them figure it out. Please do not think this is simply a matter of training or expertise. Roy has been a senior consultant for the Alban Institute for 25 years now.

Inevitably he will run into difficulties that surface when in the middle of a consultation, and he needs to call one of the other senior consultants and ask for their perspective on a problem. Congregational life is very complex. Often the presenting problem only masks a much deeper problem that is taking place within the congregation. No one should ever be flying solo where he/she does not feel free to ask for help when things get a little hairy.

This brings to a conclusion the things we have to say about Regional Bodies in their role as TRAINER/DELEGATOR/EQUIPPER. We encourage you to be spending a minimum of 20% of your time and resources in enabling and empowering clergy/lay teams to pick up dimensions of the PASTORAL CARE needs of your Regional Body. This will be time well spent. It may take years before you begin to see it pay off. There is no question in our minds that this effort is going to strengthen your system immensely. Even if the next Bishop/Executive decides not to use such a network of consultants, the skills and experiences of those people utilized during your tenure will still have long-range benefits to your Regional Body. Those people will take both their training and experience into whatever role they are called to within your system. In return, you as Bishop/Executive will be revered for years to come as a leader who was not afraid to surround him/herself with competent people and who was willing to risk having these people gain experience in actual congregational situations. Even better, you will be remembered as a Bishop/Executive who carved out time to deal with some of the IMPORTANT, NON-URGENT issues within your Regional Body. Executives who spend between 20% and 30% of their time on Important/Non-urgent issues usually make a long-term impact on their system. Within a year of your spending the time to train and delegate some of these clergy/lay specialists, you will already have bought yourself the time to set in motion some long-range redevelopment strategies within your Regional Body.

CHAPTER 4

REDEVELOPING CONGREGATIONS

Now that we have offered you some options as to how to create time for you and your staff to do the work of revitalizing congregations, it is time to offer some models as to how that task may be accomplished.

A congregation that is usually targeted for redevelopment is one that has been in a slow decline for a long time. However, it is in an area where there has been an increase in population. Such a congregation is invited into a special relationship with the Regional Body so that this trend can be reversed and the congregation can, once again, thrive and grow. To begin with, allow us to share with you some real life stories of congregations that have experienced such a redevelopment.

St. John's Church, in suburban Philadelphia

St. John's had just celebrated two hundred and twenty years of ministry in their neighborhood. The weeklong celebration, which included many former members, was a real milestone. Not long thereafter, the Council began facing the possibility that this once vital, historical church might close its doors forever. Like many faithful, but declining congregations all over the country, St. John's had suffered a series of setbacks that included internal conflict, pastoral changes and a general distrust of the Regional Body. The congregation ignored outreach and evangelism despite an influx of new residents to their community. Weekly worship attendance had dropped to an average of twenty-five or so with senior citizens comprising ninety-percent of the membership. Four children attended Sunday school and six members sang in the choir. Desperate, the congregation's leaders eventually sought help from their judicatory leadership. Today, 80 to 90 regularly worship at St. John's each Sunday, and a new healthy spirit abounds.

The turnaround came when the church leaders entered into a Covenant for Redevelopment with their Regional Body. The Regional Body required a number of things before entering into this Covenant with them:
- A willingness to engage in outreach and evangelism was needed.
- Having members who were willing to do door to door calling was important.
- Organizing and staffing a Sunday school was also needed.

The judicatory needed to know whether there was the will and determination within the congregation to do what would be necessary for them to once again become a vibrant congregation. Having passed these tests, the Regional Body appointed a Redevelopment Pastor to the congregation, and the transformation process began. There is no question in the minds of those engaged on this covenant that it is only a matter of time before St. John's becomes a program sized congregation once again.

St. Luke's, Upper Darby

In 1994 this congregation averaged forty people in Sunday morning worship. By the year 2000 they were averaging over 100 in worship. Their current financial receipts over that year totaled $125,000. They entered into a covenant with the Regional Body and were assigned a Redevelopment Pastor after the former pastor had resigned.

The new pastor developed an attractive brochure about the church and spent many hours simply knocking on doors in the community. The congregation developed a great follow up process with those who came to visit the congregation. This congregation developed a Police Appreciation Day that they sponsored once a year. All Police in their precinct were invited to church followed by a special dinner prepared by the congregation. This was a way of honoring the men and women who took on the challenge of protecting the community and enforcing the law in their area. The congregation had a similar process with the teachers in their neighborhood schools. In the process the congregation developed the ability to pull together a multi-cultural group of people who worked well together.

St Peter's, Clifton Heights

This congregation also entered into a covenant with the Regional Body to engage a redevelopment process. The first pastor assigned to them took a beating from the congregation. They really were hard on him. When he left after two years, the Bishop confronted them on their poor behavior in relationship to their last pastor. The Bishop claimed he would not send them a regularly called pastor unless they learned to treat their clergy better. After several months, the congregation came to the Bishop and sincerely asked him to send them another Redevelopment Pastor. They promised they would be good to him/her. The Bishop agreed, with the provision that he would remove the next pastor if they began to mistreat him/her.

This congregation had very little visibility within its community. The congregation began by renovating the building and putting up attractive signage. They began some creative publicity within the community. The new pastor did a lot of knocking on doors in the neighborhood. As the congregation developed a Day Care Center for children, the pastor began working with their parents.

The congregation moved from having fifty people attending worship each Sunday to having 122 in the year 2000. What makes this impressive is that, in order to raise average attendance by fifty people, approximately 150 new members needed to join the congregation. It takes about 300 to 400 new prospects to eventually have 150 people join a congregation. This congregation is now on solid footing both in its breadth of membership involving all age groups, and in financial giving.

Resurrection Lutheran Church, Inner City Philadelphia

This congregation is housed in a rough neighborhood. Many poor white members worked the surrounding factories. This congregation had experienced a high turnover of clergy. When they entered into a covenant with the Regional Body, the Synod appointed "Jake Swanson" as their pastor. Jake was a big man----a man's man. He seemed to hit it off with the neighborhood almost immediately. He often rode with the Police on their evening rounds.   Jake was single and simply spent a lot of time with people in their homes.

Jake convinced the congregation that it should renovate its old gym. He then got lots of neighborhood kids to come to church to play basketball. He became well known by these neighborhood kids.

One evening the church was broken into and vandalized.   The members of the congregation got very upset with this, and began thinking in terms of revenge. Instead, Jake went on TV and said "NO." "We are not going to match the culture by becoming violent ourselves. This made their neighborhood very happy. Many turned out to help clean up the graffiti.

Resurrection went from worshipping thirty people per Sunday in 1995 to 90 in weekly worship by 1998.

New Life Lutheran Church (Neuva Vida)

This is a story of an old German Lutheran Church in a downtown neighborhood that was closed and following renovation became a Spanish-speaking congregation. The Mission Director of the Synod found an ideal pastor for this congregation. Jonathan originally came from Minnesota, but had recently served an inner city congregation in the South Bronx. He was a very committed urban pastor. In 1986 he spent some time in Mexico City. There he met his wife. They got married and now have two children that they are raising in this congregation. They speak Spanish at home.

Jonathan made 3000 door-to-door calls in his first six month in this parish. In the process he created a stable congregation in a very transient community. What seems to be key to the success of this mission was its establishment of a community center in the old but renovated building next door to the church. Its programs were developed with the community in mind. Tutoring began to take place there. The center also developed a pre-worker program for teenagers. This enabled them to get jobs in the area. Classes were also held which included English as a second language, parenting classes, and welfare to work sponsorship. The center also sponsored an Alcoholic Anonymous and Narcotics Anonymous community.

This mission has, also, sponsored four seminary students. One parishioner who later became a seminary student was a former ex-convict. Neuva Vida Lutheran Church has now sponsored the beginnings of two additional Hispanic congregations. The Regional Body was involved in a significant way. They financed the renovation of the buildings of these old Lutheran congregations in the area and then started new Hispanic congregations in each. The Synod is now thinking of three additional Hispanic Missions as satellites of Neuva Vida, involving other Anglo congregations that are in decline. One Spanish Intern, "Angelica", is trying to do this in one of these congregations without first closing it down as an Anglo congregation. The Denomination and the Regional Body is covering her salary in this work.

Redevelopment

All the above congregations were considered "at risk" by this Regional Body. Basically, "at risk" congregations have such a low attendance that they are at risk of becoming crushed by overwhelming financial burdens. They risk losing their sense of mission. They risk becoming apathetic or angry. Often they cannot afford a full-time pastor or financing missional outreach efforts. They risk closing their doors forever.

These "at risk" congregations are in danger of descending into deep despair. "At risk" congregations don't plan to fail in their mission, they just fail to plan for mission. They cannot envision calling a bi-vocational pastor, nor can they learn to rely on trained lay leadership. Without a plan, "at risk" churches slowly, but surely die—often in areas where the population is actually growing.

At Risk Congregations

Each Regional Body will need to determine at risk factors within its own context. At risk, for the Southeastern Pennsylvania Synod, was having less than 70 regularly in worship and having a yearly budget of $70,000 or less. Using this benchmark to define congregations that might benefit from a redevelopment process, this Regional Body discovered that one out of every four congregations in the Synod met this criterion.
Without a budget of at least $70,000, a congregation is hard pressed to pay a pastor's salary, maintain a building, give support to benevolence and mission, fund parish programming and maintenance, and hold any monies in reserve for capital expenses, emergencies or additional staff. Below the benchmark of less than 70 in worship each Sunday, programs are cut back and ministry suffers. Volunteers are difficult to attract and recruit.

Experimenting with a New Approach

When this particular Regional Body discovered that 25% of its congregations could be defined as being at risk, it decided to experiment with three congregations that met this definition. The three were invited to take part in an experimental program designed to revitalize their congregation and forge a new plan for their future. They planned, prepared and prayed. When the initial three congregations did in fact respond positively to this redevelopment design, the Regional Body then began in earnest to draw other at risk congregations into this design.

Throughout North America, fully one third of mainline congregations are at or below the seventy per Sunday benchmark and are at risk, in decline, or ready to close. For these congregations to return to health, the planned partnership of lay leaders, pastors, and the Regional Body is critical. There are, of course, congregations all over the country turning around without the help of their denomination. With the support and purposeful planning of the wider church, many more can redevelop and thrive.

What might be even more devastating is that well intentioned individual lay leaders, attempting on their own to turn a congregation around without the complete picture of what all needs to happen, eventually lose the battle and end up being burnout, cynical, disillusioned, ex-church attendees. It is unlikely that they will ever again invest in assisting a congregation to revitalize itself. This fact ought to motivate Regional Body leaders to take charge of the redevelopment process, ensuring that the approach taken has a good chance of succeeding.

THE TURN-AROUND PROCESS

In general, the Redevelopment Process involves several elements. At Risk congregations seeking to turn their situation around agree to:

I.   ENTER INTO A COVENANT WITH THEIR REGIONAL BODY

This covenant or "Expectations" document, clearly spells out the responsibilities of all parties before the redevelopment process begins. Judicatory executives help select a new pastor who has the gift of visionary leadership, with special abilities and gifts in evangelism and church growth. The original Southeastern Pennsylvania Redevelopment Covenant included a three-year term call, which recently has been expanded to five years. The pastor's energies are equally divided between Outreach Evangelism and Nurture. It is folly to invite a pastor who has redevelopment capabilities into a congregation, only to have the congregation keep him/her hostage by demanding that s/he give 100% of his/her time to serving their pastoral needs. Much like a new mission developer, the pastor is equally dedicated to ministry inside and outside the current fellowship.

The congregation agrees to commit to a five-year vision plan for church growth, discipleship, and stewardship. Many at risk congregations have never considered a long-range plan. For too long, they existed from month to month, often from week to week. At the end of this chapter you will find a sample redevelopment covenant.

II.   THE CONGREGATION ASKS FOR THE COMMUNITY'S PERCEPTION OF THE CHURCH

Neighborhood visits to new residents, inactive members, and local community organizations yield valuable information about how the community perceives the congregation. Usually, this is not easy for a congregation to endure. The congregation may have to face into some painful realities about itself. It is often informative to discover whether people serving in local institutions have even heard about the congregation, much less be able to direct strangers to its location. At other times, some impressions of the congregation from an earlier age continue to linger in the minds of local community leaders. For example, they might hear something like: "Oh, you mean the church were all the rich people attend." That may have been true a couple of decades ago and no longer applies, but the perception of the church has not changed.

III.   THE CONGREGATION SOLICITS IDEAS FROM VISITORS NOTING HOW THE SERVICE COULD BE MORE WORSHIPER FRIENDLY

When someone shows up on Sunday morning for a church Service and never returns for a second visit, having a member of the congregation call that person or family to ask for some candid feedback as to why, can be tough work.   In most cases, those not returning are most willing to give their reasons for not coming back. Whether the congregation is able to assimilate information like this, and then do something about it, definitely tests their resilience in being able to take on a quality redevelopment process.
Without facing into the realities of how visitors experience the congregation, the congregation will have a hard time becoming a more inviting church. Sometimes the most candid information can be gathered simply by calling the individual by telephone.

As part of this data gathering, congregational members are also encouraged to visit other churches from different denominations and bring back suggestions on how their church could improve worship, music and hospitality.

IV.   CONGREGATIONAL LEADERSHIP ATTEND A VARIETY OF EVANGELISM SEMINARS

Regional Bodies can be an invaluable resource to all congregations, but especially redeveloping congregations, by scheduling evangelism seminars and providing grants to enable both clergy and lay leaders to attend. Ideas flow freely when pastor and people are on the same page and at the same seminar. New ideas meet with less resistance when they are heard and shared in a setting off site.

After attending a series of evangelism seminars, St. John's, in our case study above, planned several Visitor Sundays and added a "Cookie Patrol" that delivered bags of homemade cookies, a prayer and the church's worship schedule to all Sunday visitors, the very next day. A professionally crafted newsletter was mailed to area residents, and direct mail invitations for major holidays were sent throughout the year.

V. THE CONGREGATION DEVELOPS SMALL GROUPS AND INTERPERSONAL RELATIONSHIPS AMONG MEMBERS

Opportunities for social, humanitarian and hands-on service work are publicized regularly. Small-group worship, prayer chains, Bible studies, retreats and multi-generational Lenten soup suppers cultivate stronger bonds among members and visitors.

If a congregation already has a variety of small groups that have been meeting for some time, it is important that new groups be formed. It is often difficult for a newcomer to break into an existing group where the bonds of fellowship are tight. Having newcomers begin to form a group with other newcomers has a much better chance of working. The old-timers in a congregation are too well connected with fellow members. They look forward to re-connecting with those old friends on Sunday mornings. Any efforts made to connect old-timers with newcomers, however, will have long-term positive effects upon the congregation.

VI. THE CONGREGATION IDENTIFIES SPECIFIC NEEDS AND FILLS THEM

Every congregation wants to know they are making a difference in the world. Churches in decline often forget or are simply too tired to reach out. After the strength begins to return and the membership begins to grow again, a renewed commitment to losing oneself for the sake of the Gospel begins to take hold. Inviting new members to share in this kind of "hands-on" ministry makes the Gospel come alive. Assisting with meals at the homeless shelter, serving dinner for persons with AIDS, helping with Habitat for Humanity, volunteering for child or elder care at the local hospital, or hosting an appreciation dinner for the local police, teachers and/or the fire department are ways the congregation redevelops their mission.

THE REDEVELOPMENT PASTOR

The pastor's role is critical to any turn-around situation. Pastors, like parishioners, tend to spend time and energy on programs and projects that best employ their gifts. Finding talented and committed pastors who already possess gifts like evangelism, visionary leadership, teaching, preaching, and hospitality is a key first step for the Regional Body. In some situations, working with the existing pastor to develop his or her skills to make the turn around is possible. We will be pursuing this idea in a later chapter as we talk about a weeklong seminar involving not only the pastor but also several key lay leaders as well. This is then followed up by monthly telephone consultations with an Alban Redevelopment Specialist. When a pastor is not naturally gifted in this way, sometimes a team approach accompanied by some outside coaching really does work.

Within the model we are currently exploring, however, we have found it most effective to wait until there is a pastoral transition. It is during this transition that the Regional Body may begin interacting with congregational leaders about their desire for redevelopment, and whether they would be open to entering into a covenant with the Regional Body which would have the Regional Body choosing the Pastor who would serve them for the next five years. The Regional Body would guarantee that the pastor they appoint would possess the gifts and graces for redevelopment.

The process of recruiting Redevelopment Pastors to your conference, synod, diocese, district, or region is the single most difficult tasks for the Regional Body. Pursuing excellence at this level will reap benefits for years to come. The search begins by asking clergy, known to be transformational leaders, for names and personal recommendations. A transformational pastor is more likely to have friends and associates who already embrace this kind of vision. Dossiers are sorted by interest in evangelism, noting continuing education and seminars attended. Did the previous parish grow under the pastor's tenure? What kind of recommendations and references were included? What personal characteristics are mentioned most frequently? Promising candidates are called to the conference office, verifying the accuracy of the dossier's claims.

Next, the candidate is invited for an interview. If possible, the ministry area is visited and the pastor is asked to describe and discern the ministry field. What do they look for when assessing possible growth factors? Many judicatories utilize a deliberate process called the Structured Interview. Basically, the Structured Interview assumes that the best indicator of future behavior is past behavior. Questions are formulated with the intention of discovering where the pastor has performed well, and where areas of weakness exist. Little time is spent chatting with the interviewee. Most of the interview is devoted to identifying ministry skills. This process typically takes a minimum of three hours, and can easily extend to six hours. Obviously, the Regional Body Executive, concerned with recruiting and attracting qualified redevelopers, will need to devote several days a year for such structured interviews. Please refer to the chapter on Leadership for some sample questions used in such a selection process.

SUPPORT/EDUCATION

When beginning a Redevelopment Process in your judicatory, it is best if three or four congregations are involved in the process at the same time. The pastors and the congregational leaders benefit greatly from the support, encouragement, and fresh ideas others bring to the same work. Pastors should meet monthly or bi-monthly for discussion and education. Periodic meetings with the vestries or councils support the redevelopment process. If possible, set aside some grant money for continuing education events for use by both clergy and laity. When Claire Burkat held the position of Mission Director for her Synod, she regularly met with her Redevelopment Pastors one month and her New Mission Planters on the alternate month. In this way, she was able to stay in touch with how this work was affecting these clergy, and to what they were devoting their energies. What usually turned out to be the best part of such meetings was the sharing that took place between the clergy deeply involved in these distinct, yet similar undertakings.

When the Southeastern Pennsylvania Synod went on a Capital Funds drive to raise money to support new missions and redevelopment, these funds were rarely used in subsidizing the salary of redevelopment clergy. There is a down side to this type of "welfare" which should be avoided, if possible. Much of the money was used, however, in making possible educational opportunities for the clergy and laity within these congregations so they were continually learning new ways to bring their congregations to a new level of health and vitality.

ASSESSMENT

The process of redevelopment begins as the judicatory staff, or conference of deans, carefully analyzes how many congregations are currently at risk, whatever the benchmark may be. This is often a truly shocking number. Many Regional Body Executives do not consistently and thoroughly evaluate the health of the congregations they serve. Often much time is spent moving from one crisis to another. One way to evaluate is to collate congregations by size (e.g. family/pastoral/program/corporate). Now add two more categories, new missions (which may be less than 50 on Sunday morning but growing) and congregations that are in danger of dying in the next few years. Some in this last category are not good candidates for redevelopment because they might already need "life support." The redevelopment process needs to have a healthy core of at least five good leaders and some realistic hope of survival to begin the transformation process.

An invitation to participate in the program comes next. The congregational leaders look at the Regional Body Redevelopment Covenant and speak candidly with other lay leaders from other churches that have already begun the process of redevelopment. They will decide at a congregational meeting whether to accept the challenge of renewal. Often a congregation backs out at this point. It is a rare denomination where there are not many more congregations fitting the criteria for risk than might be approached. It is absolutely necessary for all parties to agree upfront on the work plan before them.

After a congregation agrees in principle and has reviewed the expectations, five other assessments are used to determine viability.

I.   DEMOGRAPHIC STUDY

It is essential for a congregation to carefully assess the present and future possibilities for ministry in the community in which the congregation resides. Often this is the first time since the planting of the church that this kind of examination has been done. Congregations tend to want to placate the denominational staff person and seek to get the quickest, cheapest material available. Resist this attempt at all costs. Observing the sincerity with which congregational leaders truly are open to seeing their community in a realistic light and not by their outdated perceptions is an assessment in itself. Often one or two key people think they know the community very well, and speak up frequently to give their opinion on the direction the church should go. It may be that their observations are correct; however, all observations should be backed up by data in order to neutralize the bias of information sources.

Census data is available through the Internet, www.census.gov and often free through denominational research and information offices. Check with your denomination for current data before proceeding.

Increasingly, denominations are turning to professional demographic information provided by para church companies mentions in Chapter 3 (Percept and Visions/Decisions).

These packaged materials are more comprehensive and easier for the average person to read and understand, because the maps illustrating the community service area are colorful, and all the demographic and lifestyle data are in one place. Often, only a few lay leaders enjoy sorting through census information and are capable of painting a picture of the community using statistics. This leaves a great number of people out of the planning who really should be involved if possible from the beginning. Just asking the simplest of questions, such as how many people are counted in a mile radius of our congregation, will bring blank stares. The kind of information and color maps provided by Percept runs about $200.00. This is a legitimate cost for the congregation in transition to pay. Many denominations offer a grant to help defray the costs. For the money, a congregation would get information on population distribution: age, gender, race; lifestyle information: working class, white collar professionals, educational level, income, charitable giving patterns, denominational preferences, percentage of unchurched in that neighborhood, and types of housing and transportation preferences, to name just some of the important information to help parish planning. One city congregation at risk, considering redevelopment, discovered they had 1,200 children under the age of five in a half-mile radius of the church and they had no Sunday School or outreach to children whatsoever.

II.   COMMUNITY INQUIRY

To complete the picture of the potential for mission outreach, a small group should be deputized to interview community leaders, such as school superintendents, local principals, realtors, teachers, police and fire officials, newspaper editors, and crossing guards. Very often they are very happy to share their views with your leaders. After all, they have dedicated their working life to bettering the community. Questions that might be asked are:

- Who are the new people in this community?
- What are the people in the community most concerned about?
- What is your greatest challenge?
- What needs do you think a church in this community might meet?
- How can we help you with your work in this community?

III.   PSYCHOLOGICAL ASSESSMENT

Next, and the most unique, is a psychological assessment of the congregation conducted by a team of professionals who interview people in the congregation and take a deeper look into the dynamics of the congregation's history. Like all systems, congregations have personalities and stories to tell that make and mold their ministry. Like people, congregations who have been traumatized in some way often act out their distrust in invisible yet powerful ways through the years. This can take its toll on lay and clergy leaders! The assessment team may include psychologists, social workers, and organizational consultants. A report, including recommendations, is drafted for judicatory and congregational discussion, and this report is shared with all pastoral candidates considering a call to redevelop this congregation. The team carefully looks at the spiritual core of the congregation: repentance, healing, and openness to change.

Since this assessment is expensive, running in the neighborhood of $2,500-$5,000, there may be a temptation to bypass it. Claire has found, however, through bitter experience that a Regional Body can go to a lot of expense trying to redevelop a congregation that has some truly dysfunctional patterns that they are not willing to relinquish. It has been these dysfunctional patterns that have kept others from wanting to join them throughout the years. It is very difficult for a quality redevelopment pastor to encourage new people to join an unhealthy community. The people in the congregation have no intention in getting well. They get some type of satisfaction from their pathology and that's what keeps them going. No skilled pastor can take on that pathology while at the same time getting new members to commit to be members of the congregation. In the long run, it is money well spent. An example of one of these collaborative care reports, done by a professional group called Physis, operating out of Philadelphia, is contained in the appendix.

IV.   CONGREGATIONAL STUDY

A congregational study, the kind usually done by the denomination during a time of transition, is also conducted. Its results are shared with the congregation, the denominational transition staff, and all candidates for the position of pastor. This study is similar to the one recommended in the book, "Discerning Your Congregations Future," in the Chapter on "Congregation Self Assessment." The process recommended in that book has every member of the congregation being invited to someone's home to reflect on two basic questions:
- What do we like about ourselves as a spiritual community?
- What concerns do we have about ourselves as a spiritual community?

Generally there is someone at each home meeting taking notes. These note takers then spend an evening together, collating the data they have collected and pulling it together into a written report.

V.   PROPERTY

All the work and good intentions will be futile if the church property is not in good shape. Early on, an inspection, like a home inspection for a house sale, is important. Often cosmetic improvements like new plastering, painting, lighting, and landscaping are good motivating projects for a congregation considering redevelopment. How they accept this challenge early on is a good indicator of what kind of resistance one can expect in other areas even more threatening, like worship style and the Sunday morning schedule. Perhaps the small endowment some congregations have squirreled away for a "rainy day" can be used now to make necessary property improvements.

SAMPLE CONVENANT FOR REDEVELOPMENT

Expectations and Responsibilities of a Pastor/Congregation under the Synodical Appointment Process for Redevelopment

PREAMBLE: As the redevelopment of this congregation begins, it is essential that the partnership and the accountability structure be clearly understood by all parties. The active participants are the CONGREGATION (represented by the church council), SYNOD (through the bishop, staff person, or mission director), and the PASTOR/REDEVELOPER.

PART ONE – Term of the Call and Subsequent Call

The Call to serve as a pastor/redeveloper of the congregation comes from the Synod Council of the Southeastern Pennsylvania Synod of the ELCA (with the advice and consent of the congregation). The call is extended for a term of five years. During the term of the call the synod will conduct annual ministry reviews with the pastor and the congregational council. At the conclusion of the fifth year of the term call, with the consent of the bishop, the pastor, and the congregational council, the congregation may call the pastor/redeveloper to continue serving as pastor.

PART TWO - Basic Expectations of the Pastor

The primary role of the pastor/redeveloper (in addition to being preacher/teacher and spiritual leader) is that of evangelist. It is expected the 50% of the pastor's time will be dedicated to the task of evangelization, which includes visitation, incorporation, faith formation for new Christians, and training of the laity for sharing the task of evangelization.

The pastor/redeveloper and lay leaders are to participate in a minimum of two Evangelization Conferences during the first three years.

The pastor/redeveloper will be responsible for the following:

- Cultivating a hospitable climate for growth;

- Making creative use of worship services for the purpose of inviting new members to the congregation, and adding services as needed to maximize outreach;

- Developing, in consultation with the Mission Director and the Council, a five year vision for church growth with significant increase in worship attendance;

- Filing reports with the Mission Director and the congregational council.

The Mission Director is the individual appointed by the Regional Body to oversee the work of redevelopment within the Regional Body. This is usually a staff person with a particular passion for outreach and evangelism.

PART THREE – Basic Expectations of the Congregation

The congregation commits itself to a program of intentional growth in worship attendance and financial support. With the clear understanding that 50% of the pastor's time will be given to the task of evangelization, the members of the congregation promise to be partners with the pastor/redeveloper in this new ministry. This partnership is expressed by a commitment to:

- Provide adequate salary and benefits to the pastor and family;

- Relieve the pastor of excessive committee meetings, with the exception of regular monthly council meetings and other significant meetings as determined by the laity and clergy leadership;

- Provide specific prayer, support, and programs that directly encourage the work of evangelization;

- Provide for the routine administrative tasks of the congregation;

- Change the existing ministries and programs as suggested by the pastor/redeveloper in order that redevelopment of the mission of the congregation can take place;

- Provide quarterly reports to the Synod from the president of the congregational council;

    Review and if necessary revise the present mission statement of the congregation;

- Share in visitation of the prospective new members identified by the pastor and congregational members;

- Develop a five-year vision for church growth in conjunction with the pastor.

PART FOUR - Basic Expectations of the Synod

The synod commits itself and its resources to supporting the congregation's redevelopment efforts through the following:

- Identifying, screening, interviewing, and recommending candidates to serve as pastor/redeveloper. Persons so identified and recommended will have the gifts, skills, and proven experience in revitalizing and redeveloping congregations;

- Assisting congregations with financial support, as needed, to enable redevelopment, to the extent available to the synod;

- Having the Mission Director coordinate and conduct continued training with the pastor/developer for the duration of the call;

- Having the Mission Director meet at least quarterly with the pastor/redeveloper;

- Conducting an annual ministry review with pastor and congregational council.

PART FIVE - Support of the Pastor and Family

As noted above, it is the responsibility of the congregation to provide adequate and just compensation to the person serving as Pastor/Redeveloper of this congregation. Therefore, attached to this agreement is a four-year budget projection indicating the extent of the financial support given to the pastor's compensation package.

Also attached to this agreement are the statements of salary, allowances, and benefits proposed for the initial year of the term call.

_____   _____
Bishop   Congregational Council President

_____   _____
Mission Director   Pastor/Redeveloper

_____
Date

REDEVELOPMENT EXPECTATIONS
(SUMMARY)

BISHOP
- Letter of Call
- Five-year term call

PASTOR   FIRST MONTHS:
- Visiting congregational members
- Building relationships
- Attending Evangelization Conference
- Monthly reports first six months
- Share evangelization plan with Mission Director and congregation
- Initial calling and/or direct mail campaign in ministry area
- Develop brochure
- Time responsibility - 50% pastoring - 50% evangelization

MISSION DIRECTOR
- Meet initially with Council
- Coordinate Evangelization training for pastor and people
- At least four times a year gather redevelopment pastors for support and training.
- Review pastor's reports
- Provide evangelization resources as needed
- Provide demographic assistance

SYNOD STAFF
- Once a year visit with Council
- Maintain supportive contact with pastor, Mission Director, and congregation

COUNCIL AND KEY LEADERS
- Financial projection – salary projection (4 years)
- Attend retreat with Mission Director and/or other Pastor Evangelists
- Support pastor in ministry
- Develop five-year plan for mission
- Explore evangelization possibilities for congregation
- Share visitation of prospective members
- Help with faith formation of new members

<u>REVIEW OF REDEVELOPMENT MINISTRY</u>

Annual ministry review that includes:

- Pastor
- Council
- Representatives from Mission Development Committee
- Plans/goals/finances/mission statement
- Mission Director

CHAPTER 5

LOCATING AND NURTURING REDEVELOPMENT PASTORS

Having just reviewed one proven method of redeveloping congregations, the key ingredient to this process is finding the right Redevelopment Pastor for each situation. This is a disciplined process that will require a major time commitment by someone on your staff. The Bishop/Executive of the region will need to give this work some priority. Everyone on the Regional Body staff will need to be on the look out for clergy who have the special gifts of turning around a congregation. In this particular model, it is in locating those clergy with redevelopment capabilities that are key to your success in becoming a Transformational Regional Body, where much more emphasis is placed on turning around dying congregations than on simply maintaining the system.

One of the best places to begin such a search is to be in touch with those clergy whom you know have proven redevelopment capability and are currently engaged in such a process. These are people who have a particular gift for evangelism, whose congregations are growing, who are engaged in innovative worship, who are effective in reaching out to younger believers, and who are on the cutting edge of technology and music. These are also people who are good at marketing and who are comfortable doing initial calling in a neighborhood. Other characteristics to look for are people who have developed a significant volunteer core, and who equip lay leaders for ministry. These are the people whom you want to challenge to seek out within their congregation lay leaders with proven transformational skills whom they can challenge to consider the ordained ministry. More on that subject in the chapter entitled, "Recruiting Transformational Leaders for Tomorrow's Church."

When you have identified, from among your current clergy roster, people who are gifted in some of the ways listed above, you might invite them to come together for a luncheon meeting. Share with them your vision of assisting your Regional Body becoming a transformational one. Ask for their ideas in ways they might participate in such a venture. Explore with them some workshops they might be willing to lead, sharing with others their particular gift in ministry. The main reason for the meeting, however, should be to enlist their aid in locating people like themselves who have the capacity to take a dying congregation in a growing area of your region, and turn it around so that it becomes a thriving, growing congregation. Possibly they know of classmates who are serving in other regional bodies. Since these are most likely the people in your region who attend continuing education events, ask them to assist you in looking for these kinds of people at these events. In your own way, you can deputize them to be your recruitment officers within your regional body. Simply initiating them into this task will not be enough. Call them together at least once a year to reaffirm your vision for your region, and your dependence upon them to assist you in finding capable, caring, committed transformational leaders who can be recruited to your Regional Body for redevelopment work. Continue to explore with them, also, ways they feel they can participate in helping your Regional Body become a Transformational Regional Body. Keep holding out that vision before them. These are your foot soldiers in your war against status quo ministry within a mainline setting. Remind them of how important they are in this ministry. Continue to affirm them in their ministries to keep them from being stolen out from under you to other regions of the church. Promise them that whenever they feel their work is completed within one setting that you will find them another challenging situation to turn around.

The next step is to put in place a structured interview process that will be effective in identifying prospective redevelopment clergy. In 1994, the ELCA Division for Outreach developed a comprehensive screening instrument. The primary consultant used in this project was Dr. Charles Ridley, of the University of Indiana, Counseling Psychology Department. The Division for Outreach adapted original material from his book, "How to Select Church Planters." It was with his permission that this material was made usable for the ELCA environment. All ELCA synods may use the material in the selection manual developed. Several times a year, training events are conducted by the Division for Outreach staff to assist synodical leaders in using this selection methodology. Other denominations may work directly with Dr. Ridley in adapting his methodology to their situation, or receive training from the Division of Outreach of the ELCA. His material is copyrighted and we are under some limitations in sharing his complete process in this document.

Although this material was originally used for the selection of new church planters, the structured interview process can be helpful in assessing the giftedness of potential redevelopment pastors. Once a denomination has received the rights to use this methodology, they can coach congregations, in an abbreviated way, to better prepare them to interview candidates. We would also recommend using this methodology within your screening process, as you select potential candidates for the ordained ministry.

Several assumptions are operative in this process.
- The church needs to minimize poor selection processes.
- No one element is sufficient to make a decision whether to accept or reject a candidate.
- Talented, motivated, and committed leadership is needed in fulfilling God's mission.
- Recruiting, cultivating and selecting appropriate mission leaders is sound stewardship of human resources.

Here are some of the most common denominational errors committed in the selection process:
- Selecting from a limited or local candidate pool
- Inadequate or nonexistent position descriptions
- Incomplete investigation procedures
- Ineffective interviewing techniques
- Unclear, unspecific selection criteria.
- Mismatching the candidate to the ministry context.

These are the seven principles that should guide the interview process:
- The best predictor of future behavior is past behavior.
- Behavioral performance is significantly more important than work experience.
- The focus is less on single behavior, more on a group of behaviors.
- Indirect observation of behavior by the interviewer is central to the interview.
- The interviewer needs to maintain decision uncertainty.
- Selection is a mutual decision-making process.
- Effective selection is a function of making a match between the person the place, and the call.

In general, the interviewer needs to be capable of following a disciplined process. Extraverts, who are tempted to engage in dialogue on subjects that are of interest to them, may not be well suited to this process. Between three and six hours of uninterrupted time needs to be set aside for this interview.

The interviewer takes care to make the candidate comfortable and explains the process completely before the interview begins. Interviewers are to listen to the answers to the questions, and try to be nonjudgmental in their manner. It is advisable to have a second interviewer in the room. One person concentrates on the oral questioning, while the other takes notes and notices the dynamics of the situation. One of the interviewers should be of the same culture, gender, race or language of the candidate. This is especially important when it is time to give feedback to the candidate on whether or not s/he is chosen for the position.

Once again, it is important for the interviewer to listen more and talk less. They are advised to ask a question another way, rather than giving the answer they had hoped to hear. The interviewer should try to complete all the categories they need to cover in order to make an informed decision. The interviewer should avoid getting stuck in one area, or allowing personal preferences guide the discussion. Chatting and socializing should be done over lunch or on a field visit to the ministry area. It is important to keep the interview going in a structured and controlled time frame, so everyone will feel the day was spent well and the interview session was complete.

A bedrock principle in this interview process is to consistently ask the candidate to give examples of their behavior in a particular situation. Hypothetical questions are to be avoided. Remember the best predictor of future behavior is past behavior, not wishful thinking. As the candidate is describing a situation, try to visualize the scene as best you can, like a video camera, in order to ask all the questions that will give you the fullest picture. Try not to correct or engage in a discussion of a subject, no matter how interesting or relevant it was to your ministry. This is the behavior, on the part of the interviewer, that most often gets everyone off track. In addition, it is important to ask the questions in a manner that does not telegraph the answers you seek. Maintain objectivity as much as possible. Often, when an interviewer "clicks" with a candidate a "halo" effect occurs whereby the interviewer hears the rest of the discussion in a favorable light and is not aware of red flags along the way.

Some sample interview questions are listed here:

Personal motivation
- Describe some of your most important accomplishments. How did you go about reaching your goals?
- How do you go about making yourself more effective in your work?
- Describe conflicting demands on your time, and how you go about resolving them.
- What energizes you in ministry?
- What depletes your energy?

Building Body Cohesiveness
- Describe a ministry situation where you felt particularly successful in accomplishing a goal important to you and the church?
- Describe how you helped new members become part of the congregation.
- Describe how you build corporate identity around the church and among the people.
- Think back on your ministry and tell me about a time when you confronted a person or group of people who were undermining the unity of the church.
- How do you feel when someone takes over your idea and changes it?
- What have you done in such a situation?

Visioning Capacity
- Describe your current vision for the ministry you serve. How did others capture the vision?
- Tell me about a time you built something from nothing?
- Describe for me a time when you felt most clear about the ministry you were performing and what you were doing in the midst of that ministry.
- Describe a situation that was stagnant or failing and how you stepped in to revitalize it.

Reaching the Unchurched
- Describe how you typically associate with unchurched people in your community.
- Tell me about an adult you introduced to the faith. How many adults have you baptized in the last two years?
- How do you convey a positive Christian witness without demeaning unchurched people?
- What does Jesus mean in your life?
- What training or guidance do you give church members who are willing to reach unchurched people?
- Tell us about a time you went knocking door-o-door.

There is a great deal more that could be said about this process. In general, one needs to practice the method before attempting to interview a candidate. Often there are lay people available who do this sort of interviewing in their work, who could be recruited to help train others for church interviewing. Not everyone has the ability to be effective at this type of interviewing. The denomination should train at least ten to fifteen people and see who does it well. Then have them do the interviews for a while before they train others.

You have now recruited several fine pastors, interviewed and placed them in appropriate call situations. However, your job is not finished. How will your Regional Body support and show its appreciation of these people, so they stay committed and energized for the long haul?

Sound a clear trumpet! People want to be part of an important and compelling mission. If your Regional Body has such a mission, people will be honored to have a place in making it a reality. Let everyone know where they are all headed in this endeavor and then thank, recognize, and celebrate all who take part. Make continuing education opportunities a reward for excellent work. A very cost effective way of recognizing and equipping pastors is to pay for their participation in a cutting edge event. Then ask them to teach the model or concept to four other churches when they return. Provide scholarship grants to lay people who also want to increase their ministry skills. Begin to become a Regional Body that rewards risk! Highlight those who have tried something new, even if it didn't work out perfectly. Pray for the people who are vital to your Regional Body vision. Send them notes when they are on your prayer list.

Making your denominational newsletter inspiring can be a vital part of your work and ministry. Tell stories of congregations that are making a difference in people's lives. Highlight transformational ministries. A colleague of ours, The Rev. Jill Hudson, Executive Presbyter of White Water Presbytery, makes it a point to ask at every Presbytery meeting, "Which congregations had one or more adult baptisms this month?" At first when she began asking that question, there was usually a stunning silence in the room. After several years of being persistent in this question, she now reports more and more congregations speaking up after this question. Now, they not only give a number but want some time to tell the stories of how one adult baptism let to another one. When the congregations under her care realized she was serious about this question, as she continued to hold it up as important, more congregations began to take evangelism seriously and became congregations that were in the business of changing people's lives. It is a great example of how a Regional Body can positively influence congregations in their care to become transformational communities of faith.

Chapter 6

ESTABLISHING NEW MISSIONS

Besides redeveloping at risk congregations, a transformational Regional Body consistently looks for opportunities to plant new congregations. We live in a land where population shifts seems to be an ever-moving target. Ideally, a Regional Body will have in its long-range strategic plan identified areas within their jurisdiction where demographers predict future growth. With creative funding, parcels of land are purchased ahead of time before their price skyrockets. Without a plan, Regional Bodies are always behind the eight ball, knowing where a new church start should have begun years ago.

There may be times when a congregation is ripe for redevelopment, but before it launches into a covenant with its Regional Body to do that, it needs to decide whether to stay in its current location, or sell their current property and move to an area where numerical growth will be a much easier process. A good example of this took place in 1999 when Roy was invited to consult with St. Martin's Anglican Church in Calgary, Alberta. Going into the consultation was a prior agreement that Roy would include as part of their developing a strategic plan, taking the congregation through a discernment process as to whether it should stay in its current location or become a core group that would establish a new mission church further out in the suburbs. After nine months of work, St. Martin's decided to sell its current property to a Korean congregation that was already using its facilities on a rental basis. They are now in the process of establishing a new mission much further west of Calgary where demographers predict will be the new building boom. In this case, the Regional Body, the Diocese of Calgary, tried to stay in meaningful dialogue with this congregation as it wrestled with this decision. The Diocese was clear that it had too many Anglican churches in the area where St. Martin's was located. All of those congregations within a five-mile radius of each other were small, struggling pastoral sized congregations. The Diocese assured its support should St. Martin's decide to sell and move further out.

Claire had a different experience with a struggling congregation in center city Philadelphia. St. Simeon Lutheran Church was established just after the turn of the 20th century to meet the spiritual needs of the German Lutheran immigrants arriving at a new home. By 1980 the community had changed ethnic populations several times, and was again changing from African American to a more African Caribbean and Latino population. The congregation struggled to reach out to the community, and had actually developed a fairly successful community center and diverse membership before crushing financial pressures forced the small congregation to close its doors in the spring of 1997. Here sat a wonderful stone building, in disrepair but in basically sound structural shape, in one of the most crime ridden and poverty-stricken areas of the city of Philadelphia, Hunting Park. The choice for the local Lutheran synod was to sell the building to another denomination or agency or to renovate and reopen the building as a new mission. It elected to renovate. It took almost a year for the Synod to refurbish the building and to find appropriate pastoral leadership to establish a new ministry in the old but changing neighborhood. With a $100,000 loan from the Mission Investment Fund of the Evangelical Lutheran Church in America, the renovation began. Asbestos removal, new electrical wiring and plumbing, cement work, plastering, painting, and a new alarm system were some of the basic needs to be addressed before a new ministry could begin. After all was finished, the cost of the renovation came to $140,000.00, and that still did not include air-conditioning, which is a future goal.

Nine possible mission pastors, fluent in Spanish, were interviewed during the year of renovations. For many reasons, some of the most experienced urban pastors were not able or willing to take this assignment. Finally, a lay leader in the neighboring Latino mission church emerged through the support and encouragement of his home pastor, and began seminary studies and mission training under a new "alternate route" process developed in cooperation with the various divisions of the national church, including the local seminary, Synod, Division for Outreach, and the Division for Ministry of the ELCA.

This new mission, named Eglesia Luterana Esperanza or Hope Lutheran Church, illustrates the hope, the opportunities, and the challenges for mainline denominations in the twenty-first century. The mission field is ripe for planting. Increasingly, the vision and encouragement for new missional activity for inner-city starts will need to come from the denomination, but initiated mainly by the Regional Body.

Another mission start of this Regional Body occurred when Claire, discovered through her study of Percept demographic data, that there was a Russian enclave in a particular neighborhood in Philadelphia. They were not currently being served by any denomination. Today there is a Russian Lutheran Church in that neighborhood. The synod located a female Russian Doctor who was willing to take on seminary education as she went about forming this new Russian church.

Congregations do not live forever. Some die, prematurely in the first year. Others live to early childhood or adolescence. Still others live to middle age, and some to a ripe old age. In the same way that children of God are born, grow, and die in varying lengths of years, so the congregations of Jesus Christ are also born, grow, and die.

When did we lose our joy for planting new congregations? When did the announcement of a new mission signal competition or fear among other churches instead of blessing and generosity?

Unlike much of Europe, where many congregations have consistently held worship services for hundreds of years, here in the United States most congregations have a vitality and growth potential similar to the active years of the normal life span of a twenty-first century human being. Unless a new congregation dies early on, the rapid growth spurt is in the first twenty years. After that the congregation often becomes comfortable and complacent for another twenty years. If there is no mission renewal during this time, many congregations begin a slow and steady decline until death, merger, or consolidation. Exceptions do occur. Some congregations with large memberships continue to remain vital through a constant revisioning process. Some congregations have wonderfully prominent locations and seem to have a steady stream of newcomers joining their ranks. These seem to be the exceptional ones. We are also aware of some congregations that have huge endowments to help stave off the inevitable even when there is no mission renewal. Unfortunately, many mainline denominations now have congregations that are only viable financially because people over sixty years of age are funding them. It is all too obvious what will happen to these congregations in the next ten to twenty years. They will either find a way to reach out and engage younger families, or they will experience a slow decline until they are closed.

At the turn of the twentieth century, many mainline denominations experienced a huge "baby church boom." Immigrant believers from Germany, Ireland, Scotland, Wales, Scandinavia, Italy, Russia and other European countries birthed new mission outposts to meet the language and denominational affiliations of the newly arriving population. These growing congregations in turn birthed new missions as parishioners moved to other parts of the United States. Often pastors were recruited from the "old country" in order to preserve the traditions and language of the people.

After the second and third generation, young people typically identify more with the culture and country of their birth than with their parent's legacy. The 1950s and 1960s focused organizing principles for new congregations less on language and more on such considerations as denominational loyalty, new suburban growth, larger families, expanding highway systems, and the culture of Sunday as a day with little secular competition. Mainline denominations in the 1960s and 1970s would often buy land early in a growing suburban area, perhaps even build a first unit and then watch as people showed up for worship and education. "Build it and they will come" was the underlying motto. Back then this worked.

The next twenty years saw a decline in church starts among so called mainline denominations as the urgency for social ministry and justice issues took priority. In the meantime, nondenominational, independent conservative, and Pentecostal churches experienced a growth spurt, as the traditional churches experienced a lag in fertility. Whereas in the past mainline denominations grew by immigration or procreation, today's new missions reach out to the unchurched in their neighborhoods, many of whom are lapsed Lutherans, Methodists, Episcopalians, and Presbyterians. While traditional churches were declining in size and trying to redefine their mission and purpose, conservative churches were organized around mandates for personal evangelism. A "successful" evangelical church was one that was fertile. Often a mother church would birth several satellite congregations in the first twenty years of its life.

Theologically conservative, they were nevertheless technologically on the cutting edge, and made good use of computers, electronic music, direct mail, telemarketing and sophisticated sound systems. All this while the mainline churches battled over new hymnals or prayer books. These conservative and Pentecostal churches were tuned into small group ministry early on, less clergy centered, which in turn brought a higher commitment of the laity to their ministry. As we turn the corner into the twenty-first century, there are as many immigrants arriving in America, as before, only these immigrants are predominantly Hispanic and Asian in descent. Inability to adjust to this new immigrant population further increased the decline within mainline churches as the dozen plus denominations, which make up the mainline, began to compete with each other for the same middle class, Euro-American families.

It doesn't take a math expert to note that in order for a denomination to grow, more congregations need to be planted than closed. In addition, more congregations need to grow in size rather than decline. A serious examination of all the congregations in a conference, synod, diocese, or presbytery, needs to be the first step in planning for a healthy future. How many congregations are growing? How many are declining? What are their sizes? Which will close? What will happen to the buildings? And what are the possibilities for new church plants in the next ten years? Sadly, very few mainline denominations are seriously planning for the inevitable decline of many congregations and the opportunities for new starts in other places. For the most part we see Regional Bodies wanting to keep their head in the sand, oblivious of the changes and opportunities that are going on around them.

Below is a sample of recent statistics for several mainline denominations. Even though the reporting and counting of new starts differ; the numbers do point to possible direction for the future.

UNITED METHODIST CHURCH
1990: 57 churches organized; 44 mergers (88 churches merged);
    184 churches discontinued
1991: 45 churches organized; 61 mergers (124 churches merged);
    127 churches discontinued
1992: 57 churches organized; 45 mergers (94 churches merged);
    146 churches discontinued
1993: 47 churches organized; 54 mergers (111 churches merged);
    124 churches discontinued
1994: 30 churches organized; 65 mergers (132 churches merged);
    192 churches discontinued
1995: 37 churches organized; 40 mergers (84 churches merged);
    156 churches discontinued

PRESBYTERIAN CHURCH
1990: (N/A) new church developments; 14 mergers (29churches merged);
    53 churches dissolved
1991: (N/A) new church developments; 18 mergers (35 churches merged);
    57 churches dissolved
1992: 45 new church developments; 14 mergers (29 churches merged);
    32 church dissolved/dismissed
1993: 28 new church developments; 6 mergers (12 church merged);
    34 churches dissolved/dismissed

1994: 25 new church developments; 14 mergers (26 churches merged);
28 churches dissolved/dismissed
1995: 23 new church developments; 16 mergers (30 churches merged);
24 churches dissolved/dismissed
1996: 17 new church developments; 13 mergers (26 churches merged);
50 churches dissolved/dismissed
1997: 23 new church developments; 14 mergers (29 churches merged);
53 churches dissolved/dismissed
1998: 16 new church developments; 23 mergers (44 churches merged);
48 churches dissolved/dismissed

CHURCH OF THE NAZARENE

1990: 62 new church developments	53 closed/merged
1991: 44 new church developments	40 closed/merged
1992: 41 new church developments	67 closed/merged
1993: 54 new church developments	40 closed/merged
1994: 38 new church developments	42 closed/merged
1995: 40 new church developments	61 closed/merged
1996: 32 new church developments	35 closed/merged
1997: 35 new church developments	49 closed/merged
1998: 37 new church developments	54 closed/merged

EVANGELICAL CHURCH IN AMERICA

1990: 33 new churches organized
40 churches disbanded/removed/withdrawn/merged
1991: 28 new churches organized
49 churches disbanded/removed/withdrawn/merged
1992: 30 new churches organized
51 churches disbanded/removed/withdrawn/merged
1993: 25 new churches organized
57 churches disbanded/removed/withdrawn/merged
1994: 36 new churches organized
60 churches disbanded/removed/withdrawn/merged
1995: 24 new churches organized
53 churches disbanded/removed/withdrawn/merged
1996: 25 new churches organized
61 churches disbanded/removed/withdrawn/merged
1997: 27 new churches organized
62 churches disbanded/removed/withdrawn/merged
1998: 23 new churches organized
44 churches disbanded/removed/withdrawn/merged

Southern Baptists intend to start between 1000 and 1500 new congregations each year. In 1998, the Southern Baptist Mission Board declared a goal of 2000 new churches a year. Independent congregations are growing at the same astonishing rate; although clear statistics about disbanded and dissolved congregations are difficult to assemble.

Fundamentalist and Pentecostal denominations also have many congregations that are merged, disbanded, or closed. They simply have a greater resolve to start more congregations than are closed. This is why these denominations continue to grow in numbers of members served while mainline denominations continue on a slow and sometimes not so slow decline.

In order for a denomination or a Regional Body to grow, there needs to be more church births than deaths. Too often, however, the majority of Regional Body executive's time and budget is spent on troubleshooting, rescuing, and counseling congregations in mid-life crisis, rather than on birthing new missions or coaching young congregations. As we learn from scripture, the harvest is ready, but where are the laborers to go and reap the harvest. It is estimated that the mission field here in North America is the fourth largest in the world.

- Thirty million people have had no contact with any church.
- Forty million people have become unchurched.
- Fifty million people are currently inactive due to a move of more than thirty miles, a crisis like divorce, job loss, abuse, addiction, or a complaint with church leaders about something they did or didn't do.
- Eighteen million people move each year. It takes two years to find a church and that's if you are taking the initiative.
- Less than 30% of the so-called Gen X population are churched. The Baby Boom Generation forgot to pass on the torch that was given to them by their believing parents.

From our perspective, the challenge is rather simple. It is not a poverty of resources that is keeping mainline denominations from doubling or quadrupling the number of new churches planted each year. It is rather a poverty of vision and leadership. We do not buy the notion that our current members are unwilling to give sacrificially to establish growing congregations. They simply have not been offered a clear challenge; with a sound blue print as to how each of our denominations is going to reach out to unchurched people with a message of hope, fulfillment and commitment. There is no question that the Holy Spirit continues to call people into a faith relationship with Christ. It is rather a question of which Regional Body is going to equip and support its members, both lay and clergy, to be the catalyst through which that call can be actualized in caring and inviting congregations. More than ever, it is clear to us that the growing need in this country is not a social, economical, or cultural one. The ever-increasing need of people in our culture is a spiritual one. In many cases, people know this to be true for them. However, many carry some wounds of former congregational experiences, or remain cynical about the simplistic solutions promoted by some congregations. What they are looking for is a faith that has spiritual depth and intellectual integrity. People are afraid they are going to have to sacrifice their minds in order to receive spiritual nurture. We, mainline denominations, have this to offer, but we remain the "best kept secret in our neighborhoods." It is time for leaders within our Regional Bodies to recognize this, and step up to the plate and take some risks for the sake of the Gospel.

It is so obvious to us that such leadership would breathe new life into our Regional Bodies and get everyone excited once again about the great things to which we had committed ourselves.

New Thinking about New Congregations

The movement for planting new congregations emerged as a key subject of interest in the work of the Indianapolis Center for Congregations. How to do it well and successfully? What models work? What are the trends in thinking? In response to these questions, the Indy Center and the staff of the Alban Institute in Bethesda sponsored a two-day consultation in December of 1999. On the first day about a dozen new congregational leaders from Indianapolis area gathered to share their experiences, and to say what resources that they found most helpful and what they most needed. On the second day, a similar sized group of leaders in the new church planting movement from around the continent gathered to respond to the questions raised the first day and to share insights about trends.

The congregational leaders, some ordained and some lay, who attended the first day of the consultation represented something of the diversity situations of congregations involved in new church starts. In spite of this diversity, there was remarkable unanimity on at least two points.

The best resource is a good mentor. In the past decade a variety of good resources have emerged. Those who attended had used and found useful various resources—Percept demographic data, Lyle Schaller's books, Bill Easum and Kennon Callahan's workshops, books by these people and others. However, there was wide agreement that the most useful resource in new congregational development is a colleague that was somewhat further down the same road. It matters little whether the mentor was from the same denomination. There were some advantages to having it be of another denomination. The mentor experienced in new church starts is important for support but also because most published resources and workshops needed to be adapted, often radically. Each new start is different, and furthermore many of the new crop of resources are largely based on the experience of a few exceptional congregations such as Willow Creek or Saddleback. While there is much to learn from these congregations it takes creativity of adaptation, application, and even re-creation to use it well. A good mentor is most helpful at this.

Careful discernment is needed before entering this ministry. Starting a new congregation is an exhilarating, exciting ministry but it is not for everyone. It is hard work and takes special gifts. One person reported that to set up in their rented building took over an hour and another hour to take it down. One pastor reported knocking on over 700 doors. Furthermore, there is a great deal of pressure in this ministry. The thought that it might not succeed is ever present. One pastor said: "Failure in new church development is the wolf outside the door." Another called it her "sword of Damocles." Finally, those in this ministry must have a gift for serving the new groups they want to serve. When things are working well, this is balanced by what some reported as the fun of new church development—the license to be outside the box. As one person said, "I like this because I can't do boring."

The second day of the consultation confirmed and extended the discussion of the first day. Again, about a dozen people assembled, this time those who either had the experience of a number of new congregation starts or who were creating programs of new church planting in their denominations. While there were many differences in this group and even disagreements, a surprising consensus again emerged on a number of points.

Leadership—as much as location—is key to success of new congregation starts. Negatively stated, more new starts fail for lack of adequate leadership or adequately prepared and supported leadership than lack of an ideal location. Gone are the days, as one person said, when the Bishop would site a new church where the Wal-Mart or McDonald's went in. Much of the creativity in work in new starts has in recent years been in helping leaders do a better job of discerning whether this ministry is for them, as well as in training teams of key leaders.

New ways to select and train new congregation planters needs to be developed. Few theological schools and judicatories do a good job in nurturing church planters. Indeed, some felt that most current systems favored those whose abilities were in system maintenance, not change. Entrepreneurs, who are the ones best able to start congregations, often are not the ones who excel at fulfilling requirements. One participant said that he would like to tell candidates for ordination that to be ordained they could either meet all the present requirements or build a new congregation to the point that it had 250 members.

Creativity in applying models is as important a factor in the success of new congregations as the model that is chosen. Congregations planted by denominations often suffer because it is hard to work through a bureaucracy not familiar with the demands of new congregation starts and because those who don't know local conditions make key decisions. These problems are mitigated when one congregation sponsors another or when a group of established congregations sponsor a new start. However, these models have problems of their own. New congregations sponsored by other congregations need to take great care to maintain their own mission and avoid duplicating their parent congregations. What works best varies considerably by social circumstance. In new immigrant communities new congregations often grow out of ministries such as English as a Second Language programs. A search for a formula of success was probably illusionary. A fairly high level of failure needed to be considered normal and expected whatever the model. New church starts are a high-risk venture. This portion concluded by agreeing with the discussion of the previous day: Whatever can be said in general about models of new church start, flexibility and adaptability are key elements.

Intentionality works. Intentionality in new congregation starts works at a number of levels. Intentionality works in the first place in that after a decade of experience in the new congregation planting movement, indications are that at least some judicatories have succeeded in increasing the number and vitality of congregations through focused attention on new church planting. Intentionality also seems to work at a second level. Intentionality in choice of specific mission of new church starts work. It seems to be more effective aiming a new congregation start at a specific group (e.g. baby boomers, GenXers, Hispanics, Blue collar workers, etc) than simply opening the doors and inviting all comers. Paradoxically, it seems that this is often true even when those who are attracted are not those at whom the new congregation is aimed. The new congregation whose mission was to serve Spanish-speaking community finds itself with a large group of Southeast Asian immigrants. The congregation aimed at GenXers finds itself with grandparents. Intentionality and focus of mission seem important.

While it is hard to say how far it might be possible to generalize the conclusions distilled from two days of freewheeling discussion, they represent interesting straws in the wind concerning the direction of a movement crucial to the future of congregations.

CHAPTER 7

DEVELOPING SEPARATE STRATEGIES FOR EACH SIZE OF CONGREGATION

Ever since Arlin Rothauge wrote his little red book on "*Sizing Up Your Congregation for New Member Ministry*," this categorization of four basic sizes of congregations has remained firm. Some people would argue with his numbers. Others have developed alternative models, keying off of the Rothauge model. For the most part this theory so reflects reality that no matter from what angle we look at it we learn something new about congregational life. Most recently, Alban Institute Senior Consultant, Alice Mann has taken this theory one step deeper in her book, "The In-Between Church."

Having advocated strongly that each Regional Body ought to have its life oriented around a strategic plan of some sort, we wish to recommend that there be a separate strategic goal for each size of congregation. One size does not fit all. Strategic goals will not fit each size congregation in the same way. An analogy that comes to mind is that of General Motors which has a Minivan Division, a Sports Utility Division, a Luxury Car Division, and a Truck Division. General Motors has oversight of all Divisions, and may set general policy that effects all Divisions, but assisting each Division to capture a strong market share in each category of vehicle is another matter. General Motors individualizes its approach to each of its Divisions since each has a unique set of challenges in the world market. In similar fashion, each of your four sizes of congregations entrusted to your care need a unique set of strategies for them to thrive in this culture. The following is our bias as to what would be some worthwhile goals for each of these four sizes of congregations.

PATRIARCHIAL/MATRIARCHIAL CONGREGATIONS
(Average Sunday attendance of 50 or less)

For the most part, these small membership congregations have been subjected to a strategy that has not worked well for 50 years, namely that of continually sending them seminary trained ordained clergy. If we would study the history of these congregations the majority would describe a whole series of short pastorates.

There is something destructive about continually experiencing short pastorates. One pastor comes in an tries to jerk them in one direction. When that fails, that pastor leaves and another comes in and tries to jerk them in another direction, etc, etc. Eventually, these congregations get tired of being jerked around and a certain Patriarch or Matriarch rises to take charge of the congregation. As Lyle Schaller told us years ago, the shorter the pastorate the more powerful lay people become; the longer the pastorates the more powerful clergy become. With such high turnover and there being such a long interim period before they are sent another pastor (unless they are United Methodist), it is natural that some lay leader will need to give guidance to this congregation. The implicit message now to any new clergyperson coming to serve the congregation is, "please give us quality pastoral care; conduct worship for us, marry us, bury us; but as far as giving us any leadership, we have all the leadership we need in our Patriarch/Matriarch." When new clergy get into a "shoot out at O.K. corral" with the Patriarch/Matriarch, it is clear who is going to win---and it isn't going to be the pastor. There may even be the subtle message from some congregants that they don't really like the Patriarch/Matriarch, and they would love for the new pastor to take him/her on. If the new pastor interprets this as a sign that s/he will get support for taking on the Patriarch/Matriarch they are in for a surprise. From the point of view of these congregants, all clergy are untrustworthy. They will leave them every time. These lay people cannot support the new pastor in a showdown with the Patriarch/Matriarch because when this pastor leaves they are going to have to live with the Patriarch/Matriarch and life will not be easy for them in the coming years.

What these congregations need is for someone to come in and love them for the next ten to fifteen years. Someone ordained with a seminary education has a career to think about. Devoting ten to fifteen years to a small place may simply be asking too much.

What are the ways Regional Bodies can bring stability of pastoral care to small membership congregations? This is the challenge for this size congregation. Continually yoking them with other smaller congregations and then sending them a full time seminary trained ordained person is going to continually have these congregations experiencing high clergy turnover. Each time there is a pastoral turnover in this size congregation the credibility of clergy takes another hit. Can you imagine what it is like being a layperson in one of these congregations where every few years your pastor leaves, and subtly kicks you on the way out because they thought you were a miserable expression of Christianity because you didn't like all their great ideas. It is out of this continual rejection that Alban Institute published the book "*Raising Self Esteem in Small Churches*" by Steven Burt and Hazel Roper. The self-esteem of these congregations that are always being left by clergy is lower than low. They even think of themselves as not being worthy of having any pastor stay with them for any extended period of time. When one does, they become suspicious, and wonder if they have a loser on their hands, since anyone with any gifts and graces would be stolen from them long ago.

One experiment that seems to be working with some denominations is identifying someone on location in these small churches, who has a call to pastoral ministry but who is employed full time in a secular job. They also need to have the respect of members of the congregation. A pioneer in this new way of serving small membership congregation was Bishop Stewart C. Zabriskie of the Episcopal Diocese of Nevada. What began as a pragmatic solution to the dozens of small congregations in that Diocese soon became a much fuller way of doing ministry in these places. Over time, whenever a congregation lost its priest, Zabriskie would visit the congregation and explore their readiness to take on the whole ministry of the congregation themselves. He would ask whether there was someone in the congregation who already was a respected leader in the congregation, and whether they would consider calling this person to the ministry of word and sacrament. This individual, however, was not asked to take on the whole role of priest in that situation. S/he would only oversee the worship and sacramental aspects of the congregation's life. Another respected leaders might be ordained as a deacon who would oversee the ministry to the community, visiting in its jails, finding food and shelter for the homeless. Someone else would take on the work of administration within the congregation. All would be volunteers. In short, the ministry of the congregation was turned over to the people of God who should have owned it in the first place. We highly recommend reading Zabriskie's book called, "Total Ministry," which describes this model. The role of the Diocese in relation to these congregations is that of continually offering training courses to those who have taken up these ministries. The Diocesan staff was small, but their main function was to offer training opportunities to these lay volunteers. This is one place where Zabriskie was firm, namely that those who took on these roles would continually make themselves available for continual training. This is where similar approaches often fail, namely in simply abandoning these people in these roles. Naturally, over time, those without training would get locked into status quo ministry and the congregation would suffer from the lack of challenge to continue to learn and grow.

The Episcopal Church has a special ordination for persons ordained for these part time functions. They call them Canon 9 clergy. These clergy have all the rights and privileges of a full-ordained priest, with the exception of being able to receive a call to another congregation. Their ordination applies only to that specific church. Other denominations have or are adopting similar alternative routes to ordination.

It may be time for us to realize that sending congregations of this size incompetent clergy keeps them fixated on the clergy dominated model of ministry. All the time they have to deal with an incompetent clergyperson, they sit around and complain about him/her, and when they can finally get a more competent one to replace this one. They will rarely explore the option of taking hold of the ministry of the congregation themselves, using their own respected leaders. They automatically assume that they cannot do without a seminary trained, ordained priest. Once again, when we have clergy over functioning, we have lay people under functioning. How can a full time ordained pastor in a small membership congregation not over function, leaving members there simply to receive his/her ministry. The result is their energy waning even further as they are bereft of meaningful roles within their own congregation. The clear result of clergy dominated congregations is the continual lose of energy on the part of lay people as they can only see their role as carrying out what "Father" wants us to do. Good sheep follow the lead of the Shepherd.

It is our sense of things that we continue to send these congregations seminary trained clergy and expect the results to be different than they have always been. As we move into what many perceive as a "clergy shortage," (we will argue about this later in the book) we might actually be forced to do what would be best for these congregations in the first place.

It is our sense of things that if congregations of this size had a choice between having a bi-vocational pastor or a full time pastor that serves two or more congregations, they would most often choose the bi-vocational pastor. Here is a clergyperson who stays with them throughout an entire Sunday morning experience. They are present for the Bible study period, they are present to conduct worship for them, and they remain for the coffee hour as well. With a pastor that serves two or more congregations, once they have preached a sermon they need to jump in their car and drive off to conduct worship in another congregation. One of our clear motivations for yoking congregations together is to provide ordained people with a full time salary. In this way, Regional Bodies become employment agencies for clergy. We really do not have the best interests of these smaller congregations in mind when we go this route. Having just come out of an over supply of clergy we naturally went this route. Every tiny little congregation got the services of an ordained pastor as we slapped them together with other small congregations so we could find another salary for a full time clergyperson. The model Zabriskie puts together in the book "Total Ministry," was way ahead of its time. Now, possibly, with a clergy shortage we might come around to do what would have been best for these congregations all along.

Another experiment has small membership congregations clustered together with a team of clergy serving all of them. This model does tend to have clergy staying around a little longer, but it also is subject to clergy always seeing better opportunities elsewhere, plus keeping these congregations stuck on a pastor dominated model. A variation of this model is having one full time ordained clergyperson giving oversight to a cluster of congregations, each of which is served by a bi-vocational pastor. The full time pastor is available to offer coaching and training to the bi-vocational clergy, plus pull the team together occasionally for exploration of solutions to presenting problems. The supervising clergy would also preach and teach within each of the congregations at differing times. The model is expensive and sometimes needs subsidy, but has the advantage of having a fully training and experienced pastor available to work with these bi-vocational clergy and their congregations. In Zabriskie's model, these clergy would fulfill the function of Diocesan staff that would continually offer training opportunities to these congregational leaders functioning in various roles.

One additional way to support these Family Sized Congregations is to monitor their readiness to make a size transition. This is a hurtle that must be surmounted or they will forever remain stuck as a small membership congregation. Within these congregations there is a lot of resistance to moving to the next level of size. Individuals have stakes, sometime unconscious, in keeping their congregation small. It is going to take some sustained effort to move through to becoming a Pastoral Sized Congregation. As a Regional Body, you can be on the look out for congregations that appear to be bumping their head up against the glass ceiling of size stability. Initiating an intervention with such a congregation can make the difference between them remaining stuck as a small church and moving up to the next level of functioning. Should your region have several of these congregations hitting this ceiling at the same time, you might call together their clergy and lay leadership and challenge them to make the shift. Promise them you will bring in some effective consultative assistance should they make the commitment to grow numerically. You may want to try to keep these congregations connected with each other, meeting to hear what is going on in the other congregations, and supporting one another in surmounting the hurtle in front of them. Here are some of the issues that are involved:

THE SIZE TRANSITION
–FROM GROUP-CENTERED TO PASTOR-CENTERED

To quote Alice Mann from her book, *The In-between Church*, "the movement from family to pastoral size involves a change in the way the system centers its life. The family size church feels like a tribe or a committee of the whole. Not everyone on the committee has equal influence, to be sure, but the single cell of members works things through in its own characteristic way. A student minister or part-time pastor who tries to take charge of that cell is in for a rude awakening because the family size church does not generally revolve around the pastor."

When a congregation begins to have a worship attendance of about 35 people, that single cell of membership becomes stretched. By the time it hits 50, the unbroken circle of members, the defining constellation of the congregation's life, is in crisis. In order to increase further, the system must allow itself to become a multi-cell organism, holding together two or three overlapping networks of family and fellowship. And it must establish a symbolic center around which those multiple cells can orient themselves. Typically, it becomes pastor-centered. This, of course, can only happen when there is trust in the pastor and some confidence that s/he is going to stay around for a while.

Given this movement from group-centered to pastor-centered in no way implies pastor dominated. In fact, a greater proportion of members may actually participate in decisions at a pastoral size than at a family size. To quote Alice Mann, "It may be that the heightened role of the pastor in relation to the board moves the congregation's political center from the kitchen table to a more accessible public setting and requires that the ordained and elected leaders work as a team to move projects forward. The pastor's central position as communication switchboard also allows for a great deal of informal consultation and problem solving; he or she can monitor key relationships, initiate needed conversations, and anticipate likely clashes."

As part of an overall strategy in your Regional Body, it would be well for you to identify those congregations in this size category that have the greatest potential to break through to Pastoral size. These congregations need to be challenged to make a concerted effort, with the right type of clergy in place, to make this break through. They will need the backing and continued consultative support of someone knowledgeable about change strategies, which can support and assist in overcoming the barriers that keep this size congregation from breaking through those barriers to become a pastoral sized congregation.

THE PASTORAL SIZE CONGREGATION
(Average attendance between 50 and 150 per weekend)

The clear majority of the congregations within your region are going to be either family size or pastoral size. Our informal data gathering on the subject indicates that one third of a Regional Body's members worship within two thirds of its congregations, while two thirds of your members worship within one third of its congregations. In some Regional Bodies, it is not uncommon for 80% of their membership to be contained in only 20% of their congregations.

Being pastoral size brings much more stability and continuity to congregational life. These are congregations that can afford a full time pastor. Congregational life revolves around the pastor, for good or for ill. It is highly unlikely that any meeting will occur in this size congregation without the pastor being present. If someone new comes to visit this congregation it is likely the pastor will make the follow-up call. People like the ready availability of their pastor. Whenever they have a problem they simply call up the pastor and within days, sometime only hours, the pastor is in their kitchen, drinking coffee with the congregant, listening to their problem, and offering consultative assistance and a prayer before leaving.

There are a good number of clergy who enter pastoral ministry to do exactly what needs to be done in a pastoral size congregation. They love hands on ministry. When people are in trouble, they want to be the ones that are there to offer pastoral care. There are times when clergy serving this size congregation, either because of salary needs or ego needs, decide they want to move to a larger congregation. Their assumption is that they will be doing the same kind of ministry except on a large scale. As a result, they move into a program-sized congregation and begin trying to manage this larger group of people using a pastoral model. What is likely to occur is that they will soon discover that there are too many people to manage in this way. Without some guidance and coaching, they will most likely continue with the pastoral model until the congregation diminishes to a pastoral size, and then they will be able to continue to serve the congregation using the pastoral style model.

It is here that CLERGY TRANSITION SEMINARS can become a crucial intervention in the lives of clergy who are moving from one size congregation to another. At such a seminar, this theory of church size needs to be explored in depth. When it is not, clergy are likely to continue old patterns even when the size of their new congregation demands a whole different approach to ministry. In the appendix of this book, Roy has placed a copy of a two-part article he wrote for Alban Institute's *"Congregations,"* in which he details the four distinct leadership styles required of these four differing congregations.

The issue of size change will also occur in some of your pastoral congregations. We would advise watching carefully as congregations within your region approach the glass ceiling on this size as well. In fact, we would say that if you only have time to monitor one congregational size transition, you monitor this one. Moving from pastoral size to program size is one of the most difficult and challenging of all size changes. The old pastoral model is so seductive. It hooks both clergy and laypeople. There are some clergy who feel that if they are not on an in-depth interpersonal relationship with everyone in their congregation, they are a failure. They will, as a result, break a leg to make sure they have that kind of relationship with everyone—even if it means allowing certain aspects of congregational programming to go down the tubes. Laity, on the other hand, often know that their pastor is too busy to give personal attention to everyone, and that she/he needs to be selective as to who gets their time and attention. However, every layperson wants to be the kind of special person for whom the pastor will drop everything and come to see them when they are in difficulty. Can you see why this pastoral model is hard to leave behind? It is doubtful whether any pastoral size congregation will be able to make this transition without careful planning and with that plan make a concerted effort to break through to program size.

As a Regional Body you ought to have available the statistics on all congregations, regardless of size. We particularly recommend that you isolate all your pastoral size congregations and track their attendance records over the past 20 years. More than likely you will have a significant number that have pushed the upper limits of pastoral size, only to fall back into to worshipping 140 or less. You should also monitor what is happening to the clergy within these congregations as well. You are likely to observe a whole cadre of clergy who have burned themselves out, trying to assist these pastoral sized congregations make it into program size. Laypeople don't mind their pastor spending large chunks of time developing both quality and variety of program offerings, just as long as s/he is available to them whenever they require some pastoral attention. As a result you have clergy carrying water on both shoulders. They are madly trying to take care of everyone's pastoral needs, while at the same time devote the necessary hours needed to get special programs off the ground. After they have hit the glass ceiling a number of times, they simply give up in exhaustion. Some simply leave. Others develop serious illnesses. Some may do something unwise, like act out in a sexually inappropriate way, which gets them kicked out of the congregation. (We rarely view clergy sexual malfeasance as an unconscious cry for help on the part of clergy, and maybe we should. This in no way makes the behavior excusable. Clergy who get themselves in trouble in this way may be quite different from a sexual predator's profile.)

Why go to the effort of moving these congregations to program size? From our perspective, pastoral size congregations are among some of your more vulnerable congregations. Yes, they promise individuals quality pastoral care from a trained professional. However, they have so little going for them in terms of quality programs that they will often have dozens of people visit them over the course of a year, only to decide that the quality and variety of program offerings are not sufficient to attract them to stay. This will be especially true of younger couples with children. What GenXers want, first of all, is something of quality for their children. They will want to have some musical options in terms of choirs, musicals, etc, plus quality educational offerings, plus some time for social bonding with other Christian children their age. Often a pastoral size congregation cannot provide all these options. As a result you see the majority of your pastoral size congregations being supported mainly by people with gray hair who have been loyal to this congregation for years, and who receive quality pastoral care— something they value highly. The older the congregation gets, the more difficulty it will have in attracting younger families who will mature to assume leadership roles within the congregation.

THE SIZE TRANSITION
--FROM PASTORAL TO PROGRAM SIZE

A simple graph developed by Alice Mann explains why moving from pastoral to program size is the most difficult transition any congregation has to make. Take a moment to look at the implications of this diagram.

Size Transition "N-Curve"

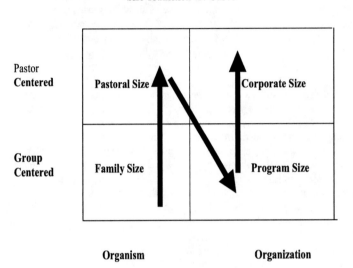

We have just discussed the difficulty of the transition of a congregation from being group centered to being pastor centered. Now the transition must move, not only from organism to organization, but it must simultaneously move from being pastor centered to being group centered once again. This is, likely, why the transition from pastoral to program size is the most difficult and the most hazardous. It is not uncommon for some members to leave in anger during some phase of this transition.

Family and pastoral size churches resemble an organism more than an organization. Both sized congregations tend to be relatively homogeneous in make up. Each revolves around a central relationship. The one centers on the relationship within a small group; (family size) the other revolves around a relationship between the sole ordained leader and the congregation (pastoral size). When you ask each of these congregations who they are as a community, in the first case they may simply introduce you to the people in the gathered circle. In the second case they would talk about the relationship the congregation has with its pastor, and the way the pastor and key leaders work together to maintain the system.

In program and corporate size congregations, the variety and complexity of relationships requires conscious attention to matters of identity, purpose, structure, role of leaders, etc. Neither the members nor the pastor can intuitively grasp the wholeness of the system. The larger membership and the rich variety of programming will only cohere well if leaders construct a clear identity for the church---often expressed in a mission statement, a vision, or a strategic plan.

As attendance approaches 150, the congregation must become more group-centered once again because the pastor can no longer carry the whole system in his or her head. There are too many individual pastoral needs to track. The relationships among projects and leaders are becoming too complex to be coordinated solely though board discussion and pastoral diplomacy. As a spider web, the center of this leadership network does not consist of a single point (the pastor) but of a small circle (half a dozen key program leaders—paid and unpaid, clergy and lay) led by the pastor.

Even though the pastor is still the center of this congregation, this pastor needs to begin functioning in radically different ways. S/he needs to have skills in planning the best programs that will meet people's spiritual and social needs. S/he will need to find leaders for those programs—train those leaders, and see that their spiritual needs are adequately met, as they must now become the spiritual nurturers of those committed to their care. These programs need to be the right ones, not too many, not too few. If the congregation misjudges and plans too many programs it will burnout its lay volunteers. If it doesn't plan enough programs, there will not be the quality and variety of programs needed to feed member's spiritual needs, plus hold newcomers who come exploring what this congregation has to offer.

When a congregation appears to be struggling with this shift, it is important that someone from the regional body makes an intervention and invites the pastor and governing board on a weekend retreat to explore all the dimensions of a size change. When you ask a congregation if it wants to grow, the answer will usually be "yes!" The follow-up question needs to be: are you willing to pay the price that growth will require? With this second question the response will usually be muted. WHAT! YOU MEAN THERE IS A PRICE TO GROWTH? The answer then ought to be, "YES, there is a steep price for growth given your particular size. Should you want to explore this let me suggest that we go on a weekend retreat to explore all the dimensions that growth will entail." This may be the motivation you will need to get them to commit to spending a weekend exploring this size transition.

Once again, this need not be something that your regional body staff needs to do by themselves. Hopefully, you will have in place a pastor or lay leader who has been part of a congregation that has just gone through this size transition. Assisting these pastors and lay leaders reflect in a disciplined way on all the things they did which helped facilitate that transition, plus all the mistakes they made, will in effect develop them into the kind of resource persons you will need to work with other congregations desiring to make this transition.

The more congregations you can facilitate moving from pastoral to program, the more congregations you will have saved from the edge of extinction, and the healthier your regional body. Once again, this is the type of pro-active stance we are encouraging you to take as a regional body. A well timed intervention into the life of a pastoral size congregation can make the difference between them killing each other, clergy included, through acrimony and dissention or their becoming a healthy program congregation which will have a much easier time growing now because they have surmounted this huge hurtle. Their growth will occur more easily because they have a model of ministry whereby adding programs merely requires finding the resources to hire part-time staff to manage that new phase of ministry, or training a key lay leader to take on that new program offering.

PROGRAM SIZED CONGREGATIONS
(Average attendance between 150 and 350 per weekend)

Staffing your program-size congregations will remain one of your key challenges as you offer oversight to this size congregation. The lead pastor of this size congregation needs to have a cluster of the right skills in order for this size congregation to thrive. In addition to being a people person, adept at inter-personal relationships, and a good preacher, this individual will also need group and organizational skills. Much of his/her time will be spent in meetings, planning and coordinating the variety of program offerings to the congregation. In addition, this individual needs to have the capacity to choose, train, supervise, and evaluate other staff members and key lay volunteers. This latter skill sometimes remains an underdeveloped aspect of this person's ministry. Quite likely, this individual was chosen to head up this program-sized congregation because s/he had done well within a pastoral sized congregation. Now this individual needs to take things s/he has done well in the past and turn them over to someone else. When they foul up or don't do it the way the lead pastor would do it, taking a deep breath and giving guidance is needed. When someone does not have experience at working collegially with other staff and key lay leaders, we often see them sacrifice on the altar of experience two or three staff members before they come to realize they need to function much differently in a supervisory role.

There is no training program provided by the Church, which equips someone to become the lead pastor of a multiple staffed congregation. The best and only training ground is for this individual to have served as an Associate or Assistant Pastor within another setting. For clergy who have not come to this office by this route, you might think in terms of having him/her team with an experienced lead pastor who might act as a coach to this individual. We at Alban Institute have come to highly value the role of coach for church professionals. We believe congregational life is so complex that it takes more than one person to figure out what is transpiring within a congregation. This is no time for a pastor to be flying solo. Possibly, you have already identified church professionals within your regional body whom you think would make quality coaches to other church professionals. This type of linking together of individuals can become another key way to do preventive maintenance within your system.

One of the places where someone new to this role can founder is in the hiring of appropriate staff. As a generalization, clergy do not do well at hiring fellow workers. When Roy does workshops with lead pastors of larger congregations, he often asks if any of them have had to fire a fellow staff member. Usually, about one third to one half of the group indicates they had to fire a staff member. He then asks how many of them have had to fire someone they themselves hired. There are usually a third of hands that go up in response to that question. Up to 80% of ordained clergy test "Intuitive" on the Myers/Briggs/Type Indicator. This statistic flies in the face of the fact that only 24% of the general population tests "Intuitive." The remaining 76% of the population test "Sensate." Sensing types usually have their feet firmly planted in reality. They are the ones that will thoroughly question an individual before they hire them. They also check out all reference as to this individual's performance in other settings. Intuitives often make choices based on their hunches about a person. Since Intuitives are bored with detail, they may miss asking all the questions needed or check out all the references. In the process they place their congregation in great jeopardy. When the wrong person is hired as the congregation's first full time Associate Pastor, the congregation and lead pastor lose big time. It will usually take two or three years to remove this person from this role. The cost to the congregation will be over $200,000--possibly more if a severance package is included. All the while the congregation has to deal with the acrimony between pastors. The program support that was supposed to result from this person being hired does not materialize. At the end of three years you have a demoralized congregation not sure it wants to experiment with another attempt at hiring another Associate Pastor. If the congregation is at all open to it, we would strongly recommend that you as a regional body explore the congregation hiring a Search/Call Consultant or a Transition Companion when they begin the process of hiring their first full time staff member.

THE RIGHT STAFF SIZE

As Program Size Congregations increase their average weekend attendance at worship, they will also need to be increasing the size of their staff. The question will usually arise, what is the right size of staff given our size of active members? The rule of thumb we at Alban have used for years (I believe we adopted it from Lyle Schaller), is ONE PROGRAM STAFF PERSON FOR EVERY 100 MEMBERS AT WORSHIP. The formula has proven to be an accurate gauge for staff/active member ratio. By a PROGRAM STAFF PERSON we are talking about someone who is hired for a program specialty that is adding quality and variety to the congregation's program offerings. The Senior Pastor constitutes one program staff person. People who are not counted in the formula are support staff personnel. By support staff personnel we are talking about secretaries, custodial staff, bookkeepers, business managers, etc. An on-going argument is whether the individual playing the organ or piano on Sunday morning is a support staff person or a program staff person. Certainly if they are putting in time to lead choir practice during the week so that there is quality choir music on Sunday morning, they should be counted.

This means, for example, if your congregation worships 275 and that includes children, you can be staffed in three ways: staffed for decline, staffed for maintenance, or staffed for growth. In the case of this particular congregation, they will be staffed for decline if they have two and one half program staff members or less. They will be staffed for maintenance if they have the equivalent of two and three quarters program staff members. They will be staffed for growth if they have the equivalent of three plus program staff members.

As you are consulting with your program size congregations, it will always be important to check to see if they are "right" staffed, or staffed for growth. When they are in a growing environment, they should be encouraged to go out on a limb and hire an extra quarter to half time person who would add some additional quality and variety to their congregational offering to members. When a congregation is understaffed, they are unlikely to grow, as newcomers will engage this congregation for a short period of time, but they won't stay because there isn't the quality and variety of program offerings to hold them. When a congregation does go out on a limb and hire that extra half time person who offers program substance, within 18 months that person should be paying for themselves as their skill and presence will be enough to attract enough new members who will raise the congregation's income enough to meet this new expense. The right staff person, even if only hired half time, will take a program and significantly raise the quality of that offering, which will result in more people being attracted to the congregation.

We generally recommend that program size congregations add staff by hiring part time specialists who will focus in on one program offering. When a congregation decides to hire one full time person who will fulfill a variety of program offerings, they usually get someone who takes the job because they like about 80% or less of what is in the job description. This often leaves 20% of their job profile that they do not care for and it is going to suffer. There is, of course, the advantage of hiring an ordained clergyperson as an Associate who will be able to offer assistance in doing some of the general pastoral care work in a larger congregation in addition to offering quality and variety in program offerings. This will work especially well if the two clergy now serving the congregation full time like each other and have fun working together. It can be difficult, painful and destructive if they end up being competitive with each other, or begin undermining each other's ministry because of their differing approaching to pastoral ministry.

The disadvantage of hiring a whole series of part time people has to do with the burden upon the head of staff who must find a way of selecting, training, coaching, supervising, and evaluating each one of them. At some point, as the congregation continues to grow towards being corporate size, some full time staff will need to be hired to assist in this ministry of oversight.

CORPORATE SIZED CONGREGATION
(Worships 350 persons per Sunday or more)

Each regional body is likely to have some corporate size congregations. Some have more than others. Generally, there will not be many. These are the congregations, which will probably be contributing the largest amount of money to your regional budget. They are also the ones who, usually, get minimal in return for those large contributions to church-wide support.

In a recent piece of research involving three Lutheran Synods, and five Episcopal Dioceses on the subject of clergy transitions, Roy had the opportunity to spend a whole day with the heads of staff of 21 corporate size congregations. They were being de-briefed as to their experience of moving into this size congregation. At one point, one of the participants made the comment that he still had not had a conversation of substance with his Bishop. Having said that, the majority of other clergy present claimed having a similar experience. This raised the question of how Bishops/Executives of a region relate to clergy that offer leadership to the largest congregations in their region. For whatever reasons, Bishops/Middle Judicatory Executives appear to think that clergy in large congregations ought to be able to manage whatever difficulties they might encounter. They also assume these clergy have all the resources to do whatever is necessary with their congregation. In many ways, this is a strange way to behave with the clergy whose congregations are providing the majority of the financial resources to the regional body.

We find that clergy of our largest congregations have enormous challenges before them. Most feel quite isolated from other clergy in the region as the problems they encounter are so different than those within smaller congregations. They have very little in common. When they do run into difficulty their most useful resource is usually the head of staff of another large congregation. There is no training available on how to manage a large, multiple staff congregation.

We would recommend that each regional body executive make it a point to bring together, periodically, the heads of staff of their largest congregations and enter into dialogue with them about ways in which the region might be a resource to them. Part of such a meeting might be to explore the ways in which these larger congregations might be a resource to other congregations in the region. These heads of staff will be appreciative of being called into community with clergy from others large congregations to do resource sharing and mutual problem solving. Having the region facilitate these periodic meetings may be the thing that these heads of staff will appreciate the most.

The key to the multiple staff larger congregation is both the heterogeneity and the cohesiveness of the multiple staff. These two do not necessarily work together. The more heterogeneous the staff the more capable that staff will be in ministering to a heterogeneous congregation and community. However, the more heterogeneous the staff is the greater the challenge to cohesiveness and teamwork. How can a regional body support both of these taking places within larger congregations?

One way would be to offer these congregations superior Search/Call Consultants who can be a resource to these congregations as they search for competent staff. The second would be to periodically offer to all the larger congregations in your region multiple staff seminars. Staff issues are the key to well functioning larger congregations. When members of a multiple staff are in constant acrimony it is difficult for a congregation to grow. In addition to staff members undercutting one another, and staff morale remaining low, it is upsetting to congregational members that their full time leaders cannot get along with each other. In one sense it is hypocritical to be preaching peace, love, forgiveness, mercy, and justice from the pulpit when people in the congregation know the staff itself is not operating this way. The medium is the message as Marshall McLuhan taught us years ago. No one wants to invite their friends to a church were the staff keeps fighting with one another. On the other hand, when the multiple staff is having fun working together and is good at what they do, it is contagious. That good will spreads like wildfire throughout the congregation. People want to get on board with the fun and the effective work.

This is one place where larger congregations can use assistance. To hold periodic seminars on multiple staff issues, run by competent leaders, is one way to strengthen the ministries of these larger congregations. In actual fact, multiple staff seminars really need to be sponsored locally if they are to be financially viable. For a congregation to send its team of six staff members to a seminar half way across the country is almost out of the question financially. Better to bring in competent leaders who will hold the seminar locally where congregations can have their staff team drive to the conference center for the seminar. In some urban locations, the seminar can be held at a central location from 9:00 a.m. to 5:00 p.m. daily with members commuting to the seminar from their homes. A big money saver! As there are many issues to be dealt with within a multiple staff, you could hold such a seminar yearly, each time developing competence in a new area of staff development. However, even with different subject matter each year, some priority would need to be given to having teams confront some of their internal issues with the help of a trained professional.

The following are some of the subject areas for seminars on the multiple staff:
- Gender issues on the Multiple Staff
- Gifts Differing—How we can capitalize on our differing typologies while minimizing the conflict such typologies might create?
- Conflict Styles---How we choose to differ with one another?
- Models of Staff Structures---Which model are we actually using and which model might best serve our needs and opportunities?

In terms of seminar design, Roy has often used a fishbowl methodology where one multiple staff is in the center working on an issue while one or two other staffs are outside the circle observing. After the facilitator calls time, those in the center circle move outside while those observing move to the inner circle. Those inside the circle now talk about what they like and value about how this staff is functioning and what concerns them about how this staff is functioning. In seminars where this methodology has been used, it often is the high point of those attending. Multiple staffs seem to value at least seeing how other multiple staffs' function.

Underlying all these suggestions related to assisting staffs of larger congregations to function effectively is the basic premise that all multiple staffs will need continuous work to remain healthy and productive. This implies that every larger church needs to have a budget item for staff development. As regional body personnel work with these larger congregations they may need to be an advocate for boards of trustees placing an item in the budget for staff development. Often lay leaders do not see the need for this. Their basic assumption is that clergy/religious professionals ought to be able to work together effectively. After all, they have God on their side. Besides, aren't deeply spiritual persons by nature peace loving and harmony creating types? Little do they realize that those who attend seminary are trained to be lone rangers. In actual fact, the corporate world has more training and support for collegial working relationships than religious professionals working in a congregational setting.

SUMMARY

Hopefully this will get you started in developing a separate strategy for each of the four size congregations in your Regional Body. These congregations are very different from one another. One program strategy will not fit all four sizes of congregations. It is time we take seriously these differing sizes of congregations and began relating to them in ways appropriate to their size. Consider having your staff look at all the congregations within your care in their differing size categories. Begin to question, which congregations are not behaving in ways that are appropriate to their size. This might merit a staff intervention. A congregation that is one size numerically, but functioning like another size psychologically is probably heading into serious trouble. Both clergy and lay leaders need to be coached as to what it will take to have them functioning true to their size. Sometimes it is clergy who know only one way of functioning as a pastor, regardless of congregation size. In other cases, you may have clergy trying their best to function in an appropriate way to the congregation's size, but congregational leaders are holding them captive to functioning in another way. Either way, these congregations need some outside assistance to gain perspective on what is transpiring in their midst.

It has been our experience at Alban Institute that Regional Bodies are not doing nearly enough in making this theory of congregational size known to both clergy and lay leaders within their care. When both clergy and lay leaders come to understand this concept, certain lights will go on, and they will never be the same again. It is a linchpin theory when thinking about congregational change and growth.

Once again, rather than having Regional Body staff making these interventions, some clergyperson or lay person, knowledgeable and experienced in size transitions, can be directed to work with these congregations. Another option is to invite a specialist in church size theory be one of your presenters at your next clergy conference.

CHAPTER 8

RECRUITING TRANSFORMATIONAL LEADERS FOR TOMORROW'S CHURCH

For congregations in decline to once again become thriving, growing communities of faith, they will need transformational leaders at the helm. Caretaker clergy, as good hearted as they might be, generally do not have this capacity. When we ask Regional Body Bishops/Executive what percentage of their clergy have this capacity, we fairly consistently get the response of about 10% to 15%. For the immediate future we will need to discover who those clergy are within our system and utilize them judiciously. This will only last so long. We are going to have many more congregational situations that will require re-development than we will have clergy with that capacity available to us. True, we can try to steal some from neighboring Regional Bodies who have not yet taken re-development of congregations seriously but that also has its limits. The same can be said for "poaching" such pastors from other denominations.

Eventually we will need to set in place a process, which has specific congregations, and specific people constantly on the lookout for lay people with this potential, especially younger people. We will then want to challenge them with the possibility of entering training for the ordained ministry. This will be the toughest challenge we place before you in this book. We have yet to discover a Regional Body, with the exception of Southeastern Pennsylvania Synod, which has the kind of recruitment program in place, which is consistently raising up the kind of transformational leaders we will need for tomorrow's church. We ask that you not be naive about the heat you will take as you limit into the ordination track only those who have transformational capacity. You will have well meaning clergy and lay leaders becoming quite upset with you when you do not accept into the ordination track those who may be wonderfully spiritual people, exemplifying many wonderful traits, but who simply do not have the necessary skills to take a dying situation and turn it around to once again become a thriving, vital congregation.

In one sense, we will need to admit that we have changed the rules for our existing clergy as well. When most of us entered seminary we thought we were entering a profession where we would inherit healthy congregations and our role would be to continue to nurture them in the faith, preaching the good news to them every Sunday, providing them with quality educational opportunities, and dealing with people in crisis who needed pastoral care. In short, we thought we would be "caretaker" type clergy who would care for God's people in whatever way they needed us. As we entered the post-Christendom era and noticed many of our congregations were in decline, we suddenly needed different types of clergy. These needed to be clergy with a certain type of charisma, men and women who had an entrepreneurial spirit about them. These are people who have had a track record to making things happen no matter what their age or context. As children these were the people who initiated the soft ball games on the vacant lot, or structured the type of imaginary game that they and their friends would play. In High School they were the team leaders who rallied the troops when their team had a tough challenge. In college they may have developed a home repair business to help pay for their tuition. We have some of these people in the ordained ministry today. No matter what situation you place them in things begin to happen.

In another sense this seems so obvious, yet our pattern continues to be that of accepting into the ordained ministry a very small percentage of these type of people. Some of this, we believe, comes from our unconscious belief that we still live in a Christendom era, in which the culture does our work for us in bringing people to faith and calling some of them to the ordained ministry. In other cases it is simply a lack of vision. When Roy was doing the research on denominational screening or candidacy committees, he would often ask whether the committee ever was handed a mandate from its Bishop/Executive or its Executive Board/Council. That is to say, having someone with executive responsibilities at the Regional level who would give some thought as to where the denomination was heading, and make some projections as to the type of clergy they would need in order to meet the demands of their Middle Judicatory some ten years down the road. The most he ever got from a Bishop was the stipulation that future candidates for ministry would need to "have the capacity to carry the freight, and play in the traffic." With this vague exception, the answer received from the screening committees within a variety of denominations, was "no." In other words, clergy and lay leaders appointed to serve on a screening or candidacy committee, whose purpose it was to decide who got approved for the ordination track, were simply shooting from the hip. In most cases this approval was given to individuals prior to their beginning Seminary education. At no point did this committee get a visit from their Bishop/Executive who would outline where the Regional Body wanted to go in the next ten years, and, consequently needed certain kinds of personnel to assist it meeting those goals. Instead, these committees were made up of individuals, both clergy and lay, who each had their own assumptions about what kind of clergy the denomination needed, and would make decisions on that basis. For the most part, decisions were made on subjective data. In the majority of the screening committees interviewed, few would clearly turn down candidates who came to them. As marginal as a candidate would be, s/he would be sent away with an assignment, to get into some therapy, for example, and then return for further examination. Even when denominations in the study had a surplus of clergy, many marginal candidates would continue to be approved for ordination. The assumption is "if he/she thinks they are called to the ordained ministry, who am I to say 'no,' even if I think they are miserable passive dependent people. God or the seminary or somebody else will fix them."

What would direction from the Regional Body look like, if it did decide to give the screening committee under its care some direction? An example might be the Bishop saying to this committee, "it is our clear intention to be a much more multi-cultural Diocese/Synod/Presbytery/Conference by the year 2010. In order for us to get there I need you to be screening into the seminary track one minority candidate for every non Hispanic white candidate you accept." Another admonition might be an Executive Presbyter saying to the Committee on Ministry, "We are sensing a crying need from our smaller congregations to have more bi-vocational clergy to serve them. Within the next couple of years, could you initiate a search for people who would be willing to serve a small congregation part-time, while they continued in their chosen profession? Instead, what Roy found was a group of individuals who all had their own ideas about who would make a good pastor, and they were using subjective judgment to decide who got screened in and who got screened out. All this under the very general mandate to "get us the best people you can." Everybody on the committee had a different idea about what "the best people" looked like

How did we get this way? For the longest time we simply hoped against hope that our declining numbers would cease and by some magic, things would be different. In many cases the problems we are facing are so daunting that we became immobilized into trying anything different. As a result we continued to do the same old things but expecting different outcomes. Isn't it strange that we human beings can keep on doing what is known and familiar to us, yet expecting the results to be different.

With regards to the recruitment of clergy, from approximately 1970 to 1990, mainline denominations experienced a surplus of people wanting to enter the ordained ministry. In the late 1970s Bishop John Walker of the Diocese of Washington reported to Roy that he had on average one layperson per week coming to see him about changing their vocation and becoming an ordained priest. This diocese had so many applicants that the Screening Committee of that Diocese had to construct higher and higher walls for people to climb over if they wanted to be considered for the ordination track. This Diocese soon required a year-long internship within a congregation (working at least ten hours per week) during which they were evaluated as to their potential for the pastoral ministry. The Diocese of Atlanta adopted a similar year long pre-seminary requirement before people would be accepted for seminary training, three months spent in a congregation, three months in some sort of chaplancy situation, and three month in some type of street ministry. All along people were evaluating them to see if they had clergy potential. In Roy's research on the screening processes of denominations, he came to see that these overly stringent requirements at the front end of the ordination track did screen out the worst candidates, but it also screened out the best. The more requirements you lay on people before they can even begin to consider a vocation in the ordained ministry, the more you will have passive, dependent types who will endure any requirement you put before them. Your entrepreneurial types, your natural leaders, your self-starters, look at all these requirements and say to themselves, "who needs this? I'm heading out to join the Peace Corps, or I'm going to go for a Ph.D. in psychology, etc."

This was all in a time when the role of the ordained clergy still carried with it a sense of honor and dignity. Ordained clergy were held in high esteem. As we enter the 21st century, the role of being an ordained clergyperson has far less appeal. As we move further into a post-Christendom era where we are experiencing a more neutral environment at best, and some hostility at worst, we are seeing people, especially young people, who do not view the church as a way of making an impact upon society.

This may be coupled with the fact that many of our current clergy are burning out from the relentless demands some congregations place upon them, and the growing complexity of their role. As Roy travels around the country doing between 30 and 40 seminars with clergy each year, he is finding between 30% to 40% of clergy experiencing burnout, with a good 15% experiencing extreme burnout. It is highly unlikely that burned out clergy are going to have the interest, much less the capacity, to convince their more talented young people to consider the ordained ministry as a life's vocation.

Another factor to consider. Over the years clergy ranks have often been enriched by "PK'S"—preacher's kids. These people often had experience and knowledge of church systems. They also were in touch with the human/family dimensions of clergy life. Today, overworked, underpaid, low-status clergy are less enthusiastic about recruiting their own children and/or relatives for this vocation.

This then gets at some of the challenge we face as we begin to go after those people who have a strong commitment to Christ, and who are the type of born leaders who will make any situation they take on into a growing, thriving organism.

SOME BASIC ASSUMPTIONS

I. There appears to be a shift in what both baby boomers and baby busters are looking for in congregational life. For the most part, these are more consumers than they are people who remain loyal to institutions or denominations. The time they begin to look for involvement in congregational life is when they begin to have children, and they desire that their children be exposed to some education in spiritual matters and ethical living. Being consumers, they will look around for the congregations that will offer them the best quality of religious education for their children and themselves. It is our larger congregations that have the most resources to provide that kind of quality and variety of religious programming those Boomers and Busters want. Our smaller congregations are clearly disadvantaged in this regard. The congregations most capable of offering great variety and quality are the larger congregations within our denominations.

> The actual statistics of one middle judicatory supports this basic assumption. The North Indiana Conference of the United Methodist Church conducted a study of its membership losses between the years 1975 and 1990. In this conference there were 612 congregations serving a membership of 124,889 members, 376 of those churches averaged less than 100 members in worship each Sunday morning.

Loss of members between 1975 and 1990

Average Attendance	Percentage loss of members attending
80-99	17%
50-79	28%
0-49	35%

We need to anticipate that our smaller congregations are going to lose ground in the years ahead. We need to focus our resources and energies on those congregations that have some reasonable chance of providing the kind of services for which religious seekers yearn.

II. The face of America continues to change with minorities continuing to expand their percentage of our population. By the year 2050, only 53% of the population of this country will be non-Hispanic Whites. By the year 2050, 23% of our population will be Hispanic. 14% Afro-American, 10% Asian American, and 1% Native American. Even by the year 2010, Hispanics will make up 14% of the population compared with only 13% Afro-American, and 5% Asian American. Yet Asian Americans remain the fastest growing racial group in the country. (Reference: *Changing Face of America*, Chicago Tribune, Wednesday 29, 1993).

Implication: When only 53% of our population is non-Hispanic White, and that is what most denominations on the continent are capable of attracting, then all mainline denominations will be competing for this much smaller percentage of the general population. There is no question in our minds that the denominations that continue to cater only to Euro-Americans are going to continue to be in decline. The implication for recruitment efforts is that we will need to be recruiting one racial/ethnic minority person for every Euro-American we recruit.

III. The decline in church attendance will continue on into the future. Key factors:
   - Growing secularism with less time devoted to spiritual matters.
   - Increased demands on the time of Boomers, Busters, GenXers and Millennials leaving less time for spiritual growth.
   - Continuing change in personal values in which the desire to be well off financially supersedes the desire to develop a meaningful philosophy of life.
   - Spirituality is "in" and organized religion is "out," ala Wade Clark Roof's book, "Spiritual Marketplace." (*Spiritual Marketplace ----- Baby Boomers and the Remaking of American Religion* by Wade Clark Roof Princeton University Press, 1999).

Result: Fewer people active in congregational life in the future. Instead, people will be seeking to meet their spiritual needs by focusing in on forms of spiritual expression that are independent of traditional religious groups, remaining uninvolved for any length of time in a single spiritual path or any given community.

Once again we need to remind ourselves of the fluke in history when we in this country had more people attending church than any other country in the world. No one knows quite why we became the most religious country in the world. However, we will continue to berate ourselves when we cannot get our numbers back to where they were in the 1950s and 1960s. Possibly we should continue to remind ourselves of one of Jesus' sayings, namely that the kingdom of God is like some yeast hidden in the dough. When God has a faithful remnant to work with, he is able to transform the whole loaf. Maybe, rather than focusing so much on numbers we need to focus on faithfulness to Christ, and depth of commitment.

IV. Congregations that cannot afford their own full time pastor would much prefer to be cared for by a part-time, bi-vocational pastor than be yoked with one or more

other congregations in order to share an ordained pastor. What these smaller congregations want from a pastor is their presence for the full Sunday morning experience that includes a Bible Study, a worship experience, and a coffee hour. When clergy serve more than one congregation, they need to deliver a sermon in one congregation, have to jump in their car to go serve another congregation. Most congregations this size hate that dimension of being yoked with another congregation. This implies, for us, recruiting far more bi-vocational clergy than we are currently.

V.   The size and type of congregation in the growing years of potential candidates for ministry greatly shapes the size and type of congregation in which they will serve best (i.e. clergy raised in a program size congregation will do their best work in program sized congregations).

VI.   The clergy who will be most capable in recruiting transformational leaders for the ordained ministry are the ones who are themselves transformational leaders. This implies a strategy of Regional Bodies being selective about the people and congregations it engages to recruit transformational leaders for tomorrow's church.

VII. Given the shift of these next generations away from smaller congregations towards larger congregations, we are going to need substantially fewer ordained clergy and far more program oriented staff specialists, with the capacity to work as part of a team (e.g. Youth Workers, Directors of Religious Education, Small Group Specialists, Associates with special skills in spiritual formation, persons specializing in working to and with Older Adults, persons adept at developing alternative worship options, etc.).

VIII. The need for "caretaker" type Anglo clergy is going to be substantially reduced, as our most pressing need will be for entrepreneurial type clergy.

Should we be on target with these assumptions, we ought to look at the ethics of our continuing to accept into the ordained ministry track non-Hispanic White, caretaker types, who assume we will continually provide them with congregations they can serve full time until retirement. Most challenging will be the task of recruiting one racial/ethnic minority person for every Euro-American person we admit into the ordination track. Equally challenging will be a strategy for recruiting people with proven leadership capacity, screening out most but not all "caretaker" types. It is for this reason that we see this aspect of becoming a transformational Regional Body as being the most difficult and the most challenging.

It takes approximately seven miles to turn around a huge ocean liner. We need to think in similar terms when we consider coming to terms with the above realities. Consider the time it takes to identify young adults who have proven leadership ability and challenge them to consider the ordained ministry. Once recruited, what additional time will be needed for them to shift their major in college, put them through seminary, give

them a few years experience as an ordained person to get their feet wet, and then place them in the type of challenging situation for which we recruited them in the first place. We are talking here of between 6 and 10 years. It is for this reason that Regional Bodies need to begin immediately to put together the type of strategic plan that would enable them to have the right type of clergy leadership to meet the demands of the 21st century.

It might help to see some actual estimates of the number and type of clergy we will need in ten years by re-visiting our tale of two Regional Bodies. This time we will look at the clergy roster in our best-case scenario and in our worst-case scenario. You will recall our generic Regional Body. It contained 100 congregations:

> 7 Corporate-sized congregations serving 3930 members
> 16 Program-sized congregations serving 3843 members
> 33 Pastoral-sized congregations serving 3960 members, and
> 44 Family-sized congregations serving 1980 members.

Given the fact that all Corporate size congregations have at least two ordained persons on staff and the same being true of some of the Program-size congregations, we would estimate that this Regional Body in the year 2001 would be employing approximately 95 full time ordained clergy.

You will also recall that **WISE VIRGINS SYNOD TEN YEARS LATER had**:

- Two congregations declined yet changed their identity to become minority congregations (one becoming an Afro-American congregation worshipping 210 per Sunday, and the second becoming a Hispanic congregation worshipping 250 per Sunday).
- Four remained stable and grew slightly and one became a mega-church worshipping 2450 per Sunday.
- A new mission started by the Synod grew to corporate size in eight years and worshipped 385 per Sunday.

The number of members these eight Corporate size congregations grew from 3930 in 2001 to 5395 in the year 2011.

Now let us review the shift in their clergy roster serving these corporate size congregations in 2011.

In the year 2001 they had fourteen full time Anglo clergy. In the year 2011 they had a total of nineteen clergy serving Corporate size congregations, yet of these nineteen, two were Afro-American, one was Hispanic, and one was Korean, leaving fifteen being non-Hispanic whites. (The mega church employed an Afro-American clergyperson and a Korean clergyperson.)

Of the sixteen Program size congregations in this Regional Body:
- Three declined to Pastoral size.
- Seven held their own, three doing so by inviting in a minority group to develop a ministry to their own people within their congregations, one Hispanic, one Korean, and one Afro-American.

- Five grew in size, two by developing a Korean congregation within their existing congregation.
- One grew to mega-church size, which worshipped 1823 per week.
- Four mission congregations started by the Regional Body grew to 250, 185, 210 and 280 respectively, two serving an Anglo congregation, one serving an Afro-American congregation, and one a Hispanic congregation.

The number of members served by these seventeen Program size congregations rose from 3843 in the year 2001 to 9155 in the year 2011.

Lets now review the clergy roster, which serves these 9155 active members. This Regional Body went from having twenty Anglo clergy in 2001 to thirty total clergy in 2011. Of these thirty clergy, three were Korean, two were Afro-American, and two were Hispanic, with the remaining twenty-three non-Hispanic whites.

Of the thirty-three Pastoral size congregations in this Synod:
- Five declined badly and eventually closed their doors and sold their buildings.
- Twelve declined to family size and were served by part-time clergy.
- Sixteen congregations targeted for re-development grew to Program Size, four by becoming Hispanic congregations.
- Five new missions were started in this Regional Body and developed to Pastoral size. (One mission was developed to serve Hmong congregants, another served only Cantonese members and a third served only Mandarin people. The remaining two served Anglo members.)

The number of members served by these Pastoral size congregations grew from 3960 in 2001 to 4320 in the year 2011.

When we look at the clergy roster serving this size congregation, we have twelve congregations being served by part-time Bi-vocational clergy. Of the remaining fourteen full time clergy, two are Afro-American, two are Hispanic, one is Mandarin, one is Cantonese, and one is Hmong, with the remaining seven being non-Hispanic whites. It is here that we have the greatest drop in our need for Anglo clergy. We drop from thirty-three non-Hispanic whites in 2001 serving full time to seven non-Hispanic whites in year 2011 serving full time.

Of the forty-four Family size congregations in this Regional Body:
- Thirty closed their doors and sold their buildings.
- Ten remained open with six being served by part-time Bi-Vocational clergy, and four becoming yoked and serviced by one ordained clergyperson and two Bi-vocational clergy.
- Two grew to Pastoral-size.
- Two inner city congregations closed and then re-opened, one to become a Hmong congregation serving 120 and the second to become a Hispanic congregation serving 90 people.

Total number of members served by these Family size congregations dropped from 1980 in the year 2001 to 730 in the year 2011.

When looking at the clergy serving these Family size congregations, we have eight part-time Bi-vocational clergy, plus five full time clergy, one Hmong, one Hispanic, and three non-Hispanic whites. In this category the Synod went from needing twenty-two non-Hispanic white clergy in 2001 to needing only three in year 2011.

SUMMARY OVERVIEW OF CLERGY SERVING WISE VIRGINS SYNOD
This Synod went from having 95 full time clergy on its roster in 2001 to 77 full time clergy in the year 2011. Of these 77 full time clergy, six were Afro-American, eight were Hispanic, four were Korean, 1 was Cantonese, 1 was Mandarin, and 2 were Hmong, with the remaining 55 being non-Hispanic whites. This was a drop of 34 non-Hispanic white clergy within a ten-year time span and an increase of 14 Bi-vocational part time clergy.

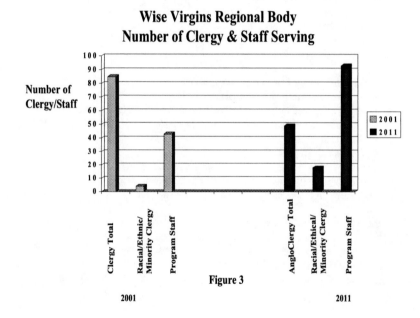

Figure 3

FOOLISH VIRGINS SYNOD TEN YEARS LATER

Of the seven Corporate-size congregations in their care:
- Two experienced modest growth.
- Three held their own and grew slightly.
- One declined to program size
- One was hit with a clergy scandal and dropped to pastoral size.

Total number of members served dropped from 3930 in 2001 to 2910 in the year 2011. In reviewing the number of clergy they employed to serve these 2910 members in 2011, this Synod dropped from fourteen full time clergy to twelve full time clergy, all non-Hispanic Whites.

Of the seventeen Program size congregations in their care:
- Five declined to Pastoral size.
- Eight held their own.
- Three grew to corporate size.
- One new mission grew to 280 per Sunday.

Total number of members served dropped from 3842 in 2001 to 3360 in the year 2011. The number of clergy they employed dropped from twenty-six Anglo clergy in 2001 to nineteen Anglo clergy in 2011.

Of the thirty-three Pastoral size congregations in their care:
- Thirteen closed their doors and sold their buildings.
- Thirteen declined to Family size with five clergy serving ten congregations and three Bi-vocational clergy serving the remaining three congregations.
- Six held their own.
- One grew to Program size.

Total number of members served by their Pastoral size congregations dropped from 3960 in the year 2001 to 1010 in the year 2011. The number of clergy they employed in Pastoral size congregations dropped from thirty-three in the year 2001 to twelve in 2011.

Of the forty-four Family sized congregations in their care:
- Thirty-six closed their doors and sold their buildings.
- Eight congregations remained Family size, currently being served by three full time and one part-time clergyperson.

Total number of members served dropped from 1980 in the year 2001 to 320 in the year 2011.

The number of clergy they employed to serve these 320 active members dropped from twenty-two clergy in the year 2001 to three full-time and one part-time clergyperson in the year 2011.

SUMMARY OVERVIEW OF CLERGY SERVING FOOLISH VIRGINS SYNOD

This Synod went from having 95 full-time clergy on their roster in the year 2001 to 44 full time and 4 part-time clergy in the year 2011. This Synod was employing 51 fewer full time clergy in 2011 than they were in the year 2001.

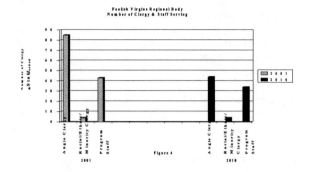

Figure 4

COMMENTARY

If we are anywhere close to predicting the future of Christian Churches, a number of things are obvious.

I. Becoming multi-cultural denominations is key to becoming vibrant, growing denominations. The faces of people populating this continent in the future will be many hued. The languages and dialects that will populate most of our states will continue to multiply. Roy has a niece, LeAnn, who teaches first grade school in the Toronto, Canada area. LeAnn is your classic blue eyed, blonde haired, Germanic young woman. Out of twenty-two children in her class, only one has blond hair and blue eyes. When LeAnn has a parent/teachers meeting, she requires seven different interpreters for her to communicate with the parents.

Recent census data, as reported out in several newspapers makes this point even more vivid:

Item 1: The population of Montgomery County in the state of Maryland now has 40% of its residents being Hispanic. This is one of the more affluent counties that is a suburb of Washington, D.C.

Prince George's County, which is a neighboring suburb is made up of 50% Afro-American. Both counties are growing, but Montgomery County is growing at a fast pace. What would be the prospects of any mainline denomination starting a new Euro-American mission in Montgomery county when 40% of the residents are Hispanic. Starting a Hispanic mission would make much more sense. Hispanic missions are not likely to succeed unless we have transformational Hispanic clergy to send into the mission field. *Data: Washington Post, March 21, 2001.*

Item 2: Califomia has become the first big state with no ethnic majority. What is predicted for this country in the year 2050 has already taken place in California. Census 2000 figures show that California's non-Hispanic white population shrank to 46.7% of the states 33,871,648 residents. California is home for one out of eight Americans. Since 1970, the state's Hispanic population has more than quadrupled to 10.9   million   from 2.4 million. Its share climbed from 12.1% of the population to 32.4%. Nearly one-third of all Hispanics in the USA live in California. Only two much smaller states, Hawaii and New Mexico, have no racial majorities. What would be the prospect of any mainline denomination starting an Anglo Mission in one of these three states?
Data: USA Today, March 30, 2001

Item 3: Hispanics surpass blacks as Florida's largest minority. The trend is so pervasive that no county in that state saw an increase of less that 30% in its Hispanic population. Orlando's Orange County itself saw a 159% increase in the Hispanic population --- or nearly one in five people in the county. In Broward County, the story was no less gripping: its Hispanic population grew by 151% or 17% of the population. The number of non-Hispanic whites dropped from 75% in 1990 to under 60% by year 2000. *Data: The Miami Herald, March 28, 2001.*

In the March/April 2001 edition of Alban's magazine called, "CONGREGATIONS," The entire edition was dedicated to the church's current dilemma of recruiting younger people into the ordained ministry. It appears as though all mainline denominations are experiencing a shortage of clergy under the age of 35. The following chart gives us some perspective on this problem.

LOOKING AT THE AGE GAP: NOW AND THEN

DENOMINATION	NOW			THEN	
	Year 1997			Year 1982	
American Baptist	64.5% reporting	4,000 clergy			
	35 & under	230	6%	14%	
	55+	1,519	38%	36%	
	Year 1999			Year 1979	
Disciples of Christ	Total	7,113		6,724	
	35 & under	260	4%	227	3%
	55+	1,071	15%	931	14%

	Year 2000			Year 1974	
Episcopal	Total	7,721		8,532	
	35 & under	303	3.92%	1,655	19%
	55+	3,072	39.78%	1,918	22%

	Year 2000			Year 1981	
Lutheran Church	95% reporting	5,783		5,702	
Missouri Synod	35 & under	446	8%	1,009	18%
	55+	1,775	31%	1,287	23%

	Year 1999			Year 1975	
Presbyterian Church (U.S.A.)	Total 8,667 (estimated)			9,151	
	35 & under	607	7%	2,241	24%
	55+	2,600	30%	1,769	19%

	Year 1999			Year 1975	
Roman Catholic	Total 27,000			30,785	
	35 & under	1,650	6%	4,926	16%
	55+	18,681	69%	9,851	32%

	Year 2000				
Southern Baptist Convention	(700 Churches sampled)				
	35 & under		11%	not available	
	55+		29%		

	Year 2000		
United Church of Christ	81% reporting	5,141	
	35 & under	207	4%
	55+	1,877	37%

	Year 2000			
United Methodist	Total	12,061		
	35 & under	740	7%	not available
	55+	1,877	37%	

	Year 2000			Year 1975	
Unitarian Universalist	Total	1,171		521	
Association	35 & under	95	8%	95	18%
	55+	419	36%	108	20%

The implications of these statistics for recruiting persons for the ordained ministry are enormous. When young people no longer see the Church as a place to make an impact on society, how are we going to present our need for their skills in a way that is both challenging and convincing. What could be some possible contexts within which we might engage young people in such a dialogue? Do we first need to develop meaningful worship and educational experiences for this younger generation before they can sense and experience the relevance of this calling? Are we doing enough to bring to consciousness the possibility of this calling to our children, before they reach their teen years? Do our current youth ministries present this vocational option to our teenagers in ways that are attractive and appealing? Possibly we need to review the curriculum of study we offer younger people, seeing to it that depth and commitment of faith is called for much earlier in life.

We also need to address our needs for a more multi-cultural approach to recruitment. It is our conviction that one out of every two people recruited for seminary training should be a racial/ethnic minority person. If our seminaries remain lily white, how are we as mainline denominations going to be able to reach out to half of the population on this continent by the year 2050? Even today, doing mission work in certain states and certain counties without racial/ethnic minority clergy is foolhardy. When all of us are going after that same shrinking population of Euro-American people, there is no way we can continue to grow and thrive.

Most of our denominations were immigrant churches at one time. We were good at it. Roy's father was a bilingual Lutheran pastor. Every Sunday he preached one German sermon and one English one. Translating that into today's world, our congregations should have one sermon in English, and one in Spanish, or Korean, or Cantonese, etc. preached in church every week. The children of these ethnic parents would be attending the same Sunday Schools as their Anglo friends. As the years go by, gradually these children will want to worship with the remainder of the congregation in a contemporary English Service.

Some suggestions about how we might do a better job at recruiting minority candidates for the ordained ministry:
a. Have someone from your Regional Body visit one or more of the interdenominational seminaries or Bible Colleges in your area of the country. Take a minority person from your denomination with you. Minority students often populate these seminaries and Bible Colleges. Many of them come from Community Churches or Store Front Churches and they have sensed a call to the ordained ministry. Talk to them about becoming an ordained pastor within your denomination. The advantage of bringing a minority person with you from your denomination, whether they serve on your National or your Regional staff, is that you are clearly communicating that serving in your denomination does not mean being relegated to some of your poorest churches in some inner city setting. We need to be able to communicate that our denominations are open to having minorities serving at a variety of levels of authority within our systems.

It should not surprise us that these types of students would be interested in serving as a pastor within a mainline denomination. We have the type of order and structure which would allow them to serve in a variety of capacities. If they don't join a mainline denomination, their only other choice is to begin a church on their own. Sometimes that works, sometimes it doesn't. If it does they will be stuck with that church for the rest of their ordained ministry. These students can clearly see the advantage of belonging to a denomination that can provide them with many more options of service. This approach may work best when going after Afro-American students.

There is one major caution that must be heeded when using this approach. When recruiting minority students in this way, they will need to spend enough time within your system, both learning it and serving in it, before they are ordained. It is important to build up some denominational loyalty in this person. Otherwise, you may give this person a congregation to serve, and he/she will take that congregation out of your denomination and make it an independent church.

b. In the cases where we are going after a potential candidate for ministry who is fluent in Spanish, Japanese, Korean, Chinese, etc., we may need to make a trip to one of those countries, locate a talented pastor already working in a congregation, and explore with them the possibility of coming to North America to serve here. Many of these foreign pastors are fluent in English and would have little difficulty in communicating with people on this continent. More than likely, the pay package and perks you can offer would be sufficiently higher than what they are receiving in their indigenous country. Mainly appeal to their sense of mission. Let them know that the "fields are ripe, but we do not have laborers who will gather in the harvest".

c. Sometimes it is advisable to develop a national strategy for going after minority candidates for ministry. When we are collaborating with other Regional Bodies, we can develop separate task forces made up of clergy from a given minority group. Before we assign them the task of recruiting people for the ordained ministry from among their own people, we will want to explore the level of satisfaction they have in serving within our denominations. We may need to do some hard work at improving the way these people are treated within our system. Do they feel valued and appreciated by our system? When they are happy campers, they will be motivated to go after capable people from their race or ethnic group to see if they are open to a call to the ordained ministry within our denominations.

II. Every second person you recruit for the ordained ministry needs to be a minority person with transformational capacity. In addition the majority of Anglo persons recruited will need to be a transformational leaders as well. Yes, we will need some "caretaking" type clergy, but we will not need many. We will have more than enough of those kinds of clergy coming to us to gain entrance into the ordination track. We now have the technology available to us in the Charles Ridley methodology of interviewing that we can determine who is and who isn't a transformational leader. This six-hour interview process is explained in greater detail in Chapter five. Once again, if we are on target with our predictions about the future of the Christian Church on this continent, we are not going to need that many Anglo clergy. If this is the case, why not hold out for the people who can take a dying situation, turn it around, and make it into a thriving congregation once again. To be sure, we will need some "caretaker" type clergy. We are going to find that a good number of the congregations under our care are not interested in either growing or ministering to the crying needs of their community. These are congregations made up mainly of older adults, who simply want their church to be around to bury them when they die. Beyond that, they have no investment in their congregation surviving to serve the generations that follow them. It is no use burning out transformational leaders on congregations that maintain this attitude. These are congregations that generally have little opportunity to grow anyway. They can be in a location that is declining demographically. Some may not have adequate facilities to thrive and grow. These are the type of congregations that could use a warm, caring, loving pastor who is quite willing to give them palliative care as they slowly die.

Hopefully, the majority of situations within our Regional Bodies will not resemble congregations of that nature, but will, instead, appreciate a more dynamic clergyperson. If we were using the Ridley method to ascertain which clergy within our Regional Body have transformational abilities, it would be prudent to train your Screening Committee or your Committee on Ministry with this interview method. Not everyone this committee interviews and approves will have this kind of leadership capacity. However, the committee should be aware of the ratio of these types of candidates for ministry that it approves as opposed to the care-taking types they are currently approving. The Governing Board of your Regional Body ought to be able to receive a report from this task force on this ratio, which will update them on the kinds of people going to seminary in any given year. This should apply to all candidates for ministry, including your minority candidates.

CLERGY SHORTAGE?

Within the last 5 years most mainline denominations claim they are experiencing a clergy shortage. Each denomination can detail how many call vacancies they have. They speak in terms of having 500 to 800 situations that could use a Pastor and there are none to fill these pulpits.

On the surface this implies that we need to search the highways and byways to get more people ordained to fill these vacancies. However, the problem as we have defined it grows out of our having a clergy surplus for the 20 years prior to this time. When in a clergy surplus, any little church with Sunday attendance of 50 or more got a Pastor of their own---that is, if they could afford it. When they couldn't afford it, we yoked them with another small membership church so that between the two of them they could afford a full time Pastor.

Now, as we look at this so-called CLERGY SHORTAGE, we still are thinking in terms of having an ordained person serving all these places. Referring back to the polarity:

CLERGY DOMINATED------------------LAITY DOMINATED
CONGREGATION   CONGREGATION

we can see why we are CLERGY DOMINATED.

We should look with interest at the Roman Catholic Church that has experienced a major clergy shortage over the last 20 years. Have they declined in membership as a result of that shortage? No! As a matter of fact, the Roman Catholic Church in this country has been growing while all mainline denominations have been in decline. Do they have an ordained Priest for all those small congregations? Not by a long shot. Possibly we need to be talking with our Roman Catholic brothers and sisters to understand how they have accomplished this feat. How have they continued to grow with such a clergy shortage?

What may be needed here is a paradigm shift within mainline denominations. A parallel situation may be our observing the decline of dairy farmers in this country. Hundreds of dairy farms close down every year. They simply cannot survive given their size and the price of milk in this country. Do we see anyone in panic saying, "We have got to go out and recruit a whole new lot of dairy farmers. We are not going to have enough milk to support our needs in this country." Nothing could be further from the truth. We continue to experience having more milk available to consumers than is necessary, which keeps the price of milk so low that the small dairy farmer can no longer make a living wage.

Our old mentality thinking on this issue has us believing that we have a clergy shortage. This has us allowing into the ordination track any warm body that is willing to go to seminary. Recently, Barbara Wheeler at Auburn Theological Seminary conducted a study entitled, "Is There A Problem?" (Center for the Study of Theological Education, Auburn Seminary, 3041 Broadway at 121st St, New York, N.Y. 10027 Telephone 212 662 4315). The report involved 2512 entering master's level theological students in a variety of seminaries around the country in the spring of 1999. The finds are based on an examination of the responses of these entering seminarians.

Her figures indicate that in that year seminaries accepted into their student membership 87% of all applicants. To quote the summary of that study, "Theological schools are not highly selective (data from other sources show that half accepted 87% or more of those who apply). A majority of students apply to only one school. Only a handful says that they were not accepted by their first choice of seminary. That figure should alarm us. For example, most medical schools in the country normally accept less that half the students that apply. It implies that we are accepting into the ordination track a large number of marginal students, many of whom do not have the capacity to lead a congregation to greater health and vitality. To be sure, we might still have warm bodies to place into all those marginal congregations within our Regional Bodies, but let us not have any illusions about those situations becoming vital centers of faith and outreach. We would probably be doing those congregations a favor if we simple told them that we did not have clergy available for them and that they needed to find a way of remaining a viable spiritual community without the presence of an ordained Pastor. That would place the responsibility back where it belongs. When we send in an incompetent Pastor to those situations, the membership of those congregations remains stuck in an old paradigm. They will simple sit around and complain about the Pastor and when they can get another one who might be better than the one they have. They will remain a CLERGY DOMINATED congregation, where it is the Pastor's job to make things happen.

To be sure, the shift from one way of using clergy within our Regional Bodies to another will not be an easy or painless process. At first it will feel like we are going to die. Can we possibly see the hand of God in all this? Can we learn from the Roman Catholics that God did not abandon them when they became seriously short of Priests?

We believe that it would be prudent and wise for mainline denominations to adopt a policy of only allowing into the ordination track transformational men and women who possess the charisma of gifted leadership. Using the Charles Ridley method of interviewing potential candidates for ministry, we promise to ordain only people who are entrepreneurial in nature. These are people who have had a track record of making things happen, regardless of their context, and regardless of their age. In the long run we will be much further ahead than our current trend which is to open wide the gates and allow into the ordination track any warm body capable of seminary academics.

In all this, we may need to reconsider how we view seminary education. Is it possible to postpone approval for ordination until after people have graduated from seminary? In other words, we should not deny anyone in their desire to obtain a seminary degree. We would, therefore, not be cutting the lifeline of seminaries as well. Allow seminaries to recruit students with abandon. Having more people trained in Bible and Theology might be an advantage to our congregations. In this scenario, the call to the ordained ministry would come towards the end of such an education, possibly following an internship within a congregation. We would make no promises to ordain anyone who graduated from seminary. For the majority of students, the call to the ordained ministry would occur only in conjunction with feedback from seminary faculty, fellow students, and the supervising Pastor in a year long internship. The exceptions would be those people we had intentionally recruited because of their racial/ethnic makeup or their proven transformational capacities.

The Auburn study indicates that this is happening already. "Students come to theological schools in pursuit of numerous professional goals. Though 80% say that their goal is a "religious" profession or occupation, fewer (60%) plan to be ordained, and ministry in a congregation or parish is the primary goal of less than one-third of students.

This study also confirmed the lack of racial/ethnic minority students entering seminary. "Compared with their presence in the general population of North America, both African-Americans (less than 9% of the theological student population) and Hispanics (only 3%) are significantly underrepresented."

One approach, cited in this study, which deserves exploration, is the creation of standards for "premium" programs of ministerial education that have higher entrance and completion standards. Such programs, which might take the form of honors tracks within existing programs, would not require any school to exclude from its basic program students who are sent to them by their sponsoring religious body. Honors tracks would, however, produce some graduates who are identified as especially promising religious leaders. This approach would accommodate Regional Bodies who invested much into recruiting transformational leaders, especially those representing racial/ethnic minorities. These students would be placed immediately in the honors program, which would guarantee them a call to the ordained ministry upon graduation. At the same time, anyone interested in pursuing a theological education would be welcome to enroll.

III. If the ratio mentioned above is to increasingly tilt towards candidates that are entrepreneurial leaders, we will need to stop being passive and more aggressively go after the brightest and the best within our congregations. Currently we would guess that less that 10% of all Regional Bodies within mainline denominations have a proactive process in place that actively recruits quality ordained leaders for tomorrow's church. It is our sense of things that 90% of all Regional Bodies are still stuck in a passive mode, simply screening the people who come to them with an interest in the ordained ministry. We think this is true for a number of reasons:

a. A Christendom mentality still pervades many denominational bodies. We seem unable to get out of this orbit and open our eyes to the realities of a Post Christendom time. We all know we are not getting the right kinds of candidates for ministry entering seminary training, yet we simply hope that next year's crop will be different. Once again, doing the same old thing but expecting different results.

b. The specter of mounting a pro-active recruitment process is so daunting that we simply avoid thinking about it. In many cases it is a lack of conviction on our part that the mission and work of our congregations is worth asking a young person who has a promising career in such professions as Law, Medicine, or Corporate Management to sacrifice that career and give their life to serving the Christian Church as an ordained person. We may need to structure some time to explore this matter in a variety of settings to become clearer about our theology of call. It is not we who call these people into this ministry, this is the Spirit's doing. Yet, does that mean we should simply remain passive and expect the Spirit to do all the work? No, we believe we do have a role in this. The Spirit may need our conviction and our passion for Christ and His Church to call some people into this type of service.

c. Church systems are slow to change. Many Regional Bodies still have in place screening systems that were meant for another era. Back in the 1970s and 1980s when we had a plethora of people coming out of the woodwork wanting to be ordained, we had to set up screening processes which were designed to slow these people down and put them through some challenging tasks to allow them to see more clearly the demands of the ordained ministry. For many Regional Bodies, these systems still are in place --- even though they don't fit for this time and situation.

d.   For many Regional Bodies, there is little motivation to begin a dynamic recruitment process. The policy of their National Church discourages it. Currently, we are fussing with one mainline denomination about its policy related to seminary graduates. The way this system works is that all Bishops/Executives come together with their needs for seminary graduates. The system works like the NFL draft. Each Bishop/Executive gets a turn each round to choose one of the graduates from all the seminaries in that denomination. This policy solves one problem, namely making sure that the more frontier Regional Bodies get their share of graduates, but it creates another one. What would be the motivation for a Regional Body to do the hard work of recruiting a quality minority candidate for ministry, only to have that candidate picked off by another Bishop/Executive upon graduation? We can't think of a better way to discourage Regional Bodies from being pro-active about going after the brightest and the best. Best to sit on your duff and benefit from other people's recruitment efforts. This denomination counters this argument by saying that every Regional Body gets the first chance to call candidates from their own Region. Yes, that may be the case, but what will be the choice of the candidate when another Regional Body offers them an opportunity and pay package that you cannot match? We can just imagine the anger of a Regional Body, say in the Philadelphia area, which has nurtured a talented Afro-American student for years, only to have the Regional Body in Chicago give them an opportunity and pay package that candidate could not refuse. What would be the motivation for that Philadelphia Region to go after other talented Afro-America students following that experience? Unless this denomination changes this policy, we do not see any Regional Body within this denomination ever putting much effort into the recruitment process.

IV.   Recruitment of quality people for the ordained ministry needs to happen at the Regional level. There is an important role that National Structures can play in this effort. One is to produce a variety of audio-visual materials that Regional Bodies can use in their recruitment effort. We can also visualize a National Body having a concerted effort to recruit racial and ethnic minorities to the ordained ministry. This may involve the National Body hiring racial/ethnic minorities to focus all their attention on attracting people like themselves to consider the ordained ministry within that denomination.

In addition, we are witnessing some seminary graduates who begin their ministry within a congregation with a huge debt from their years of training in college and seminar. Some graduates have as high as $60,000 in college and seminary debt upon graduation. This clearly limits the places they can agree to serve as an ordained minister. They will need to hold out for the highest paying positions in order to pay off that debt. We need to think long and hard about what must transpire in a newly ordained person's mind when they are being paid the denominations minimum salary and need to pay off such a debt. Even a $10,000 debt may appear awesome to some of these clergy. We are aware of one denomination, the ELCA, which has hired a full time person to work at raising an endowment to financially assist candidates for the ordained ministry. The goal of the ELCA is to raise an endowment of between $112,000,000 and $120,000,000 to assist candidates for ministry. The Presbyterian Foundation now will grant $10,000 debt payment to a seminary graduate who will serve 5 years in a small congregation.

Beyond the above mentioned roles, it is the Regional Body which needs to take on the challenge of recruiting the kind of people it will need ten to twenty years down the pike, to assume pastoral responsibility within its congregations. It is the Regional Body that has direct access to local congregations. Any recruitment process ought to grow out of the strategic vision of a Regional Body. **Since no two Regional Bodies are alike with regards to their cultural make-up and demographics, the specific needs for certain kinds of candidates for ministry is unique to each Regional Body.**

It is for these reasons that we direct this challenge to all Regional Bodies. If we do not develop an effective recruitment process, we should not expect this to be done for us anywhere else. In some denominations, seminaries are charged with the task of recruiting candidates for the ordained ministry. Are we able to see politically why they may not be the best people to be recruiting people for the ordained ministry? The majority of denominations have too many seminaries. Each is trying to survive. These days, seminaries get such a small proportion of their budget from their denominations that they must function as independent entities. Most mainline seminaries are financed by large endowments, financed by wealthy individuals who can clearly see the need for quality people in the ordained ministry. They also have alumni who remain faithful to their alma mater. We are often amazed at how seminaries can raise such large endowments when we cannot do the same for other mission projects within a Regional Body. The only way seminaries can justify asking funders to finance their operations is if they have students. Can we see how, psychologically, they are not in the best position to recruit candidates for ministry? Their very survival depends upon them having students, even mediocre students will do. We know they would like to have the best interests of the wider church in mind as they do their recruiting, however, there is no way they can be objective about who gets screened in and who gets screened out when their very life depends upon them having a large number of students go through their doors every year.

It is the Regional Body that has its finger on the pulse of what the Church needs in terms of ordained personnel. **Please accept this challenge.** Do not anticipate that you will receive much help from other places in the church as you take on this task. You alone have access to the people who need to be doing this work on your behalf, namely the clergy and lay leaders of the congregations under your care. Set a process in motion, a variety of procedures, involving your must committed clergy and lay leaders which will remain focused on this task of attracting the kind of clergy you will need to keep your Regional Body on its growing edge. This will only happen when Regional Body executives express their passion about the importance of this work. These executives, then, need to continually support and provide resources to the cadre of people who can meet this challenge head on. Down the line their successors will thank them for the effort they made in this regard.

RECOMMENDATIONS FOR WAYS TO GET ON WITH THIS TASK

I. We recommend separating your recruitment task force from your screening committee. Your current Screening Committee is too overwhelmed with its current task to take on another one. It is like asking these volunteers to do twice as much work this year than they did last year. For the most part, this group will stick with what they do best, namely interview and screen those brought to them by the system.

We encourage you to structure a separate task force who's sole job is to challenge the most capable people within your system to consider a vocation in the ordained ministry.

We would recommend that this task force and your screening committee meet together periodically to discuss their joint responsibilities. These people need to pray for one another and respect the difficulty in each group's responsibility. Each should be aware of what the other group does and how it intends to go about its task. It is not difficult to see how these two groups could become frustrated and angry at one another. If, for example, the recruitment task force spends two years courting a minority student into considering the ordained ministry as a vocation and the screening committee ended up giving this individual a hard time, we can see how frustrated and angry the recruitment committee might be with the screening committee.

II.   Earlier in this chapter we surfaced the idea that the people most able to recruit transformational leaders are other transformational leaders. The implications of this may give a scare politically, but it means calling together a select group of clergy, commending them on the innovative work they are doing in their congregations, and challenging them to find candidates for the ordained ministry that could do what they are doing. This group should be called together at least once a year where they have a chance to talk about the difficulty they are experiencing in challenging those people with good leadership potential to consider the ordained ministry. These annual meetings, plus frequent mailings, will help this group stay focused on this task.

III.   For the remainder of your congregations, but especially your larger congregations, ask if they would be willing to appoint a "Silent Recruiter" to work with your Recruitment Task Force. These need to be mature lay people who have a love of the church and are committed to mission outreach. Once identified, invite these people to attend an all day training seminar where this challenge is laid before them. At the seminar explore with them the needs of the church for quality men and women to enter the role of ordained clergyperson. Be as simple and clear as you can be about the qualities they need to look for from within their congregation. We would suggest limiting the key characteristics to look for to no more than five. Any more than five makes the task too complicated for people with limited training. Explain to them the concept of being a "Silent" recruiter. By silent, we mean that no one else in the congregation knows that they have been appointed to this task. Their job is to quietly, yet persistently, ask capable people if they had ever considered the ordained ministry as a profession.

This approach can be especially effective with young people. These Silent Recruiters approach capable young people and inform them that they think they would make a good Pastor. Over the years, they stay in touch with these young people, sometimes asking them if they have given some thought to the role of ordained minister. Sometimes they may ask these people to continue to be in prayer about this. When these young people go off to college, this Silent Recruiter may drop them a card occasionally, staying in touch with them. If appropriate, this Silent Recruiter may say that s/he is praying for this person, asking God to assist this person become clearer about their calling in life. This is a long-term task and generally has long-term pay-off. If everyone knows this lay recruiter has been given the task of challenging people to consider the ordained ministry, they can write this person off too easily. In order to keep these silent recruiters on task, they need to come together periodically to be thanked for their efforts, and for them to share how effective they feel at this task. A simple newsletter would help to remind these people that they are part of a much larger effort to re-vitalize the Church. If they succeed in only getting one capable person to give seminary a try, they will have achieved a lot.

IV. We may need to resurrect the whole idea of church camps as being an ideal place to challenge young people to consider this vocation. At some church camps this still is taking place. After a great week together, sitting around a camp fire and singing all their favorite songs, having someone lay out the need for committed people to care about leadership within church can touch these young people in a profound way. The time and situation is ripe for asking everyone present to seriously consider whether God is calling them to this vocation.

V. In a bygone era we asked campus pastors to be on the lookout for committed, capable college students as possibilities for the ordained ministry. Should your Regional Body employ campus pastors at colleges and universities within their area, the Recruitment Task Force should call these people to a meeting once a year to inquire about their work, and to remind them to be on the lookout for specific types of people in their daily contacts with college students.

Over the years, campus ministry appears to have lost its vision for ministry to and with college students. In many cases, the money has dried up which normally went to support these campus pastors. Quite possibly, with a renewed vision of how these campus workers could play a significant role in the recruitment of potential church workers, we might think again about investing in these types of ministries. These campus workers, when they get to know students well, often find themselves talking with students as they struggle with what they should be doing with their lives. Because they are able to be present for these students during these times of struggle, they can be the catalyst in steering these students into leadership roles within the church. In addition, whenever they lead students in a worship opportunity, they have a captive audience to which they can occasionally pitch an invitation for these students to consider a vocation in the church.

VI. Wesley Theological Seminary in Washington, D.C. engaged congregations within Conferences located near it in a program they call "Ministry Sunday." The program encourages every congregation to set aside one Sunday a year for a "Ministry Sunday." The day is dedicated to talking about God's call. Wesley Seminary will often provide the preacher for such a Sunday. Within the context of considering God's call to ministry, members are asked to respond by placing the name of a person within their congregation whom they think has the gifts needed for the ordained ministry. They have discovered that there are usually thirty plus names that are written on cards and placed in the offering plate. The seminary then follows up on these names with a letter of invitation to come to visit the seminary and be in dialogue about the Church's need for full or part-time professionals.

This program was written up in Wesley's Newsletter called: *Partners in Ministry*. The Rev. David McAllister-Wilson, executive vice-president of the seminary, has preached at twelve Ministry Sundays. "It's the most remarkable thing I've seen at Wesley during my time here," he says. "It's like a dam that's about to burst. All you have to do is talk about it and give people the opportunity to respond."

Another Wesley graduate, the Rev. Larry Tingle, pastor of Mt. Olivet United Methodist Church in Arlington, Virginia, was one of the pastors who, on behalf of the seminary, entered a resolution at his conference asking all congregations to have a Ministry Sunday at least once a year. At his church's first Ministry Sunday, held November 12, 2000, McAllister-Wilson preached. The congregation turned in 36 names of people they thought had a special call to ministry. Tingle forwarded the names to the seminary, which sent each person a letter. Two of those named are now enrolled at Wesley.

The Rev. Jim Driscoll, pastor of Great Bridge United Methodist Church in Chesapeake, Virginia said that as a result of Ministry Sunday held at his church in January, a number of people had come to him to discuss the possibility of pursuing ordained ministry. "There is a stirring of interest, which is good to see." Said Driscoll. "That hasn't always been the case in my previous congregations."

Not all people answering this call are planning to be ordained. Many are taking courses in Wesley's newly established Equipping Lay Ministry program so they can become effective lay leaders in their churches and workplaces.

The names of people submitted within these congregations often ranges from the teens to the fifties. To quote another United Methodist Pastor who had 36 names forwarded to the seminary as a result of Ministry Sunday, "I have to think that for teenagers especially, to be notified that they have gifts for ministry, that they could be a pastor, that must be a powerful message."

In one of Roy's seminar conducted on behalf of Alban Institute, he had an informal conversation with one young clergyperson who had had before him an exciting future in the field of economics. When asked why he chose the ordained ministry instead of that exciting, alternative profession, his only reply was: "Because I was asked." This response sent light bulbs flashing in Roy's mind. Of course! It was so simple! No one is really asking young people today to consider a vocation in the ordained ministry. We have completely under-estimated the power of simply asking.

This is often the way Fortune 500 Corporations recruit some of their most talented personnel. They send recruiters onto college campuses who identify some of the best students in that college. Then they ask them if they would consider a vocation in their company, as a specialist of some sort. When college students often struggle with what to do with their lives, having someone identify them as having particular gifts to advance them in certain careers, these students are often drawn to those vocations like a magnet.

Do we still have the conviction of faith to ask bright, capable students who could have exciting and successful careers in other fields, to consider the ordained ministry? This may boil down to the kind of passion we have for Christ and the Church, which has us asking people of ability to sacrifice their future in another field because the Church has need of their gifts right now.

"Natural Church Development," a company founded by a German, Christian A. Schwarz, which has tested its theories in 27 countries, has identified eight essential qualities of healthy churches. In North America, the company functions out of St. Charles, Illinois. They have developed a questionnaire, that when given to 30 members of any congregation will surface which of those eight qualities that church scores lowest. They claim that simply raising the quality of their lowest scoring characteristic will significantly improve the health of the congregation. The eight qualities are:

1. Empowering leadership
2. Gift oriented ministry
3. Passionate spirituality
4. Functional structures
5. Inspiring worship services
6. Holistic small groups
7. Need-oriented evangelism
8. Loving relationships.

With remarkable consistence, the one function that most mainline congregations score as their lowest is Number 3--Passionate Spirituality. This is a very telling statistic when considering the subject at hand. We will not be recruiting some of our brightest and best people for the ordained ministry if we do not have the passion to ask them to consider this vocation. At stake here is our sense of how important this one task is to the future of the Christian Church. We may need much more Bible Study and prayer, much more soul searching, to get us over this hump. It is our very passion for the faith that is, in itself, the key ingredient that has someone consider giving their life to the ordained ministry. Is there a place or a way you can locate this kind of passion for Christ within your Regional Body that will produce the people you need to be on your recruitment task force? The future health of any

Regional Body may be dependent upon its ability to find these people, and finding them soon.

In summary, it is the Regional Body that has the greatest potential for recruiting transformational leaders and, also, recruiting racial/ethnic minorities for tomorrow's church. In order to do so, however, there needs to be a dramatic shift in how much attention a Regional Body gives to this task. In addition, most Regional Bodies need to reconsider the kinds of people it needs to recruit to this task. It will be difficult to remain diligent to this task. For most Regional Body personnel, this task is so daunting that they would rather live in denial and ignorance than face this challenge head on. Unless the Bishop/Executive of the Regional Body has a clear vision of the importance of this task, little of significance will take place in this regard. We remain convinced, however, that Regional Body leaders, with vision and passion, can make a significant impact upon their system by tackling these issues directly. Even if it is the only thing these Regional Body executive do well, it still will have long lasting impact on the future health of their system.

Chapter 9

REDEVELOPING CONGREGATIONS
...AN ALTERNATIVE APPROACH

Redeveloping a congregation takes hard intentional work. We are mainly referring here to congregations that have been on a steady membership decline and wish to reverse that trend to once again become a growing, thriving congregation. Such a reversal rarely happens in the absence of conflict.

The model for redeveloping a congregation that is most likely to succeed is the one outlined earlier in this book, namely waiting until the congregation has a change of pastors. During this transitional time, the Regional Body enters into a contractual arrangement with that congregation whereby the regional body appoints the congregation's next pastor for a five-year term. The regional body then secures a pastor for that congregation with proven skills in redevelopment. There are many other things that go into such a contract with this congregation, which allows for the greatest possibility for such a turn around and success.

Most recently, Alban Institute has been working on alternative models for redevelopment. The preferred model as outlined above has its limitations, the biggest one being able to find enough Redevelopment Pastors who have the capacity to turn around a congregation experiencing a membership decline. We became curious about the possibility of working with clergy who were faithful, caring Pastors but lacked the leadership capacity to turn around a declining situation. What would it take to move such a Pastor from merely being a caretaker type Pastor to being a transformational leader?

We had some skepticism about the training model that we employ in so many other courses in our Educational Department. Taking a Pastor out of his/her context, filling them with a lot of great ideas, and then sending them back to their congregations, has its limitations. We find that these clergy often become overwhelmed by all the challenging ideas they have been given, and they do not know where to start to communicate this with their lay leaders. To begin with, lay leaders do not have huge chunks of time to sit and listen to all the ideas that the Pastor has brought back. The Pastor needs to choose carefully what to share and when. What we discovered is that these clergy slip back into crisis mode and begin responding to all the people who have need of their pastoral care. Over time, little of what was learned at the seminar gets translated into action.

The other approach is the consultative model. In this model, someone with knowledge and insights into church renewal consults with a congregation over the course of several months, trying to get both clergy and core lay leadership to act in concert with one another in bringing about the changes that are needed in order for the congregation to begin again to engage in its primary task of changing people's lives and moving them to surrender their lives to Christ. This would also include equipping their members to become an inviting congregation, reaching out to the unchurched in their community. The drawback of this model is the intensity of labor that is required by an outside consultant working with congregations one at a time.   Additionally, is such a model cost effective? Most congregations cannot afford to pay an outside consultant to work with them over the course of months and, perhaps, years.

It occurred to us that we might consider a combination of the above two approaches. What if we combined both training and a consultative model in working with a cluster of congregations? We began to play with the idea of having clergy and lay leaders experience the same seminar together, along with someone from their Regional Body staff. Was it realistic to expect that a congregation would have the kind of key lay leaders who could take a week off from work to attend such a seminar? It crossed our minds that we might begin such a five-day seminar on Wednesday afternoon, ending on Sunday late afternoon. This would limit the days a lay leader would need to be excused from their job in order to participate in such a venture.

We began experimenting with this combination in the Fall of 1997. Senior Consultants Roy Oswald and Alice Mann invited eight congregations into an experiment involving a weeklong training seminar, combined with a year of consultative follow up.   We developed a set of criteria that would determine the kinds of congregations we would engage in such research. We needed congregations that had the potential for becoming turn around congregations. The following are some of the items that went into our contract with these eight congregations:

- A pastor who has been with the congregation at least a year.
- A church plant that is in reasonable repair and is debt free or close to it.
- The capacity to pay for the full time salary of a pastor plus benefits.
- The unanimous approval of the governing board to enter such a transformational effort.
- The ability to send the pastor plus at least one lay leader, preferably two, to the training seminar.
- Having someone from the regional body present at the training seminar with this team of pastor plus two lay leaders. This was to ensure that the congregation's Regional Body was supportive of this congregation entering into this type of contractual arrangement, and also knew what it was attempting to do.   .
- The congregation needed to invest in some type of professional demographic analysis of their community and bring that analysis with them to the training seminar.
  (This professional analysis is completed by companies such as "Percept", or "Visions/Decisions.)

In addition to conducting a weeklong training seminar with four people representing each congregation, we contracted to remain in contact with each participating congregation for at least a year.   This contact included eight conference calls with members of the redevelopment teams, plus quarterly reports which received an individual Alban response, plus participation in a internet chat page devoted entirely to this project.

As is obvious, we are approaching redevelopment through a team approach. The reason we insisted on having someone from the Regional Body present throughout this training event had to do with having upset people end up in the Regional Body Executive's office demanding this effort to cease. Once again, without conflict little transformation work takes place. We could foresee several powerful lay leaders, who did not like what was going on in their congregation, ending up in their Regional Body Executive's office, putting pressure on him/her to put a stop to the changes that were taking place in their congregation. With a representative from the Regional Body present in the training, they would expect some upset people to be coming to them, and have a ready response for them. The Regional Body representative also engaged in on-going consultation with this congregation throughout its redevelopment effort.

We are into our fifth year of experimenting with this approach. Roy now teams with Claire Burkat in conducting these transformational events. Alice continues to work with congregations in the New England area using this approach with clusters of congregations. To date everyone is both surprised and pleased with the results. We have not had 100% success in every case, but we have witnessed the majority of congregations that participate in this program experience a turnaround.

It is our sense of things that the strongest element in this approach is insisting that the participating pastor bring several lay leaders with him/her to the training seminar. Because of this, they review important theory pieces and strategies together. Throughout the week they are engaged in review and planning as a team. This team has been assured of support by the congregation's governing body. The on-going telephone contact with the Alban consultants continues to re-enforce the need to stay with their strategy for redevelopment, even when the going gets rough.

Heavy use is made at the seminar of the demographic data, which the participants bring with them to the seminar. They are instructed how to maximize the information assembled in that profile. We encourage them to work with the STRENGTHS and WEAKNESSES within their congregation as this relates to OPPORTUNITIES and THREATS in the external environment. Teams are encouraged to develop a strategic plan as to how they will match a STRENGTH within their congregation with an OPPORTUNITY in the environment. At the same time they are to plan ways they will minimize the THREATS in the environment while at the same time addressing their WEAKNESSES within.

Of particular importance in the seminar is addressing any type of size transition they are facing. Alice Mann's latest book, "*The In-between Church*," has produced some new insights into the difficulty and complexity of moving from one congregational size to another. She has taken the Arlin Rothauge size categories in his book, "Sizing Up Your Congregation for New Member Development," a quantum leap deeper. She has identified the forces at work, which naturally keep a congregation stuck within a size category. When a congregation reaches the glass ceiling of a particular size, it's more than likely going to shrink in size rather than break through to the next size. Participating congregations are instructed as to the cost of moving to another size, plus given strategies as to how to break through to the next size. What follows is a demarcation of the various sizes with an accompanying identification of the transition phase. When we refer to size in this theory we are referring to the average worship attendance on a weekend, including children.

> Transition phase   500 – 600
> > Corporate size congregation worshiping 350 to 500
>
> Transition phase 350 to 400 average worship
> > Program size congregation worshipping 150 to 350
>
> Transition phase 150 to 200 average worship
> > Pastoral size congregation worshipping 50 to 150
>
> Transition phase 50 to 80 average worship
> > Family size congregation worshipping 0 to 50 per Sunday.

Another strong element in the training seminar is the emphasis that is placed upon strong leadership, especially leadership styles as people face into difference and conflict. Several survey instruments are utilized to give participants an accurate picture of their current leadership style, with a clear identification of alternative leadership styles and conflict utilization styles that might be used. As pre-work to the conference, we have each participant have three lay leaders within the congregation complete an assessment of them with regards to their capacity to be a VISIONARY LEADER. They then were able to compare how they rated themselves with regard to being a Visionary Leader over against how three lay leaders rated them on the same scales.

Participants are also challenged to review their spiritual autobiography to ascertain the key elements in that autobiography that they might use in inviting others to surrender their life to Christ. Time is spent on various aspects of human transformation and the conditions under which a spiritual conversion might take place. Related to this, we encourage each team to manage the Discipleship Polarity, putting into place both an easy process for people to become a member of the congregation, and a challenging process, which would engage inquirers in a yearlong catechumenate. With two processes in place for how people can join their congregation, they are able to ascertain the readiness of people for moving into a surrendered relationship with Christ. Some are scared away by a yearlong discipleship process. To these people you offer a much shorter new member class, yet always holding open the possibility for them to go deeper with a more involved process down the line. For some, however, the longer, more demanding process is exactly what they are looking for. Without this more demanding process in place, all we have to offer people with genuine spiritual hunger is something shallow and overly simplistic. To their dismay, they go away still hungry for something of substance. We should not be surprised when they leave to explore the Buddhist approach to spirituality, or the rigid demands of a high commitment denomination such as the Mormons, the Jehovah Witnesses, or the Church of God. With two equally accepted ways of becoming a member of a congregation, an easy process and a challenging process, people are given a choice as to which appeals to them most. Even when people opt for the easy process the congregation is able to say to them that at some point they would hope they would go through the more challenging process, as there is more to the Christian faith than they are able to give them in four new member classes. This way the faith is not trivialized by communicating to newcomers that we can teach them the faith in four easy lessons.

Accompanying this is a study of the congregation's assimilation process with survey instruments to assess the extent to which they are an "inviting church." Related to this is the exploration of adding an additional worship opportunity as a way of engaging more people and differing types of people in worship.

Participants leave the seminar with a 12-month strategic plan, which is the first step to a five-year plan.
Contained within that plan are:
- How they will create a sense of urgency within the congregation, which will motivate it to embrace the changes that are needed within the congregation for it to once again become a growing, thriving congregation.
- How they intend to put in place a guiding coalition, which will actively pursue positive change strategies. They are also to identify the power people who must be part of that guiding coalition if it is to succeed.
- The short-term wins that will be visual reminders to the whole congregation that change is underway and is succeeding.
- What specific goals are to be accomplished within this first 12 months.

The seminar ends with contracts related to times the teams are to check in by telephone conference call on their progress related to identified goals, problems or difficulties they have encountered, and what next steps are planned. Consultants are in dialogue with four congregations at a time in these conference calls. In this way, that cluster of congregations gets to hear what is happening in three other congregations. The whole cluster engages in problem solving when one congregation is experiencing difficulty.
The redevelopment team from one congregation comes to realize that they are not the only ones that are struggling within their congregation. Each hour-long consultation with four congregations ends with prayer. Congregations are encouraged to pray for one another while going through this year of transformational activity.

Consultants are usually in touch by telephone once a month for the first four months, with conference calls being spread out thereafter. Agreements are also made as to the quarterly reports that will be submitted to the consultant, with a specific response to each report being promised.

As we have evaluated this approach to redevelopment of congregations, the feedback we receive from participating congregations emphasizes the foundation work they are encouraged to complete before they launch any change effort, plus the support that is offered throughout the following year.
Lately, Roy, Claire, and Alice, have been contracting with specific Regional Bodies to replicate this entire process within their given Regional Body. Regional Body Executives

are realizing that it is much more cost effective to have this seminar conducted on their territory over against sending a team of four people somewhere else in the country.

This approach is clearly a new way for Alban Institute to relate to congregations. We have usually kept our Educational Department and our Consulting Department at arms length from one another. However, this model has us combining the two in offering a quality seminar to teams of people from within congregations, and then following it up with consultative support for at least one year. The results have been promising. If you are interested in this approach, be in contact with Alban's Educational Department, which will assist in setting up such a yearlong redevelopment program within your Regional Body. We usually begin these seminars on Wednesday and end them Sunday afternoon. In some cases we have allowed lay leaders to come in on Friday evening and remain with us through Sunday afternoon.

In a recent project using this model that Roy contracted to do for a Presbytery in North Carolina, we built into the training design an afternoon of house-to-house calling on behalf of a Mission Congregation in that Presbytery. The Mission Congregation developed a special brochure for participants to leave at homes receiving such a call. For most of the participants in this training event, this was the first time they had ventured out to do initial calling on homes in a given neighborhood. There were many participants who expressed anxiety about doing this. By the end of an afternoon of calling, done in pairs, the group returned to debrief the experience. Most found it much less threatening than expected. There was surprise as to how well they were received by the people on whom they were calling. At least one of the seven congregations in this particular project continued to do cold calling within their own neighborhood when they returned home.

Two years ago, Roy took five congregations within the Sierra Pacific Synod, ELCA through this process. All members of the synod staff were present for the whole week of training. Now, two years later, it has become clear that three of the five congregations have increased their average weekly attendance at worship. One congregation has shown signs of growth, but not as clearly as the other three. The one remaining congregations ran into some unexpected challenges and continues to struggle. Improvement in four out of five congregations is not bad.

One additional positive outcome of this approach, which was a surprise, was the way in which a given cluster of congregations within a Regional Body became invested in each other's success. Having spent a week together in the training seminar, they remained in touch with each other through the conference calls that were held monthly. As they listened to what was being attempted in each congregation, they were able to offer support and counsel to one another. Several of the congregations would include in their Sunday morning prayers, petitions on behalf of the other congregations in this venture with them.

As we continue to look for models of congregational redevelopment within Regional Bodies, we believe this option has real potential. We continue to fine-tune the model as we contract with other Regional Bodies for such work with selected congregations.

CHAPTER 10

THE REVOLUTION TAKING PLACE IN TEXAS
THE DIOCESE OF TEXAS SHOWS US ANOTHER WAY

In February of 1994, The Right Reverend Claude Edward Payne became the Seventh Bishop of Texas after serving sixteen months as Bishop Coadjutor. In the six years since this election, the Diocese of Texas has increased its average Sunday morning attendance by 18% from 26,651 in 1994 to 31,441 in 2000. Confirmations, receptions, and adult baptisms have increased from an annual plateau of 1,800 in 1994 to 2,416 in 2000, a 14% increase. Operating Revenues have jumped 60% in this time period, from $32,789,924 to $54,445,745. Today the Diocese contains 11% of the fastest growing congregations in the Episcopal Church. It is the fourth largest Episcopal Diocese in America, but ranks first in church-school membership, in children in parochial schools, in adult education, and in the number of members confirmed.

The story behind this exciting explosion of energy within a single Diocese is not a simple one, but it is a clear demonstration of the power a compelling vision can have on a system. It is also an example of how a courageous and risk taking style of transformational leadership can make an impact upon a Regional Body. All of this is documented in a book recently published by Jossey/Bass entitled *"Reclaiming the Great Commission."* The authors are Claude E. Payne and Hamilton Beazley.

Whether the model is replicable within other Regional Bodies may depend upon a Regional Body's commitment to explore such a vision and the commitment of a visionary leader at the helm. It may also depend upon the type of mandate given to such a dynamic leader coming into that office. Prior to his election as Bishop of the Diocese of Texas, the Rev. Claude Payne had laid out a vision for moving the Diocese from a maintenance mode to a missionary mode. He was very clear he would not accept an election to the office of Bishop if the Diocese did not approve of his moving in this direction. "If you want business as usual, do not elect me to this office" was his stance at the Diocese's Convention to elect a Bishop. He received a strong vote of confidence for this vision by his election. Thus, having a clear mandate to make significant changes in the system at the front end of a leadership change may make a great deal of difference.

Following a year of data gathering, utilizing a specifically constructed survey instrument, plus visits with various groups within the Diocese, Bishop Payne called for a special gathering to be held June 22 to 24, 1995. He called the event "A Gathering of the Diocese." He asked that a tithe of each congregation's membership attend this convocation, that is, he wanted each congregation to bring at least 10% of their membership to this event. Over 1,500 people showed up for the event. A special tent was erected on the campus of Episcopal High School in Houston, which covered four contiguous tennis courts. It was at this Gathering that Bishop Payne laid out his vision for the Diocese. Other keynote speakers at the event included Loren Mead, founder and former President of Alban Institute, laid out the challenge before the church as it faced into the 21st century. Carol Childress, information and research specialist of Leadership

143

Network spoke of the emerging context for ministry. The genius of the conference design was its use of Open Space Technology to give everyone present a chance to voice their concerns about the vision,

Open Space Technology has been in use now for some ten years in the corporate world. An Episcopal Priest, Harrison Owens, developed it. A variety of books are available on the subject. Basically, it is a process for allowing people to meet with other people who share their concerns and have those concerns presented and heard. It begins with everyone being present in a large auditorium with those who have a concern going up to the microphone, introducing him or herself, indicating he/she would be willing to lead a discussion on their topic of concern. The title of the topic is placed on newsprint. At this convocation 81 separate group discussions took place. Once all 81 people had voiced their willingness to lead a discussion on a topic, these topics were posted on a massive bulletin board, giving a time and location for each discussion. Participants had the opportunity to attend at least two such discussion groups. Some groups were very large while others were small. A person was appointed to take minutes in every meeting, and have those minutes ready for publication by day's end. Every participant then was able to read what transpired in each of those 81 separate discussion groups. All groups had at least someone other than the facilitator present at their interest group, with the exception of one, in which one participant proposed that the Diocese return to the liturgy in the 1928 Prayer Book.

Reading between the lines plus debriefing someone who had first hand information, I (Roy) learned that the people who gathered at this event were not the old guard who had dominated Diocesan policy for decades. A serious attempt was made to get some of the more progressive thinking types to represent the various congregations within the Diocese. Plenty of groundwork preceded this event.

The vision that was presented at this gathering was not a mere tweaking of the system, but represented an overhaul so major as to represent a new paradigm. Rooted in the historic evangelism of the Christian faith, the new model restructured the relationships this Regional Body (Diocese) was going to have with its congregations, congregations with each other, congregations with their disciples, disciples with their congregations, plus disciples and congregations with the unchurched.

Taking its name from its primary purpose, the missionary model replaced a maintenance mentality with evangelistic focus. In this new model, mission in accordance with the Great Commission and the Great Commandment became the heart of the Church's work. Mission in this model is sustained by a vision. This vision of the missionary Church is captured in the purpose statement of the Diocese of Texas, which is as follows:

> The Diocese of Texas has a vision of being One Church, under the leadership
> of Jesus Christ, as a "Community of Miraculous Expectation." It is a missionary
> diocese, whose bishop is the Chief Missionary, localized in missionary outposts
> and missionary institutions, utilizing the historic catholic structure of classic
> Anglicanism, and whose purpose under the Great Commandment to love is

focused on the unchurched with a goal of growing to 200,000 by the year 2005. This is growth beyond mere numbers toward discipleship and seeks to include all sorts and conditions of people, bringing joy to those who are reaching out and to those who are reached.

The vision and model of this Diocese goes counter to some of the conventional wisdom being touted these days. The conventional wisdom tells congregations that if they want to grow they need to drop their denominational label and become a community church. Some of the mega-churches on this continent do not have a denomination listed in their name (e.g. Community Church of Joy, Willow Creek Community Church, Saddleback Ministries, the Crystal Cathedral, etc.). In the model this Diocese puts forward, it not only claims its identity as a denomination, but it actively utilizes that identity and structure for the purposes of mission. It sees all congregations of that Regional Body as missionary outposts of the one church that is that Regional Body. Congregations, rather than competing with one another, are encouraged to explore a common mission in their area.

What is so powerful is that the congregations are no longer identifying as isolated congregations but as the one church of the diocese of which they are a part. It is the powerful sense of community and belonging that's so critical.

The authors of the book *"Reclaiming the Great Commission"* acknowledge that there are certain caveats to making this model work. One of these caveats is accountability. Episcopal clergy have always been accountable to their Bishop for what they do or say. In this model, there is also accountability to the vision. Since the entire Diocese adopted this vision, and elected a new Bishop with this particular focus, everyone in the Diocese can be held accountable for its accomplishment. To quote the authors:

> " The Church is not a business in the usual sense, but neither is it immune from sound management principles. For that matter, neither is a family a business, but it is also not immune from sound business practices such as budgeting, planning, and using its resources in the most effective ways possible.
> Those clergy members who have not been held accountable for how well they serve their congregations may bristle at the thought, but the rest of us should be buoyed by the idea that the goal of the Church is to be as effective as possible in the lives of its members. For very good reasons, the notion that keeping our jobs might be dependent upon the quality of our performance is an everyday experience for most. This kind of accountability, in which the clergy accept responsibility for performing well in their assignments to the ultimate benefit of their congregations, has been historically lacking in the maintenance church. Not, however, in the missionary church."

As you can see, the model put forward is able to capitalize on the historic structure of the Episcopacy, and utilizes it for the sake of mission.

As we, the authors of this book first read about this model we had some questions about how this Diocese went about motivating certain clergy and congregations that are normally resistant to any influence by its Regional Body. This is where the basis of a mandate for change and revitalization may make the difference between this model working or not. It's important to know that one of the powerful things about the vision is that it calls people to it. Many who were not initially convinced were won over. Really, we can believe that the Holy Spirit is at work changing the hearts and minds of those who are willing to listen. Those who do not listen tend to drift away. They drift away to older model churches where maintenance is the overriding goal, but that are not really forced out. They simply go away in search of what they used to experience in the maintenance church.

One of the reasons this model may be working as well as it is, has to do with the pure momentum of events that seems to have been well orchestrated. A mass gathering involving the more progressive thinkers in the Diocese followed the election of the Bishop with a mandate, and at which anyone who had a concern could voice that concern and be heard. A single-minded Bishop who surrounded himself with a staff that was brought on board to implement this mission then held the diocese on focus. Anyone not on board soon must have felt like they were odd person out. Some early successes, such as membership and attendance increases, indicated that the model was working well. It certainly makes it more difficult to dig in one's heals and not cooperate.

For those who claim that social justice and ministry to the poor and outcast is just as important as transforming lives, the model has a key trump card to play. This model really does take seriously the Great Commandment, to love God and our neighbor as ourselves. Outreach ministries that engage congregations and individuals in service of those who are poor, sick, infirm, underprivileged, or troubled are considered a form of evangelism and an important function of a missionary church. Several innovative outreach programs within the Diocese of Texas are diocesan-wide and involve multiple congregations because their scope is beyond the ability of one congregation to handle. Examples:

- Episcopal Health Charities: a $150,000,000 charity created out of the financial reserves of St. Luke's Episcopal Hospital by Bishop Payne is devoted exclusively to assessing and enhancing community health, particularly among the poor.
- Lord of the Streets Episcopal Church: a million-dollar health care facility for the indigent and a live-in recovery center for 31 homeless men is supported by nine congregations whose volunteers take turns serving breakfast to more than 120 homeless people every Sunday.
- Community of Hope: trains volunteer lay chaplains to serve in health care settings, local congregations, and other places in the diocese. These lay chaplains provide spiritual nourishment and encouragement during times of stress, change and crisis.

A number of things utilized by this diocese in its strategic vision parallel the things we are advocating in this book. They also make good use of size theory, giving special assistance to congregations experiencing a size transition. They also make use of the John Kotter model of strategic change as outlined in his book, *"Leading Change."* Even though they don't utilize the polarity model, they state very clearly that the church needs to be about the business of both nurture and transformation. Even though they don't use the term "triage" they are using this concept in their assessment of congregations. They put it in terms of: a) those congregations who need help, b) those congregations that don't need help, and c) those congregations that can't use help. We say "yes" and "amen" to the need for a compelling strategic vision. As we have stated clearly the Regional Body staff needs to be spending a minimum of 20% of its time on congregational revitalization and renewal over against responding to crisis, the Diocese of Texas functions with at least that balance if not more. We both would agree that having Regional Body staff existing mainly to put out fires is functioning mainly on a maintenance mode. The Texas model is based heavily on the notion that we are now living in a different time, in a post-Christendom era, as does ours. We make a strong pitch regarding the need to become much more multicultural by reaching out to racial and ethnic minorities, as do they.

At the same time, our models are significantly different. Their work is specific on issues that we are not, and vice versa. As we outline the chapters in their book you can see where their approach differs from ours.

Chapter One: Introduction
Part 1: The New Apostolic Age
Denominational Crisis and Opportunity

Chapter Two: Spiritual Hunger in America
Chapter Three: The Great Commission
Chapter Four: The New Apostolic Age
Chapter Five: Denominational Crisis, Denominational Opportunity

Part II: The New Apostolic Denomination: From Maintenance to Mission
Chapter Six: The New Apostolic Denomination
Chapter Seven: Implementing the Vision
Chapter Eight: Changing Organizational Structure and Culture
Chapter Nine: Managing Change
Chapter Ten: Making Disciples
Chapter Eleven: Developing Congregations

Part III: Leaders in the New Apostolic Age
Chapter Twelve: Missionary Congregations
Chapter Thirteen: Apostolate of the Laity
Chapter Fourteen: Apostolate of the Clergy
Chapter Fifteen: Judiciary Leaders in the Missionary Church
Chapter Sixteen: Communication and Technology
Chapter Seventeen: Outreach, Christian Education, and Youth Ministry
Epilogue

As you can see, their model advocates a complete restructuring of a Diocese. Our model tends to place emphasis upon some important ingredients in a Redevelopment Regional Body, but leaves the overall structure up to each local constituency. We would encourage you to place the two models side by side and decide which one would fit your Regional Body best. We are delighted that we now have more than one model to present to you in this book. We continue to watch with interest what is happening in the Diocese of Texas. We feel their track record is looking good so far. The key has been the vision and the repetition of it over and over and over by Bishop Payne and the other members of his staff. But that new vision has led inevitably to a restructuring of the diocese and a change in its goals and culture—it can't be otherwise as people catch the vision and its possibilities. This model, developed within the Episcopal Diocese of Texas has now been adopted wholesale within the Episcopal Church in the Diocese of Albany (New York), the Diocese of Southern Ohio, the Diocese of Southeast Florida, and the Diocese of Louisiana. We now know that we have a growing number of Regional Bodies within the Episcopal Church and the Lutheran Church, ELCA that have reversed their decline in membership and participation. No one can say that turning a Regional body around is not possible anymore. There are likely many more Regional Bodies within other denominations, which have experienced a similar turn around. We look forward to hearing of them and the special ways they went about such a revitalization process.

CHAPTER 11

INSIGHTS FROM THE CORPORATE WORLD
.... ON HOW TO BECOME A TRANSFORMATIONAL REGIONAL BODY

Corporate Agility and Vitality

Another resource that was developed for the corporate world that has much insight to provide those of us working within religious/volunteer systems is the work of Dr. John P. Kotter in his article and book entitled, *"Leading Change, Why Transformational Efforts Fail"* Kotter is one of the most sought after corporate consultants in the world. He is the Konosuke Matsushita Professor of Leadership at the Harvard Business School in Boston, Massachusetts. He has consulted with some of the premier corporations in the world including General Motors, British Airways, Bristol-Myers Squibb. Over the past decade he has watched more than 100 companies try to remake themselves into significantly better companies. He claims these efforts fly under many banners, such as right sizing, total quality management, cultural change, turnaround, restructuring, reengineering, etc. In all cases the request for assistance is the same. These companies are losing their market share of business and need some help to once again become a thriving corporation.

Kotter has come up with eight reasons why such transformational efforts fail. In all the work we have been doing in the field of organizational change we have not come up with a clearer blueprint of what needs to take place if a congregation, a regional body, or a whole denomination is to succeed in turning itself around. This work was originally produced in an article in the March/April, 1995 edition of Harvard Business Review. Kotter later expanded the piece into a book by this same title, *"Leading Change, Why Transformational Efforts Fail."*

According to Kotter, error number one is:
NOT ESTABLISHING A GREAT ENOUGH SENSE OF URGENCY.
He claims that well over 50% of the companies he has watched failed in this first phase. He claims leaders often underestimate how hard it can be to drive people out of their comfort zones. If they remain in their comfort zone, they will have neither the stomach or the energy for the changes that need to take place if a system is truly to be transformed.

Here are some examples of what secular companies did to create a sense of urgency within their system as a prelude to major change:
"One CEO deliberately engineered the largest accounting loss in the company's history, creating huge pressures from Wall Street in the process. One division president commissioned a first-ever customer satisfaction survey, knowing full well the results would be terrible. He then made these findings public. On the surface," says Kotter, "such moves can look unduly risky. But there is also risk in playing it too safe; when the urgency rate is not pumped up enough, the transformation process cannot succeed and the long-term future of the organization is put in jeopardy."

What would be the equivalent of such a dramatic moves within a Regional Body? Calling a Special Assembly and have a team of people present all the charts and graphs about death and decline? Having the Bishop/Executive threaten resignation unless something is done soon to support a turnaround? Each middle judicatory is different and thus would need its own special way of calling attention to the fact that status quo is no longer acceptable. Now that we know that several Regional Bodies have in fact revitalized themselves, middle judicatory systems can no longer hide behind the hand wringing, and say "ain't it awful but there is nothing we can do about this." We now have documented proof that Regional Bodies can revitalize themselves. What may be wrong is a lack of leadership at the helm of Regional Bodies who have neither the vision nor the stomach to upset their judicatory to the point where it wakes up and realizes that business as usual can no longer be tolerated.

Error number two:
NOT CREATING A POWERFUL ENOUGH GUIDING COALITION.
Without the right people heading up the transformation effort, the move will not have the respect of the key players within the Regional Body. In addition, unless the key shakers and movers within the middle judicatory are behind the effort, it isn't going to succeed anyway. This will be especially true when it comes time to put the plan into effect by under girding it with adequate finances. No capital funds campaign is going to succeed unless the people with financial resources have an opportunity to shape what is going to transpire. When those with financial resources are too busy to participate, they at least need to know that the guiding coalition has the kind of people in it to make this thing fly.

Error number three:
LACKING A VISION
In failed transformations, you often have plenty of plans and programs, but no vision. In addition, without an exciting vision, you are not going to be able to get people to commit to it financially, or any other way.

John Kotter often talks about going into a system and asking the CEO what his/her vision is for the company. He says that when the CEO goes into a rambling thirty-minute spiel that contains some good ideas, but in the end it remains unclear where s/he is trying to take the company, that company and CEO have no vision. A great vision is one in which the chief executive can explain it to you in five minutes, and at the end of the five minutes you are drawn into the excitement of where the organization is going.

Within a Regional Body, an exciting vision would be simple, down to earth, and doable. It needs to be one that can be communicated to clergy and congregations in five minutes, with some excitement being generated each time it is shared. The following is one that might do just that:

In this Synod, we want to establish three new mission congregations each year for the next ten years. In addition, we want to redevelop seven declining congregations each year for the next ten years. We also intend to have some of the best Evangelization training available on our territory, available to every clergyperson, lay person, and congregation in our Synod. With the above, we are going to be ministering to an additional 16,000 people by the year 2011, which represent more than numbers but changed lives.

Having heard the above vision statement once, could you share it with someone else getting most of it right? You probably could!

Error number four:
UNDERCOMMUNICATING THE VISION BY A FACTOR OF TEN.
Transformation is impossible unless hundreds or thousands of people are willing to help, often to the point of making short-term sacrifices. Both clergy and lay leaders will not make sacrifices, even if they are unhappy with the status quo, unless they believe that useful change is possible. Without credible communication, and a lot of it, the hearts and minds of the membership are never captured.

In short, sending out the vision statement in one newsletter is not going to do the trick. Neither is one session at an annual convention going to do the trick. More than likely a cadre of clergy/lay teams is going to need to be sold on the vision first. These teams then need to visit every congregation within the Regional Body and request at least a two-hour session with their governing board, and whomever else in a congregation might be interested. This process would also have the effect of gaining the perspective of the congregations within the middle judicatory, which would assist in determining what barriers to the vision are out there.

Error number five:
NOT REMOVING OBSTACLES TO THE NEW VISION.
Claire talks about the difficulties that arose in her Synod when a committee brought a half-baked idea for a capital funds drive to the Synodical convention for approval. The motion failed miserably. Yet someone at the convention had the wisdom to have another motion passed, namely that the committee go back to the drawing board and within six months bring their re-worked plan to a special Synod assembly. The committee did go back and re-work their plan. They also did something very important. They shared their new plan with a variety of people and asked them, "what are the obstacles that may have the plan founder again?" After receiving all that negative criticism to their new plan, the committee got together for several more meetings and developed answers to all the possible objections that might be raised about this new plan. At the special Assembly, there were a lot of challenges to the proposal, but the committee was ready for ways in which these could be overcome. The motion passed this time. This is simply one approach to removing the obstacles to the new vision.

Error number Six
NOT SYSTEMATICALLY PLANNING FOR AND CREATING SHORT-TERM WINS
Within any religious, volunteer system, people do not see each other very often. This is especially true within a congregation, and even more so within a Regional Body. As a result, the Regional Body can have some people working hard to bring their vision into reality, but this effort goes unnoticed by the majority of people within the middle judicatory. It is why doing visible, concrete things every year to point to the fact that some important things are happening around here. These are the short term wins that consistently reminds people that the Regional Body is working on an exciting strategic vision, and what is working.

If three new congregations are established each year within the Regional Body, a big deal needs to be made of this every year at a Synod Assembly. If seven congregations each year enter into a contract with the Regional Body to become revitalized, some representative from those congregations needs to be given some air time at the Regional Body's annual convention, to talk about the good things that are happening in their congregations. Stories of congregational turnarounds need to be written up and published in a monthly newsletter that goes out to clergy and key congregational leaders. Whenever a major capital funds campaign reaches another milestone, this needs to broadcast far and wide. Both the Southeastern Synod and the Southeastern Pennsylvania Synod, ELCA produce a video each year to communicate the transformational successes taking place within their synods. Every congregation is sent a copy of the video. It is one way that short-term wins within these two synods are communicated to their judicatories every year.

Error number Seven:
DECLARING VICTORY TOO SOON
While celebrating a win is fine, declaring the war won can be a catastrophic. People throughout the Regional Body need to remain pumped up throughout the entire strategic plan. When they feel that the important things have already been achieved, their energy and prayers begin to lag. As St. Paul would have us believe, "we are not wrestling against flesh and blood, but against the principalities and the powers of darkness." Against such a foe we can never let down. When we think we have won by achieving some concrete signs of growth, it allows "the devious, deceptive one" a toe hold into the system which can signal the downfall of all that we have achieved.

Error number Eight
NOT ANCHORING CHANGES IN THE CORPORATE CULTURE
Within a religious, volunteer system, anchoring changes into our corporate culture means keeping whatever momentum we have going for us on a continual roll. For congregation's to be redeveloped, members of those congregations need to continue to be a welcoming, inviting community of faith. They don't stop being those kind of Christians just because the membership rolls seem to be growing. This is when a long term vision is more like our returning to be the kind of Christians we needed to be all along, namely contagious Christians who are always ready, like the Ten Wise Virgins, when an

opportunity presents itself for us to invite a friend or family member into our fellowship. Other changes that need to be anchored into our systems are ways of constantly being on the lookout for entrepreneurial leaders who might consider the ordained ministry as a vocation, especially ones that represent a minority culture.

To be sure, Kotter's eight reasons why transformational efforts fail are stated in the negative. However, one doesn't need to be a rocket scientist to see the positive blueprint for a change effort that it contains. When Roy first came upon this article by John Kotter in the March/April edition of the Harvard Business Review, he was so taken by it that he phoned his presiding Bishop in Chicago and asked for an audience to explore the implications of this article to some changes the Presiding Bishop had initiated within the ELCA. To his credit he gave Roy two hours, along with five or six of his lieutenants, to explore the implications of this blueprint for change on what he was attempting for the national body. Roy has been working within denominational systems for 24 years, and in all that time he had not come upon any strategy for change that matched what Kotter had pulled together in the book and this article.

It would be a mistake if any Regional Body tried to initiate substantive change within its culture and ignore these reasons why their effort could fail. A common mistake would be to take only some of these reasons for failure seriously but to skip some. It has become clear to us that any redevelopment effort will fail if it does not take all eight of these items seriously. The one that I have seen Regional Bodies ignore the most is the first item on Kotter's list, namely NOT ESTABLISHING A GREAT ENOUGH SENSE OF URGENCY. To leap frog over this one is to doom any change effort that is undertaken. This is where the chief requirement for effective leadership is risk and courage.

APPENDIX 1

What follows are two psychological assessments of congregations completed by **PHYSIS**, a counseling organization in Philadelphia, which offers these services to Regional Bodies. Physis can be contacted at the following address and phone number: Dr. Dennis O'Hara, PH.D., ABPP, Southeast PA Synod, 109 Fox Knoll Lane, West Chester, PA 19380 (610) 269-3037.

Physis Associates is an interdisciplinary group of professional men and women with expertise in psychology, pastoral counseling, social work and organizational consultation. The Greek word, physis, describes development as the process of growing and reaching one's intrinsic potential. Our goal is to supply high-quality mental-health-care services to individuals and organizations based on the unique needs, values and resources of those served.

Physis Associates work with business, educational, religious, health care and government organizations to address systemic issues, leadership training, small group conflicts and facilitation of meetings. Using a team approach, Physis Associates applies its unique Collaborative Development Program to organizations, which could benefit from a comprehensive self-study. Physis Associates conducts evaluations of existing and proposed management systems.

Physis Associates subscribe to the highest ideals of theirr professional ethical codes. Each client can be assured of confidential and culturally sensitive treatment reflective of the most current developments in the profession. Expectations, procedures and limits of responsibility are outlined during the initial session when a therapeutic partnership is formed.

These psychological assessments are not cheap, but they are clearly worth the cost considering that a Regional Body is going to invest money and personnel in a congregation. Redevelopment Pastors are hard to come by, and it is no use wasting their time and energy trying to turn around a sick congregation. In each case, the synod relied on these assessments to determine whether or not they would invest redevelopment efforts into each congregation.

We include two such assessments, as it will give you a sense of the variety of recommendations coming out of such an assessment.

CASE STUDY NO. 1

COLLABORATIVE CARE REPORT: Historic Distrust of the Synod
NAME OF CHURCH: St. Martin Lutheran Church
ADDRESS: 2020 First Ave., Someplace, USA
PASTOR (interim):   Rev. Mary Interim
INTERVENTION TEAM: CONSULTANT ONE INTERPRETER/ ANALYZER

BRIEFING SESSION:	Date	List of those present
	5/7	Council President
		Treasurer
		Building Committee Chair
		Women's Organization President
		Synod Staff Representative
		Consultants (2)
CONTACTS:	5/14	Two Group Interviews
	5/20	Three Group Interviews
		Individual Interview - Interim Pastor
		Individual Interview - The former Pastor
	5/13	Interview - Synod Staff member
	5/21	Reviewed Document: Summary of Congregational Self-Study
	5/26	Feedback to council/and interim pastor

Goals Stated at Briefing:

An objective assessment of St. Martin Church's potential for growth.

Identify the issues necessary to qualify St. Martin for re-development.

Identify the barriers to congregational growth.

Determine the level of enthusiasm for evangelizing, particularly in regard to bringing new members with young families into the church.

These goals are congruent with the congregation's projected mission goals as stated on page 16 of the "Summary of Congregational Self-Study."

Process Observations

The members who participated in the data gathering process shared their perspectives openly and with apparent sincerity. A great deal of anger and disbelief was expressed about the synod staff representative's statement to the council that "no pastors were interested in coming to St. Martin." This statement had thrown many of the congregation into confusion and entrenchment. As a result, hostility and disregard for the role of the synod was open and, at times, quite vehement. Anger with the synod was often expressed through criticism and cynicism. There was such a widespread sense of unrest and victimization that one member of the consultant team consulted later with the synod staff for clarification of the reasons for suggesting re-development as one of the options for St. Martin Church. There are approximately fifty worshiping members at St. Martin and the 75 % representation at the data gathering sessions indicates the high degree of emotional involvement with the option of redevelopment.

Issues Shared By Participants

The following section of the report reflects information that was shared during the data-gathering phase of the Collaborative Care Consultation. The views of individuals vary widely on the issues and will be presented in that fashion. The accuracy of this information is a matter of perspective and the Consultants do not "believe some and not others", as each person's experience is truth for him or her. An analysis of this data will be reflected in a later section of the report.

The issues and concerns expressed by members of the congregation may be organized into the following perspectives: historical data, the identity of St. Martin congregation, the relationship between pastor and congregation, and the mission of the congregation.

Historical Data

St. Martin congregation has been in existence since 1950. The church progressed at a fairly steady rate until the end of the third Pastor's ministry (1976-1982). He was creative and energetic and the life of the congregation expanded in many directions. The fourth pastor, who resigned after twelve years of ministry with the congregation, followed the third pastor. It was the fourth Pastor's resignation that led to the present vacant pastorate situation.

Most of the congregation recognize that they "have not been actively evangelical" for many years. Some date this back to the time of the second Pastor (1971-1976). Others acknowledged that four years into the fourth Pastor's term, "the church became stuck." This had much to do with the Pastor's style of leadership. He "was not an evangelical pastor" and there were several personality clashes between the pastor and other leaders and ministers within the church.

Identity of St. Martin Congregation

In its mission statement, St. Martin congregation described itself as "a small, friendly family of God." This statement is at the heart of the controversy about its identity. During the fourth pastor's twelve years of service and up to the time of his resignation, the congregation in general appeared to be content and have a relatively clear sense of its identity as small and intimate. However, when the synod reminded the church that the mission of the Lutheran Church is evangelism, and that it is unlikely that evangelical Lutheran pastors would desire as inward-looking a church as St. Martin, the congregation experienced something of a crisis about its identity.

After the fourth Pastor's resignation, the synod staff members at a meeting addressed serious questions about the future and viability of St. Martin with the church council. The entire congregation presented the following options to the council for its consideration and for consideration:

Make no changes and continue with a long-term part-time interim pastor. This option would maintain the status quo of the church.

The synod could find a pastor but it could not promise to supply a quality pastor as desired and needed by the church. This option would prepare the church for a "slow death" because it would mean that no planned change to the operation of the congregation would take place.

Re-development could be offered to the church if they truly wanted it. This option would necessitate ownership of evangelism and outreach programs by the congregation and would be for a three-year period. The synod would pay part of the re-development pastor's salary.

Some members of the congregation heard only the "ultimatum" of the third option while others heard only the second and third options. Only a few, mainly council members, were clear that they had been given three options for consideration. Consequently, members of the congregation felt alternatively "confused," "shocked," disbelieving," and "angry": there is a commonly held belief among church members that they have been "blackballed by the synod." Also, some feel that because St. Martin was a part of the "other" Lutheran Church before the merger forming the Evangelical Lutheran Church of America, they are "not accepted by the present synod." Many reflected that there had been no process of integration into the Evangelical Lutheran Church in America eight years ago and no attempts since then to remedy this limitation.

Relationship Between Pastor And Congregation

Another predominant issue was that of "supporting" the pastor emotionally. The fourth Pastor had emotional and marital problems during his time at St. Martin: his three marriages were interspersed with two divorces. These problems appear to have engaged much of the emotional energy within the church. Their response was to rally around the pastor with support of many kinds. Most saw this as their "Christian duty", while admitting that they were also in the position of having to support the pastor. The general response to the question of how they might respond to another pastor was "the pastor is a member of the congregation. Of course we would support him/her in the same way." According to one person, "Because we are small, we have a special relationship with our pastor."

The fourth Pastor also had "a strong personality and was very controlling." For example, he "attended too many committee meetings" and "people were discouraged from taking leadership roles." According to one church member, "He was confronted about his controlling and manipulative style, and some of the people who did this left the church." The fourth Pastor's perspective varied considerably from the congregation's. He became aware that there were certain roles in the church which were being played out by different people at different times. As he saw it, however, the underlying dynamic was that of sabotaging change. For example, when decisions are made (usually at council level) some person or persons asks for further clarification or re-evaluation. The result is that "Decisions don't stand. They are reviewed and then don't happen." Ultimately, it appears that the congregation's saboteurs, "do not want the leaders to be able to function as leaders." The fourth Pastor claims also to have been aware of his difficulty in differentiating from the congregation. However, two years before he resigned, he made attempts to differentiate but felt that "the people wouldn't let (him)" He tried to "pull back" from the congregation, but because the people wanted and needed the pastor to be their friend, he was drawn back into his old style of relating.

On one hand, people spoke positively about the pastoral style of the interim Pastor. Her sermons were good and she was personable with the people. Furthermore, she has been encouraging of leadership within the church and did not attempt to coerce people to her way of thinking. The interim Pastor reports that she was "very encouraged by the people" and feels that it is very possible to work with them" because they are warm, friendly, have good leadership potential, and are willing to look at change." On the other hand, they are not always committed to the changes, which they proclaim as values. For example, having young families join the church is seen to be good. However, when children cry in church, some express impatience.

Mission of the Congregation

In a similar vein, many do not consider the church in need of re-development. The anger that surfaced in this regard had a dual focus. First, there is the widely held belief that the suggestion/decision about re-development was made by the synod "without due consultation" with the congregation. Second, there is the belief that the document "Summary of Congregational Self-Study" presented by the synod was a "distortion of the data" submitted by the congregation and "did not account for the action of the Holy Spirit." Still others believe that the synod has no interest in St. Martin Church or the congregation: "They do not know us." "They never contact us." "They misinterpret us negatively." "We're being channeled into going in one direction only."

While several council members sympathize with many of the above sentiments concerning the synod, they are in agreement with, and committed to, the idea of redevelopment. They see this as the way to achieve their strong desire to "keep the church functioning." They also "feel strongly that the congregation is of the same opinion."

Although some members agreed that evangelism had to be a priority for the future, the reasons for such prioritizing varied. Some felt that this had been a lack in the church for many years and needed to be re-established. Some believe that evangelism has to begin with members who have stopped attending church. Others felt that new and creative forms of evangelism, consonant with today's society and various lifestyles, had to be found and implemented. There were those who clearly were prepared to be part of such an evangelism committee. Others were equally clear that "if re-development (means) knocking on doors, I want no part of it." These latter groups seemed unable to imagine other forms of evangelism. Still others felt that evangelism would have to go outside the immediate neighborhood, which is predominantly Roman Catholic.

There does not appear to be an over-arching vision at St. Martin Church which was lamented by some. Rather there are "little visions" which take the form of ideas and projects. While these are usually supported, there is not a larger vision within which the "smaller visions" may be contextualized. Also, the desire to maintain their "small, intimate church" is felt keenly by some. New members could destroy this "close family bond", and therefore, are not necessarily viewed in a positive light.

Spirituality is another area about which there are strongly varying opinions. One member believes that there is no sense of spirituality in the congregation, and that this must be top of their list of priorities. Others would agree that the fourth Pastor's sermons "lacked spiritual depth" and there was a "spiritual void" in their lives. Still others reported that the spiritual lives of the members of the congregation are not a matter for concern. Rather it is "above average" because people have a real sense of why they go to church. They "hear the word of God and get strength from that."

Analysis of the Systems Issues

St. Martin is a church in turmoil. The anger and resentment felt by many mitigates against the peace Christ came to give. The unrest and sense of rebelliousness is not unlike that of a child who believes that he/she has tried to be good by caring for a parent and finds, after several years in this role, that the efforts have been in vain. The only courses open are withdrawal (and guilt) or continuation (and further frustration and resentment). Parents who need this degree of emotional support from their developing children will continue to make demands, and the children will always feel that they are never quite good enough to take the burdens from their parents.

There was a great deal of defensiveness whenever members of the Consultant team raised this boundary issue and style of relationship for reflection. The defensiveness displayed by some members of the congregation served as a barometer for the accuracy of the above interpretation.

In the case of St. Martin Church, the degree of support expected by a pastor who is undifferentiated from the congregation and the degree of support given has caused a major blurring of boundaries. This is not an issue of Christian love but rather one of dependence and counter-dependence. Both parties have been gratified by their roles in this dynamic, since there is always interplay between the leader's issues and those of the group. In this case, the congregation appears to have derived complacency in being a "small, friendly family of God" and become unmindful of the Great Commission. In order to maintain its homeostasis, the congregation has projected its anger towards the fourth Pastor and itself on to the synod. Rather than face the challenges inherent in the process of re-development, many in the congregation have projected their shame at being so challenged into anger for "being blackballed by the synod."

It had been reported during one of the data gathering sessions that there is a resistance to effective lay leadership in the church. It would appear that there is a resistance also to the leadership role of the pastor. He is "a member of the congregation, like everyone else." In general, members do not differentiate the role of the pastor and the person of the pastor. The fourth Pastor was aware of his own limitations in this regard. This led to an egalitarian-style, but in reality an enmeshed, congregational identity with an overall blurring of professional boundaries. Church members have been unaware of this dynamic, believing instead that they have been supportive fellow church members to their pastor.

Another area of concern is the attitude towards re-development as an option for the church. Because evangelism is the primary mission of the Evangelical Lutheran Church in America, it is an essential dimension for re-development. Yet, the response to evangelization is a mixed one, just as there is an ambivalent attitude towards re-development. At the same time, church members want a strong spiritual leader. The truth is that no amount of enthusiasm or specialized training in a re-development pastor can replace a lack of motivation towards evangelism and systemic change. Even creative evangelism projects are likely to be infiltrated by conflict, discouragement and ambivalence that directly relate to the lack of spiritual motivation for change and to evangelize.

For St. Martin to be successful in re-development, it will be necessary to have the concept explained more fully to the congregation and for them to want re-development and be committed to its implementation, fully hearing what will be required of them as individuals to make it work. At this point in time, it is not clear that the congregation is sufficiently free or informed to make such a decision.

Summary and Recommendations

The first critical issue facing St Martin is that of leadership. This issue has been fraught with difficulties over many years. Because everyone cannot, nor should, know everything that is happening in an organization, a new model of leadership is needed which is more appropriate for the churches setting it needs to be one which gives authority to the lay leadership of the congregation.

1. It is recommended that the council spend a prayerful day together reading and understanding the content and recommendations of this report. It would be most profitable if a portion of this day could be led by a synod staff member so there is corresponding clarity about the three options, and their implications, as offered by the synod.

2. It is recommended that a congregational meeting be called during which the fully aware and informed council members may present the three options clearly to the congregation. It is important that the implications for each option be spelled out so that the difference between maintenance and mission is clear. It is important that the congregation understands that re-development is for spiritual growth and fulfillment of the Great Commission. People must be given an opportunity to discuss the options fully.

3. It is recommended that the congregation be given time and places for prayer and reflection prior to a vote being taken. Before the congregational meetings, the council will decide what type of majority is required before a request for redevelopment is possible.

4. It is recommended that the spiritual gifts inventory, available from the synod, be used as an essential part of the process of leadership discernment. A retreat day to identify and share spiritual gifts with each other should be arranged. From the stance of prayer and sharing, each member may decide where their gifts can be used maximally.

5. It is recommended that this style of decision-making be extended gradually to other committees so that the council and committees may become strong and clear about their identities and roles within the church.

6. It is recommended that intensive leadership training be given to members of the council and other committee leaders so that they might grow in personal and professional development.

7. It is recommended that a mentoring program be developed, using the gifts and expertise of other Lutheran churches. It is important that there be some official recognition of this process so that healthy churches are chosen as role models for the building up of the Body of Christ.

Conflict resolution is another area that gives cause for some concern within the church dynamics. It appears that conflicts are generally ignored. In the Family Therapy Model, the reason given is that the family must appear to be "together" as it shows its face to the outside world. Furthermore, because offending family members cannot be easily cast out, no interventions are made when difficulties arise - in the hope that these difficulties will "go away."

8. It is recommended that the leadership committee give attention to the choir director to help her cope with her demanding, and voluntary job and with the personality clashes which occur between herself and others in the music ministry. Because of

inadequate leadership within the church, the "buck" has nowhere to stop when interventions are needed.

9.   It is recommended that the council, with the treasurer, explore thoroughly the financial status of the church. Finance is frequently a source of conflict. The fact that land was sold some years ago has enabled St. Martin to remain solvent and financially viable. Nevertheless, this is not a true picture. It may be that some of the building fund money should also be used for needed repairs.

Good things are already in place in St. Martin Church; for example, the prison ministry, local and synodical benevolence, and vacation Bible school to name but a few. It is important that these good things be maximized and there be openness to addressing deficiencies also.

10.   It is recommended that there be focus on youth ministry (for pre-teens and older) so that more young people actively give allegiance to St. Martin Church. Doing this in conjunction with another Lutheran church in the area would allow for a combined Lutheran youth ministry under the leadership of one director or coordinator.

11.   It is recommended that the church council and congregation be creative about the lack of space for programmatic development. The suggestion of a modular classroom for Sunday school classes is one positive suggestion.

12.   It is recommended that a strong adult education program be started. This program could include such topics as:

-    Family Systems and Dynamics
-    Congregational Dynamics
-    Leadership: Roles, Responsibilities, Models, and Styles

13.   It is recommended that the council request that the seminary consider sending interns to St. Martin to help with the organization of such programs.

It is a positive and hopeful sign that the congregation has responded so well to the interim Pastor who has a completely different leadership style than the fourth Pastor. The interim Pastor is well liked and appreciated. Once the internal work above is underway and the congregation demonstrates a commitment to it, they will realize they are doing it not just to please the Pastor.

14.   It is recommended that if re-development is desired and requested from the synod that a thirty-hour a week program of evangelization begin with the lapsed members of St. Martin Church. Once members are comfortable with this approach to evangelization, more creative and courageous approaches should then be taken.

These suggestions are offered to St. Martin Church in the hope that their implementation may provide growth and greater freedom in the service of the Lord's people.

CASE STUDY NO. 2

COLLABORATIVE CARE REPORT:	A Dysfunctional Leadership Congregation
NAME OF CHURCH:	St. Timothy Lutheran Church
ADDRESS:	5050 Someplace Ave.
PASTOR(S):	Interim Pastor
CONSULTANT TEAM:	Consultant/Interpreter

BRIEFING SESSION:	February 6	Council representatives:
		Synod consultants (2)
		Synod Staff
CONTACTS:	March 4	Group interview - Church
Council		
		Group interviews - members
	March 5	Group interviews - members
	March 6	Review of Percept Study
	March 13	Telephone interview -
		Second Pastor
		Telephone interview -
		Long Term Pastor
	March 19	Feedback session

Need Stated at Briefing

The Collaborative Care Consultation of St. Timothy Lutheran Church in Transition USA was requested by synod staff of the Synod of the Evangelical Lutheran Church in America. St. Timothy is applying to the synod for Redevelopment; but it may be better placed in a Fresh Start or Ethnic Outreach category. The goal is to ascertain the dynamics present which will positively and negatively impact this process. Further goals stated at the briefing session were exploring the congregation's expectations of a pastor, identifying the impact of a small, vocal, negative minority, and exploring the reaction to the Second Pastor's ministry in light of residual issues which are likely to face the next pastor.

Process Observations

Because there are no outside lights on St. Timothy Lutheran Church and their sign is poorly lit, the church was difficult to find. The consultants and newcomers had the feeling that the church was inactive or closed. The energy level differed between groups - some very de-energized and others lively and participative. There was more energy around the issues of the Second Pastor's ministry for most participants than in articulating a vision or direction for the future. All participants seemed sincere in sharing their perspectives. The attendance was excellent. Forty-seven people participated in the data gathering sessions, which is approximately 65-70% of the worshiping members. This degree of participation increases the degree to which these findings can be seen as representative of the congregation.

Issues Shared By Participants

The following section of the report reflects information that was shared during the data-gathering phase of the Collaborative Care Consultation. The views of individuals vary widely on the issues, and will be presented in that fashion. The accuracy of this information is a matter of perspective and Associates do not "believe some and not others", as each person's experience is truth for him or her. An analysis of this data will be reflected in the following section of the report.

The issues shared in the data gathering sessions can be organized into the topics of historical perspective, present status, and challenges for the future.

Historical Perspective

St. Timothy Lutheran Church in Transition USA is filled with history. Many members shared that their fathers and grandfathers worked and sacrificed to build and sustain the church. There is a dynamic of nostalgia in this regard, as some stated as their reason for wanting the church to survive, "I can't imagine letting it die after all my family did to build it. It would be a disgrace to their names". Others commented on the family histories of baptisms and marriages in the church and stated, "I want the church to survive so that my daughter can be married in the church and her children baptized and confirmed."

Most participants described the church as a "pastor-centered" church. Members described the twenty-four year tenure of the Long Term Pastor as containing years of activity and growth, yet ending with conflict and decline. During those years, the Long Term Pastor was described as an "old-fashioned" pastor who "took charge" of church activities. Members relied upon him to carry on the work of the congregation. There is a consistent core of members who have served faithfully for many years, with a much larger group enjoying a membership characterized with rich fellowship and support for one another. Seen positively by most, a few reported that St. Timothy is often referred to as the social club of Transition. The Long Term Pastor's perspective is that the congregation has declined due to "morale" problems, but that he believes it can be "revived." He corroborated that there are a few powerful people in the congregation who vie for power in decision-making; but on the whole, it is a group of people who support one another and have a rich history together. The Long Term Pastor reportedly retired with short notice, leaving many in the congregation "in shock" and bewildered.

There are complaints from many that the synod "should have come in and helped them through the transition." Some stated that the congregation was desperate to call another pastor because they had never taken responsibility for the ongoing functions of the ministry and did not feel that "it was their job" to do so.

The ministry of the second pastor is a subject of great disparagement. Most members interviewed stated that she is an excellent "preacher." Having credited her with that strength, many and varied weaknesses were described at length. These include: not visiting the members, and when she did visit, exhibiting poor boundaries in staying past her welcome; lack of confidence; lack of involvement; poor to nonexistent leadership; inability to motivate the congregation; and many more. Some shared these in context of an overall hopeful picture, but many participants had difficulty moving from this topic to consider healthy dynamics or future direction. These seven years were culminated by another resignation with short notice. This time, however, the consensus of the participants is that it was time for the Second Pastor to leave and most attribute the decline in church viability to her poor leadership. The Second Pastor's perspective is that she was never received into the congregation as an "insider." She reports that the congregation at St. Timothy refers to anyone whose family has not helped to build the church as an "outsider" and that label includes people in the neighborhood, visitors to the church and new members. She believes that this "closed" system negatively impacts evangelism efforts and fuels an insular perspective that encourages fellowship, but does not reach out to others.

Present Status

The positive aspects of the ministry at St. Timothy reportedly includes an active Food Basket, the Aid for Friends program, a strong Sunday School, a devoted choir, the children's sermon and active Women of the ELCA group. The problems were identified as no evangelism, an aging congregation, no youth group, no membership drive, and a tired and "saturated" core group. The presence of the Community Agency in the building is seen by most as a positive use of the space; and it is hoped by a few members, that this group will become a springboard of ministry into the community.

It is reported that many families left the church due to the hurts and disappointments incurred during the former Pastor's ministry. These members left the body fractured, and many wished for their return. The issue of the age of the congregation was a frequently cited concern for its future viability. Some described a "catch 22" dynamic in that the church needs new families to survive, but many of the older members resist change and do not want to create an atmosphere to attract people if it means their comfortable traditions would change.

Many discussed the topic of music as an area of dissatisfaction. Some members feel that the hymns are "liturgically correct," yet unfamiliar and boring, and wish for an infusion of life through the music. Although some members recognize that learning new hymns is important, they feel that being forced to struggle through hymns that no one knows is not conducive to worship while singing familiar, beloved hymns facilitates worship.

A few members commented that they had volunteered to participate on committees or for projects but were never contacted. It was suggested that the "core group" resists letting "outsiders" take on vital functions. Members who have been in positions of responsibility for years saw this differently. Many feel that they practically "fall over new people" to have them feel welcome and so they can bring new blood to the church work.

When groups were asked to describe the spiritual condition of the congregation, there was often a long silence. In a few meetings, members responded, "What do you mean?" Spiritual nurture has been lost for many, as there are no Bible studies or spiritual resources other than the Sunday morning service, and the groups that do meet are purely social. Some seemed interested in this being recovered, but others seemed neutral on the issue.

In review of the Percept Survey, critical dynamics to the future direction of St. Timothy include the increasing African American population in the neighborhood, a projected overall decrease in population in the immediate area, a very high giving potential per household in the area, and a presence of large numbers of traditional family units. These predict that evangelism must include diversity, that it needs to reconsider outreach to people living at a distance, and that there is a potential for active young families to be attracted who both need ministry and are capable of financially supporting the church.

Challenges for the Future

The challenges to St. Timothy Lutheran Church are described as many. If one response is paramount, it is "leadership." Most members believe that the presence of a strong leader will give the church energy, motivation, and enthusiasm which will then bring it back to life.

When questioned about openness to welcoming others not like ourselves into the church, the first response by most members was "I think we have to." When clarified by the consultant that it is one thing to "have to" and another to have hearts open to different cultures, some members responded that their personal heart is open. In seeking to test this response for the general population, there was a difference in perspective. It can be summarized, that most members believe that there is resistance by some to "outsiders," but that they do not want those few to influence the future viability of the congregation. When pressed about the breakdown of support on this issue, one member speculated that one third of the members will be offended if the church is integrated.

Evangelism is another critical concern for a congregation seeking redevelopment. In asking each group if they were personally willing and able to add to their present commitments and take part in an active evangelism campaign, there was a total of 12-15 people who responded positively.

The future of a viable congregation will depend in part upon the development a youth program and the continuation of a healthy Sunday School. The need for young members to grow into positions of leadership is seen as essential by most interviewed.

When asked about expectations of redevelopment, responses included "holding our hands, showing us what to do, infusing us with a new energy, giving us a process to work with, teaching us how to be effective, stabilizing the financial picture until we get more giving units."

When questioned regarding expectations of the next pastor, the responses included "outgoing personality, willing to visit shut-ins, responsive to needs of the congregation, willing to get involved in church life, has a direct approach, deals with the grapevine by confronting it."

Analysis of the Systems Issues

The central problem at St. Timothy Lutheran Church in Transformation USA is the lack of spirituality. The focus on the outer layers of church function, like fellowship, leads to a diminished ability to sustain health and growth, as the mission becomes "remaining comfortable". The attitudes toward evangelism are of most serious concern. Neither consultant was impressed with a "burden for souls" or a drive to bring St. Timothy to the community. Evangelism was discussed, rather, pragmatically in relation to numbers, money, changes, and workload. No amount of enthusiasm or specialized training in a redevelopment pastor can replace a lack of spiritual concern for others. It is difficult to have a spiritual concern for others when the congregation itself is so spiritually depleted. The evangelism projects are likely to be infiltrated by ambivalence, conflict and discouragement that directly relate to the lack of spiritual motivation to evangelize.

The strengths of the church lie in the commitment of members to a continued life together and the hard work that the core group continues to do to preserve that life. Questionable concerns are: How much more can be expected from this group?; What power dynamics will come into play if changes threaten the status quo?; and, How much tenacity the members have in confronting resistance by powerful people?

St. Timothy is compromised by several critical dynamics. The age of the congregation is a concern, but a greater determinate of dysfunction is the lack of development of lay leadership throughout the years. There appear to be many members with a sincere desire to help, and yet do not know how to combat the inertia and wheel-spinning which has all but paralyzed the congregation. The inertia takes its form in blaming all the ills of the church on leadership while looking for the salvation of the church through leadership, the diminished focus on spirituality, and lack of participation in activities.

It seems clear that when the Second Pastor was called, this church had no idea of its needs, and moved quickly to have a new leader. The metaphor of the family can be used, for it is like a family left without a parent avoiding the pain and distress of being alone by quickly re-marrying. Once the decision is made, the pressure is on the new parent to fulfill these deeply felt, but not at all clearly defined holes. St. Timothy being the former Pastor's first church further complicates this. The long-standing power dynamics exhibited by families, coupled with the grief and loss of the familiar way of doing things, set up immediate tension in moving into a new ministry. It is difficult to follow any tenured and beloved pastor, and in this situation, expectation and styles clashed greatly, to the detriment of all parties.

There are interesting paradoxes at St. Timothy, in that accompanying a strong sense of ownership for the church, ("This is our church, and we won't let any pastor tear us apart".), there is a lack of ownership for the health, depth, and spirit of the congregation ("That's the pastor's job".). The dependency and victimization expressed by many of the members underlies the demands for empowerment. A strong resistance accompanies the recognition of need for diversity and change to it.

The council seems conflicted around the issues of the amount of change people will support, the extent of their inclusiveness, and the priority of things to be changed. The consultants are concerned that although a clear agreement for payment was made at a briefing session March 4, internal confusion caused the commitment to be broken by the church. Their concern focuses on process and power and the breakdown in communication and action. When a congregation is requesting to be considered for redevelopment or a fresh start, it is incumbent upon its leaders to present to both to the consultants and the synod the most unified and competent lay leadership it can muster. At this time, a breakdown in its commitment to action needs to be explored by the council and its impact on the ability to follow through on commitments understood.

For St. Timothy to be successful in redevelopment, it will be necessary to embrace diversity. An example was given of an African American woman who was welcomed into the congregation in the past as an example of the church's openness. In addition to responding openly to a person who sought the church, the congregation needs an "openness of heart" in recognizing the universality of human beings. The notion of "insiders" and "outsiders" is not compatible with inclusive membership and cannot be tolerated. It leads to what was expressed by some as "1st class members" and "2nd class members." Unless new members of all backgrounds are received as full members with rights, responsibilities and privileges equivalent to the founding members, the church will not remain viable as a mission church. This model is more akin to a "chaplaincy" church in which the members are serviced by the pastor and one another in meeting needs in an insular fashion.

Summary and Recommendations

The spiritual needs of the church are paramount. The enrichment of spirituality will provide a solid center from which to build a Christ-filled, enduring ministry. In preparation for consideration for redevelopment, it is recommended that:

1.   A healing process be formalized in the congregation around the Good Friday and Easter liturgies. Preceding the Holy Thursday or Good Friday services, brief discussion groups might focus on validating feelings of hurt and pain and include a discussion what surrender of this pain and healing would mean. The discussion groups need to be time-limited and facilitated by lay leaders in order to avoid story telling and blaming. The Easter liturgy might be used to celebrate new life and the expectation that a positive focus will be the core of building a successful future together.

2.   Bible studies, prayer groups and prayer chains be instituted and run by lay leaders under the interim Pastor's guidance.

3.   The present groups, such as the women's group, incorporate a spiritual focus into their meetings to differentiate them from a social group. This might take the form of readings; discussion of a book read together, prayer, etc.

There are significant questions regarding the motivation, ability and willingness of the congregation at St. Timothy to sustain a prolonged effort in evangelization at this time. The remnants of the recent, painful separation of their pastor threaten the success of a redevelopment pastor. There are, however, a group of people who want very much to turn the church around and to be trained in a new way of ministering. In this regard, it is recommended that

4.   A pilot project be assumed by the congregation at St. Timothy which will include an opportunity to demonstrate a singleness of purpose and ability to follow-through against whatever resistance arises. This might include the successful implementation of Bible studies and prayer groups, or the successful completion of a preliminary project designed by the synod.

5.   The Church Council undergo leadership training in order to develop skills and abilities to prepare them for the challenges of redevelopment.

6.   The Church Council enters into a facilitated internal process to evaluate decision-making, power bases, and role clarity.

Youth ministry is also a core structure for the future.   St. Timothy is experiencing the loss of children after confirmation due to lack of programming. In this regard, it is recommended that:

7.   Sunday School teachers receive training in teaching techniques and the application of spiritual principles into the everyday lives of children and young people.

8.   Lay leadership be sought to begin a youth club with 10-11 year old children who are presently active in the church. In this way, a new generation of kids will be prepared to move up into a teen group.

9.   If starting an internal youth group is not possible, collaboration should be instituted with another church in the area whose youth group is active. This will necessitate a youth coordinator at St. Timothy to be liaison and companion in youth events. A church, which takes a spiritual as well as social approach to youth ministry, is the most solid model.

Committee participation is essential to revitalize ministry at St. Timothy. In this regard, it is recommended that:

10.   A mentoring program be developed to utilize the expertise and experience of lay leaders at other Lutheran congregations to mentor and advise Committee Chairs. This might include attendance at meetings at other churches to bring new ideas and see how others face challenges.

11. A spiritual gift inventory be utilized in the congregation to help to identify areas of service best suited to each individual's gifts and talents.

The music ministry is in need of redevelopment in order to have it accomplish its purpose in promoting worship in the liturgy. Choosing music that is liturgically correct, yet practically ineffective compromises a medium with enormous potential for creating life and energy in the congregation. Consideration of a worship committee with authority to plan and implement worship is essential. It is therefore recommended that:

12. A contemporary liturgy be explored as a monthly alternative.

13. Special music be encouraged which utilizes talents within the congregation.

14. Old hymns be incorporated weekly into the worship.

The church needs to declare its presence in the community. It is recommended that:

15. Outside lighting and spring plantings be a priority in the action plan.

16. A member who is talented at PR actively promotes news of services at St. Timothy.

Should the decision be positive by the synod to enter into a redevelopment process with St. Timothy Lutheran Church in Transition USA, the selection of a pastor will be critical to the success of the program. In light of the need for diversity and the change this will create within the congregation, it is recommended that:

17. A pastor be considered who is a member of an ethnic group represented in the surrounding area. This person can model the seeking of inclusiveness while building trust within the congregation that an integrated, culturally rich group can worship together and minister to one another effectively.

If the congregation is not willing to institute these changes then the consultants would recommend that the synod propose a fresh start ministry seeking to have the present membership transferred to healthy congregations and a fresh start identifying this community as a base to start all over again.

APPENDIX 2

How to Minister Effectively in Family, Pastoral, Program, and Corporate Size Churches

From Chapter 2, Making Your Church More Inviting, *by Roy Oswald (Washington, D.C.: the Alban Institute, 1992).*

The theory of congregational size that I find most workable is Arlin Rothauge's, described in his booklet *Sizing Up a Congregation for New Member Ministry.* It was originally written to help congregations recognize the different ways different-sized churches assimilate new members. When a theory is on target, however, it so accurately reflects reality that it can be applied to other dimensions of a church's life and work. Rothauge's theory elicits consistent "ah ha's" from clergy who are reflecting, on their transition from one size parish to another. Whether churches are growing or downsizing, congregations hold on to deeply ingrained assumptions about what constitutes a dynamic church and what effective clergy do. The inflexibility of these expectations is an important cause of clergy malfunctioning.

Rothauge sets forth four basic congregational sizes. Each size requires a specific cluster of behaviors from its clergy. The average number of people attending weekly worship and the amount of money being contributed regularly provide the most accurate gauge of church size. Since membership rolls fluctuate wildly depending on how frequently they are evaluated, they cannot provide an accurate measurement of congregational size. Rothauge also holds that a church's size category is a matter of attitude as much as numbers. I knew of one congregation that averaged 700 at Sunday worship and still functioned on a Pastoral model. All the pastor did was preach on Sunday and visit people through the week. The pastor's perception of his job burned him out and eventually cost him his marriage and his ministry.

Here is a brief description of each of Rothauge's four sizes and my understanding of what members expect of clergy in each size.

The Patriarchal/Matriarchal Church: Worships 50 or less

This small church can also be called a Family Church because it functions like a family, with appropriate parental figures. The patriarchs and matriarchs control the church's leadership needs. What Family Churches want from clergy is pastoral care, period. For clergy to assume that they are also the chief executive officer and the resident religious authority is to make a serious blunder. The key role, of the patriarch or matriarch is to see that clergy do not take the congregation off on a new direction of ministry. Clergy are to be the chaplain of this small family. When clergy don't understand this, they are likely to head into a direct confrontation with the parental figure. It is generally suicide for clergy to get caught in a showdown with the patriarchs and matriarchs within the first five years of their ministry in that place.

Clergy should not assume, however, that they have no role beyond pastoral care. In addition to providing quality worship and home/hospital visitation, clergy can play an important role as consultants to these patriarchs or matriarchs, befriending these parental figures and working alongside them, yet recognizing that when these parental figures decide against an idea, it's finished.

Clergy should watch out for the trap set when members complain to them about the patriarch or matriarch of the parish and encourage the pastor to take on the parental figure. Clergy, who respond to such mutinous bids, expecting the congregation to back them in the showdown, betray their misunderstanding of the dynamics of small-church ministry. The high turnover of clergy in these parishes has taught members that in the long run they have to live with old Mr. Schwartz who runs the feed mill, even when they don't like him. Pastors come and go, therefore it is far too risky for members to get caught siding with pastors who come and go against their resident patriarch/matriarch.

Because these congregations usually cannot pay clergy an acceptable salary, many clergy see them as stepping stones to more rewarding opportunities. It is not unusual for a congregation of this size to list five successive clergy for every ten years of congregational life. As Lyle Schaller claims, the longer the pastorates the more powerful clergy become. The shorter the pastorates the more powerful the laity become. These Family Churches have to develop one or two strong lay leaders at the center of their life. How else would they manage their ongoing existence through those long vacancies and through the short pastorates of the ineffective clergy who are often sent their way?

The president of the Alban Institute, Loren Mead, began his ministry in a Family Church in South Carolina. Later in his ministry he attended a clergy conference at which he discovered seven other clergy who had also started their ordained ministry in the same parish. As they talked, those clergy realized that, in view of the difference in their styles and the shortness of their tenures, the only way that parish survived was to take none of them seriously.

One of the worst places to go right out of seminary is to a Patriarchal/Matriarchal Church. Seminarians are up to their eyeballs in new theories and good ideas. They want to see if any of them work. Even though some of those good ideas might be the ticket to their small church's long-term growth and development, the church's openness to trying any of them is next to zero. Sometimes, through the sheer force of personal persuasion, a pastor will talk a congregation into trying a new program or two. Pretty soon parishioners find themselves coming to church events much more than they really need to or want to. As they begin then to withdraw their investment from these new programs, clergy inevitably take it personally. Concluding that their gifts for ministry are not really valued in this place, they begin to seek a call elsewhere. On the way out of the church they give it a kick, letting the parish know in subtle ways that they are a miserable example of Christian community.

These small congregations have endured such recriminations for decades. The message they get from their Bishop/Executive is that they are a failure because they fail to grow while consuming inordinate amounts of time. Middle judicatories try to merge them, yoke them, and close them--mostly to no avail. You can't kill these congregations with a stick. Large churches are far more vulnerable. A Bishop/Executive can place an incompetent pastor in a large church and lose 200 members in one year. Yet the same Bishop/Executive can throw incompetent clergy at Family Churches, leave them vacant for years, ignore them all together with little effect. The Family Church has learned to survive by relying on its own internal leadership.

These congregations need a pastor to stay and love them over at least ten years. This pastor would have to play by the rules and defer to the patriarch or matriarch's leadership decisions for the first three to five years. At about year four or five, when the pastor did not leave, the congregation might find itself in somewhat of a crisis. At some level they would be saying, "What do you mean you are going to stay? No clergy stay here. There must be something the matter with you." Then the questioning might begin: "Can we really trust you? Naw! You are going to leave us like all the rest." In this questioning we can see the pain of these congregations. For a minute, let's put ourselves in their shoes and imagine an ordained leader walking out on us every few years, berating us on the way out. Would we invest in the next pastor who came to us? Not likely! It would be simply too painful. The Family Church may have invested in one five years ago, only to find that the pastor left just when things started to move. Basically these people have learned not to trust clergy who repeatedly abandon ship when they see no evidence of church growth.

I conclude that we need to refrain from sending these congregations seminary-trained pastors. History demonstrates that these churches have not been served well by full-time ordained clergy. The Episcopal Diocese of Nevada and the North Indiana Conference of the United Methodist Church are among judicatories experimenting with employing persons indigenous to the communities, providing them with some basic training to enable them to give long-term pastoral care on a part-time basis. I believe long-term tent-making ministries offer the best possibility for ministering to many of these Patriarchal/Matriarchal Churches.

If denominations and middle Judicatories persist in placing newly ordained clergy in these parishes, they should do so only after laying out this theory for these clergy, helping them discover who indeed are the patriarchs and matriarchs of the parish, suggesting some strategies for working with them. If these clergy find it simply too difficult to work with these parental figures, they need to let their Bishop/Executive know promptly. Rather than leaving these newly ordained clergy regretting that they pursued ordained ministry in the first place, the Bishop/Executive should move them out of the Family Church.

The Pastoral Church: Average Worship Attendance of 50 to 150

Clergy are usually at the center of a Pastoral Church. There are so many parental figures around that they need someone at the center to manage them. A leadership circle, made up of the pastor and a small cadre of lay leaders, replaces the patriarchs and matriarchs of the Family Church. The power and effectiveness of the leadership circle depends upon good communication with the congregation and the ability of the pastor to delegate authority, assign responsibility, and recognize the accomplishments of others. Without such skill, the central pastoral function weakens the entire structure. The clergyperson becomes overworked, isolated, and exhausted, may be attacked by other leaders. Finally the harmony of the fellowship circle degenerates.

171

A key feature of a Pastoral Church is that lay persons experience having their spiritual needs met through their personal relationship with a seminary trained person. In a Pastoral Church it would be rare for a Bible study or a prayer group to meet without the pastor being present. The pastor is also readily available in times of personal need and crisis. If a parishioner called the pastor and indicated that she needed some personal attention, the pastor would drop over to see her, probably that afternoon but certainly within the week--a qualitatively different experience from being told that the first available appointment to see the pastor in her office is two weeks from now. The time demands on the pastor of a Pastoral Church can become oppressive. However, most members will respond with loyalty to a reasonable level of attention and guidance from this central figure.

A second feature of the Pastoral Church is its sense of itself as a family where everyone knows everyone else. If you show up at church with your daughter Julie in hand, everyone will greet you and Julie, too. When congregations begin to have 130 to 150 people coming every Sunday morning, they begin to get nervous. As Carl Dudley put it in *Unique Dynamics of the Small Church* (Washington, DC: The Alban Institute, 1977) they begin to feel "stuffed." Members wonder about the new faces they don't know--people who don't know *them*. Are they beginning to lose the intimate fellowship they prize so highly?

Clergy also begin to feel stressed when they have more than 150 active members whom they try to know in depth. In fact, this is one of the reasons why clergy may keep the Pastoral Church from growing to the next larger size congregation--the Program Church. If clergy have the idea firmly fixed in their head that they are ineffective as a pastor unless they can relate in a profound and personal way with every member of the parish, then 150 active members (plus perhaps an even larger number of inactive members) is about all one person can manage.

There are some clergy who function at their highest level of effectiveness in the Pastoral Church. Given the different clusters of skills required for other sizes of congregations, some clergy should consider spending their entire career in this size congregation. Since the Pastoral Church can offer a pastor a decent salary, clergy do tend to stick around longer. If clergy can regard themselves as successful only when they become pastor of a large congregation, then sixty-five percent of mainline Protestant clergy are going to end their careers with feelings of failure. Two-thirds of mainline Protestant congregations are either Family or Pastoral Churches.

Clergy with strong interpersonal skills fare well in the Pastoral Church. These clergy can feed continually on the richness of direct involvement in the highs and lows of people's lives. Clergy who enjoy being at the center of most activities also do well. There are lots of opportunities to preach and lead in worship and to serve as primary instructors in many class settings for both young and old. Outgoing, expressive people seem to be the best matches for the style of ministry in the Pastoral Church. An open, interactive leadership style also seems to suit this size church best.

Growth in the Pastoral Church will depend mainly on the popularity and effectiveness of the pastor. People join the church because they like the interaction between pastor and people. When new people visit the congregation for the first time, it is likely to be the pastor who will make the follow-up house call.

When a congregation grows to the point where its pastor's time and energy is drawn off into many other activities and the one-on-one pastoral relationship begins to suffer, it may hire additional staff to handle these new functions so the pastor can once again have plenty of time for interpersonal caring. Unfortunately, this strategy will have limited success. To begin with, when you hire additional staff you then have a multiple staff, which requires staff meetings, supervision, delegation, evaluation, and planning. These activities draw the pastor deeper into administration. Then, too, additional staff members tend to specialize in such things as Christian education, youth ministry, evangelism, or stewardship, which tends to add to the administrative role of the head of staff rather than freeing his or her time up for pastoral care.

Clergy consider a congregation's transition from Pastoral to Program size the most difficult. One can expect enormous resistance on the part of a Pastoral Church as it flirts with becoming a Program Church. Many churches make an unconscious choice not to make the transition and keep hovering around the level of 150 active members. The two treasured features of a Pastoral Church that will be lost if it becomes a Program Church are ready access to their religious leaders and the feeling of oneness as a church family, where everyone knows everyone else and the church can function as a single cell community.

Two things can prevent a congregation from making that transition: The first barrier is found in the clergy. When clergy hold on to a need to be connected in depth to all the active members, they become the bottlenecks to growth. The second barrier is found in the lay leaders who are unwilling to have many of their spiritual needs met by anyone except their ordained leader.

It is most helpful to put this theory up on newsprint before the chief decision-making body of the church and ask where it thinks the parish stands. If they have been saying "yes, yes" to church growth with their lips, but "no, no" with their behavior, this theory can bring their resistance to the conscious level by pointing out the real costs they will face in growing. Churches tend to grow when parish leaders, fully aware of the cost of growth, make a conscious decision to proceed.

Without the backing of key lay leaders, the cost of moving from a Pastoral to a Program Church usually comes out of the pastor's hide. The parish may welcome the pastor's efforts in parish program development, while still expecting all the parish calling and one-on-one work to continue at the same high level as before. Burnout and/or a forced pastoral termination can result.

The Program Church: Average Worship Attendance of 150 to 350

The Program Church grows out of the necessity for a high-quality personal relationship with the pastor to be supplemented by other avenues of spiritual feeding. Programs must now begin to fill the role of spiritual nurture.

The well-functioning Program Church has many cells of activity, which are headed up by lay leaders. These lay leaders, in addition to providing structure and guidance for these cells, also take on some pastoral functions. The Stewardship Committee gathers for its monthly meeting and the committee chair asks about a missing member. Upon being told that Mary Steward's daughter had to be taken to the hospital for an emergency operation, the chair will allow time for expressions of concern for Mary and her daughter. The chair may include both of them in a opening prayer. If the teacher of an adult class notices that someone in the class is feeling depressed, the teacher will often take the class member aside and inquire about his well-being. Even if the teacher eventually asks the pastor to intervene, the pastor has already gotten a lot of assistance from this lay leader.

Clergy are still at the center of the Program Church, but their role has shifted dramatically. Much of their time and attention must be spent in planning with other lay leaders to ensure the highest quality programs. The pastor must spend a lot of time recruiting people to head up these smaller ministries, training, supervising, and evaluating them, and seeing to it that their morale remains high. In essence, the pastor must often step back from direct ministry with people to coordinate and support volunteers who offer this ministry. Unless the pastor gives high priority to the spiritual and pastoral needs of lay leaders, those programs will suffer.

To be sure, a member can expect a hospital or home call from the pastor when personal crisis or illness strikes, but members had better not expect this pastor to have a lot of time to drink coffee in people's kitchens. To see the pastor about a parish matter, they will probably have to make an appointment at the church office several weeks in advance.

When clergy move from a Pastoral Church to a Program Church, unless they are ready to shift from a primarily interpersonal mode to a program planning and development mode, they will experience tension and difficulty in their new congregation. It is not that clergy will have no further need for their interpersonal skills. Far from it--they need to depend on them even more. But now those interpersonal skills will be placed at the service of the parish programs.

Key skills for effective ministry in a Program Church begins with the ability to pull together the diverse elements of the parish into a mission statement. Helping the parish arrive at a consensus about its direction is essential. Next the pastor must be able to lead the parish toward attaining the goals that arise out of that consensus. To wilt in the face of opposition to this consensus will be seen as a lack of leadership ability. The Program Church pastor will also need to be able to motivate the capable lay persons in the parish to take on key components of the parish vision and help make it become a reality. Developing the trust and loyalty of these parish leaders and ensuring their continued spiritual growth and development is another key part of the cluster of skills needed in the Program Church.

For clergy who get their primary kicks out of direct pastoral care work, ministry in a Program Church may leave them with a chronic feeling of flatness and lack of fulfillment. Unless these clergy can learn to derive satisfaction from the work of pastoral administration and ministering mainly to church leaders, they should think twice about accepting a call to this size parish.

The Corporate Church: Average Worship Attendance of 350 or More

The quality of Sunday morning worship is the first thing you usually notice in a Corporate Church. Because these churches usually have abundant resources, they will usually have the finest organ and one of the best choirs in town. A lot of work goes into making Sunday worship a rich experience. The head of staff usually spends more time than other clergy preparing for preaching and worship leadership.

In very large Corporate Churches the head of staff may not even remember the names of many parishioners. When members are in the hospital it is almost taken for granted that an associate or assistant pastor, rather than the senior pastor will visit them. Those who value highly the Corporate Church experience are willing to sacrifice a personal connection with the senior pastor in favor of the Corporate Church's variety and quality of program offerings.

Sometimes the head pastor is so prominent that the personage of the pastor acquires a legendary quality, especially in the course of a long pastorate. Few may know this person well, but the role does not require it. The head pastor becomes a symbol of unity and stability in a very complicated congregational life.

The Corporate Church is distinguished from the Program Church by its complexity and diversity. The patriarchs and matriarchs return, but now in the governing boards that formally, not just informally, control the church's life and future. Laity lead on many levels, and the Corporate Church provides opportunity for them to move up the ladder of influence.

Key to the success of the Corporate Church is the multiple staff and its ability to manage the   diversity of its ministries in a collegial manner. Maintaining energy and momentum in a Corporate Church is very difficult when there is division within the parish staff. Any inability to work together harmoniously is especially evident during Sunday worship where any tensions among the ordained leadership of the parish will manifest themselves in subtle ways.

It is at this point that clergy making the transition to the Corporate Church find themselves most vulnerable and unsupported. Our denominational systems do little to equip clergy to work collegially within a multiple staff. A three-day workshop on the multiple staff is a bare introduction. Leaders in industry with master's degrees in personnel management still make serious mistakes in hiring and developing leaders for the corporation. The head of staff of a Corporate Church learns to manage a multiple staff by trial and error. Sacrificing a few associate and assistant clergy on the altar of experience is the price the church pays for such lack of training.

For the most part clergy are not taught to work collegially. In seminary we compete with one another for grades. Each of us retreats to his or her own cubicle to write term papers. There is little interaction in class. In seminary we don't really have to take each other seriously. This might change if, for example, a professor were to assign four seminarians to complete research on a church doctrine, write one paper, and receive a group grade. In that kind of learning atmosphere we would have to take one another on and argue about our different theological perspectives and forms of piety. Unless our training can begin to equip us for collegial ministry, our seminaries will continue to turn out lone rangers who don't really have to work with other clergy until they get to the Corporate Church or the larger Program Church. By that time our patterns have been set.

The clergy who are called as head of staff in Corporate Churches are usually multi-skilled people who have proven their skill in a great variety of pastoral situations. In a multiple staff, however, the senior minister will need to delegate some of those pastoral tasks to other fulltime staff members, who will inevitably want to do them differently.

Learning to allow these people to do things their own way is in itself a major new demand.

Our research with the Myers-Briggs Type Indicator shows that congregations are best served when the multiple staff includes different types. The more diversity the staff has, the greater its ability to minister to a diverse congregation. But this requirement for diversity makes multiple staff functioning more complicated: The more diverse the staff, the harder it is to understand and support one another's ministries.

Lay leaders are generally completely baffled by the inability of ordained people to work collegially. "If our religious leaders aren't able to get along, what hope is there for this world?" they may wonder. Lay leaders could help enormously by seeing to it that there is money in the budget for regular consultative help for the staff. This help is not needed only when tensions arise. Multiple staffs need to be meeting regularly with an outside consultant to keep lines of communication open and difficulties surfaced.

When the multiple staff is having fun working well together, this graceful colleagueship becomes contagious throughout the Corporate Church. Lay people want to get on board and enjoy the camaraderie. The parish has little difficulty filling the many volunteer jobs needed to run a Corporate Church.

In addition to learning to manage a multiple staff, clergy making the transition to head of staff need to hone their administrative skills. These clergy are becoming chief executive officers of substantive operations. Yet I would emphasize leadership skills over management skills. While managers can manage the energy of a parish, leaders can *generate* energy. They generate energy by creating exciting visions for the future to which lay leaders can give their energy. The Corporate Church needs leaders who know how to build momentum. Otherwise, even when managed well, these large churches run out of gas and begin to decline.

In summary, the most difficult transitions in size are from Pastoral to Program or, when downsizing, from Program to Pastoral. These are two very different ways to be church. More is required than a theoretical vision of the shift. We need to deal with the fact that a shift in size at this level just doesn't feel right to people. Somewhere deep inside they begin to sense that it doesn't feel like church anymore.

Choice Points for Clergy

It is not uncommon for congregants to want to add a hundred new members to the parish but be unwilling to change one thing about their parish to accommodate the increase. We often refer to this as the vampire theory of growth: "We need some new blood around here." Basically members desire a bunch of new people to help pay the bills and to fill up the choir, Sunday school, and sanctuary, but they don't expect to make any sacrifices related to the things newcomers want from their church.

Some of the greatest upheaval caused by numerical growth occurs when a congregation is on the borderline between two of the four different sizes of congregations described earlier. When a congregation crosses the boundary from one size and another, it needs to begin relating to its clergy in fairly radically different ways than previously. As a review of these descriptions in a group setting, ask four participants to volunteer, each to summarize the dynamics of one of the four types of congregations. At the end of each summary ask the group if it remembers any additional points. Fill in any important aspects not brought up. Briefly discuss what description best suits your parish.

Remind the group that the most difficult transition is between the Pastoral and Program Church. The following activity will help illustrate what a transition from one size church to the other might mean.

Ask participants to stand and push the chairs to the side of the room, clearing the floor.

Rather than have participants simply circle answers to prepared questions, I like to send the "A's" to one side of the room and the "B's" to the other side. You can see at a glance where everyone stands on an issue, and the two groups can talk to each other about their choices. Since the questions deal with choices clergy need to make between two competing activities, I ask any clergy present to remain silent until the other participants have answered.

Have one side of the room represent response A and the other side represents response B. Read aloud one set of A-B choices. Have participants choose their responses by going to the designated side of the room. Tally the results. Allow up to two minutes for the two groups to discuss their stance, and then go on to the next question.

Each set of questions represents a choice point for your pastor. Should your pastor have had a week full of crises and only limited time left, which response represents your preference for what the pastor should do?

A. Visit more shut-ins?
B. Prepare a better sermon?

A. Attend a wedding reception?
B. Go on a retreat with parish staff?

A. Call on prospective members?
B. Conduct a training session for church officers?

A. Visit a bereaved family?
B. Help two church officers resolve a conflict?

A. Make a hospital call on a fringe member?
B. Attend a continuing education event?

A. Give pastoral counseling to members?
B. Attend a planning event with officers?

A. Call on parishioners?
B. Recruit leaders for parish events?

A. Attend an activity with parish youth?
B. Critique a meeting with a church officer?

Once you have completed the exercise as a class, invite the pastor to share personal responses to each question. I encourage clergy to choose the activity they would most enjoy rather than the one they believe might claim a higher parish priority. The differences between the pastoral and lay responses to these questions may result in some fruitful discussion related to size of congregation and pastoral expectations.

This activity can point out several issues:

1. Congregations may be Program size yet still require their clergy to attend to all the category A pastoral activities. This is a perfect prescription for burnout. It can also lead to labeling clergy as "bad" because they don't accomplish all the tasks in the A column while they are also expected to crank out quality programs for the parish (Category B activities).

2. Clergy in small Pastoral Churches should be focusing their energies and attention on the A activities. But sometimes because their background or training is in Program Churches, they continue to concentrate on the B activities or feel guilty because they aren't doing so.

3. Clergy and laity often disagree on priorities for clergy. This exercise often surfaces those differences quickly and makes role negotiation possible.

Staffing for Growth

Some congregations do not grow because they are not staffed for growth. If, for example, you are a Program Church, expecting your pastor to assist you in developing and executing quality programs in the church, yet you also expect your pastor to do pastoral calling in homes, you probably have a pastor who is doing neither task well and is burning out trying to do it all. Unless those pastoral expectations change or you add more staff, the congregation will not grow, as members are going to be dissatisfied with both the programs that are offered and the fact that they are not receiving the pastoral care they desire.

As a rule of thumb, if you desire to staff for growth, you need one full-time program person on your staff for every one hundred active members. (This does not include support staff such as janitors or secretaries.) *Active members* refer to how many are attending weekly worship including children in Sunday School on the average year. You are staffing for maintenance if you are just slightly under that figure. You are staffed for decline if you are seriously under that figure.

(e.g. 175 average weekly attendance –staffed for growth -- two plus program staff

--staffed for maintenance –1-3/4 program staff

--staffed for decline -- 1-1/2 or less program staff.

Growing churches see that their members as well as their visitors receive adequate pastoral care during times of crisis or need. People well cared for pastorally are inclined to invite their friends and family members to become affiliated with their parish. When a new family to your area is having difficulty, having a staff member make a call to discover ways the parish can meet needs makes a deep impression. Without that call, they are less likely to think of joining your congregation. In Program churches mainly trained lay volunteers make these pastoral calls. In Pastoral churches mainly clergy makes these calls.

The addition of a paid professional (i.e., youth worker, religious education specialist, business manager) usually pays for him/herself within twelve to eighteen months. For example, a congregation with 225 active members that hires a third full-time staff member to provide better quality ministry will most likely to grow to 300 members. The increased revenue will then be able to pay for this additional full time program staff person.

APPENDIX 3

Regional Bodies & Congregations
What's the Connection? *(Draft)*
by Loren B. Mead

(Adair Lummis and her colleagues have done a lot of research on how the regional entity or "judicatory" of denominations "works," and has invited a number of judicatory executives into conversation about their experiences. She has asked me to join the conversation as one who can be a "senior consultant" in this process. Because I have worked with such judicatories for four decades in a variety of roles and have been a colleague of consultants similarly engaged, I have also accumulated a body of experience, often gathered in less structured ways. Reading over the Research Report Adair Lummis produced, and by an initial response by Bob Johnson, one of the judicatory executive from whom I have learned, I find that my experience is precipitating into a framework for thinking that may be helpful to the researchers and to the executives. This paper is a step toward such a framework for thinking.)

Introduction

The relationship between a congregation and its regional body is almost always problematical, but specifically what the problem is likely to be is hard to predict. The conversation about that relationship I find to be emotionally charged, often; with an assumption that someone is "right" and someone is "wrong."

This is a real problem. The regional entity, if there is one, or the relationship between independent congregations ought, it seems to me, exist to strengthen the work of the churches and not to be an obstruction. The relationship, whether close or distant, ought to "grease" the wheels of ministry and mission, not throw "grit" into the gears.

This paper is an attempt to tease apart the different dynamics I have discovered that influence the nature of those relationships and provide a "map" for those, whatever their orientation to these issues, who want to remove some of the "grit" from their experience and get ideas about how to "lubricate" their gears.

I. The Basic Operating Principle: A Continuum, not a Focus Point

Discussion of what is the "right" approach to the connection between congregations and their systems assumes a set of normative values that I simply have not observed in dealing with congregations.

In my experience, congregations, even congregations in the same denomination and in the same community, do not have identical relations with their regional offices or officers. I have found American Baptist regional ministers acting much like Presbyterian executives with some congregations. I have found United Methodist bishops or district superintendents have disastrous experiences when they try to do what the Book of Order says they are supposed to be able to do with congregations. I have found Episcopal bishops stymied by "congregational" attitudes in some of their congregations and treated by others as "the word from on high." Episcopal bishops wish they had the power United Methodist bishops have, and United Methodist bishops wish they had the power the Episcopalians think they have. I have seen United Church of Christ conference executives wheel and deal with congregations, powerfully influencing them in ways Presbyterian executives can only stand back and admire. The same is true from the "other" end -Baptist congregations begging for help from their system; Episcopalian congregations who have nothing to do with their bishop; Presbyterian congregations who are grateful when their executive acts with the authority no sane Presbyterian would admit to be legal.

In reality, congregations and executives are all over the map. It has been helpful to me to think of what we are talking about as a continuum from one extreme to another, with one's location on the map being influenced by many factors.

The end-points of the continuum are clear, logically.

At one end are those congregations that are totally autonomous -they have to answer to no one, relate to no one, but are totally free to set their agendas, relate to their faith in whatever way their own internal processes determine. I call this end point on the map "AUTONOMOUS." I do not mean to overlay it with any values -it is descriptive.

At the other end of the continuum congregations are totally dependent upon a structure from outside themselves -a structure that may be theological, political, or almost anything else, but that makes all critical choices of the life of the congregation based upon its being dependent upon a larger entity of faith. I will call this end point of the map "STRUCTURED." Again I intend no value judgment, just the description that relationships at this "end" exist in a tight interconnected structure with the "higher" entities having the role of empowering those below it. The word "hierarchical" is used often, but that word has taken on many emotional overtones. The word "connectional" is used often, but that word does not adequately carry the authority of the structure that belongs at the extremes. I simply mean that the people at this end understand their system to be intimately interconnected, and that by consensus some of the parts of the system have authority over other parts.

To differentiate between these two, I propose a mental map -a continuum, with degrees of connection from AUTONOMOUS to STRUCTURED. Voila:

The Mental Map

AUTONOMOUS   STRUCTURED

1   2   3   4   5   6   7   8   9   10

Every congregation can be located on that continuum. Please remember, this is a mental map, not a scientific indicator. It is to help us think about the issues and about relationships, it is not a "predictor" or an instrument of measurement.

II. Factors Influencing Location on the Continuum

It is not difficult to note the fact that congregations relate to their systems in different degrees of autonomy or dependence.

It is difficult, however, for people in different congregations or levels of one denominational system, to admit the validity of the position others take when it is different from their own.

A factor causing that difficulty is that a denomination often adopts normative language for what is considered the "correct" way to be "connectional" or "independent." Wars were fought over different ideas of polity, and feelings still run high, even though we may have forgotten why our great-grandparents were ready to fight about things that may feel inconsequential today. I know Presbytery Executive who admits that in certain issues of conflict in a parish she acts the way a Catholic bishop might have acted at the time of the reformation. She says, "If it works, everybody cheers. But if anybody ever says, 'You are acting just like a bishop!' she says, "I'm likely to lose my job." The ancient memory is strong. Some of our members are convinced that the 16th Century takes precedence over the 21st!

I see Episcopal bishops saying confidently "The smallest unit of the Church is the Diocese!" This sort of thing is most often said in a speech in which the bishop is trying to get the congregations to back his or her program ideas for the next year. That bishop rarely seems to notice the laity and the clergy rolling their eyes in disbelief. That bishop may have a point in "- the history of Episcopal polity," but the people rolling their eyes know a very different reality on the ground where they are!

I will try here not to use normative language but descriptive language. That is not to say that it is unimportant to have norms; it is only to say that when we act as if normative language really describes how people act, we can be seriously out of touch with what is going on.

Here are the eight key dynamics that influence where a congregation may be on the continuum from autonomy to dependence, from independent to connectional. My thesis is that each of these influencers affects where the congregation will be on the continuum.

> Polity/Theology/Ecclesiology
> Experience over time in that judicatory
> The character of the executive
> The character of the pastor
> The orientation of leading laity of the congregation
> The relationship to the denomination
> The nature of the other congregations in the community
> The flow of money and resources

Now let me briefly "unpack" those concepts so that they can become tools for your thinking.

A. Polity/Theology/Ecclesiology.

Congregations do bear within them the values and history of their denomination. Key theological ideas that shaped the denominations early life will be reflected in how those congregations understand what a congregation is, what the role of the pastor is, and how to value other denominational expressions of their special heritage.

Above, in my description of the bishop's idea of polity and how the laity and clergy roll their eyes at it, for Episcopalians there IS a "pull" between what the bishop was expressing and what the clergy and laity live out in their congregation. That "pull" will have an influence on how congregations understand their connection to the denomination. It will not, as I have suggested, be as convincing to the congregations and clergy as it is to the bishop. That's another story!

Because of this pull of history, congregations of a particular denomination will tend to clump together in one area of the continuum, but they will not be uniform. Within any denomination there can be a considerable range of acceptable positions. Baptists, for example, have a high stake in full autonomy of the individual's faith and of the life of the congregation. Yet no denomination has had more serious battles about the dependence of the congregation upon positions taken by the "Conference." And no denomination can match the Southern Baptist Sunday Church School Board for developing congregational uniformity in program material.

What this means is that on our mental map you will expect a denomination's congregations to be clustered in from 3 to 5 of the points of the continuum, toward one end or the other, depending upon their history and polity. But in few cases will a denomination be on only one single point. I would expect, for example, the more congregational denominations cluster between stages 2 and 6, the more connectional denominations to cluster between 4 and 8. If Presbyterians, say, hypothetically follow that observation, they would cluster between 5 and 6, probably. But in fact I wouldn't be surprised to see a few over in stage 2. You may even find one renegade flirting with stage 8 or 9.

Polity/theology/Ecclesiology is an important influence on how a congregation "fits" the continuum from autonomy to dependence, but it is not a sure guide.

In my opinion, this remains important, but is increasingly marginal for congregations who have fewer members deeply ingrained in the heritage of the denomination. Other influences are likely to increase in importance in the future.

B. Experience over time with that particular judicatory.

In the course of time, every congregation has business with its judicatory quite a few times. The executive is likely to visit from time to time, members of the congregation serve on judicatory task forces, there are celebratory events, the congregation may request resources of one kind or another, the two will negotiate financial matters.

Over time, the congregation learns what to expect from the judicatory, and either build a sense of trust or of suspicion. If experience leads to distrust, that distrust will build up like a bank to suspicion, the congregation will more and more tend to pull back, defend its turf, and not be hospitable to judicatory leadership and resources.

A complicating factor, in my experience, is the fact that congregations' memories are long. Often they are reacting to a bishop or judicatory structure from a generation ago, not their contemporary experience. I have known bishop-types whose hearts were broken by what they interpreted as the people's defensiveness or lack of responsiveness to them, when the people were simply acting out their distrust of a predecessor, perhaps even a predecessor once or twice removed.

Just as a good set of experiences can build up credits for the executive, those credits can also be transferred to the executive's successor. The reverse is uncomfortably true also. Suspicion and distrust engendered by one leader or set of experiences can cloud relations for a long time.

C. The Character of the Bishop, Executive, or judicatory system

The personality, the skill-set, the charisma of the executive or of the staff of the judicatory makes a difference in whether a congregation is pulled toward an autonomous or a structured relationship on our mental map. As indicated in # 2 above, this has to be understood in the light of the congregation's previous experience with other executives and staffs.

When a congregation recognizes, on calling its "headquarters," that the people on the other end of the phone know what they are doing and have something to offer, it builds bonds that matter. When the congregation sees productive, helpful ideas and information making sense to pastors and lay leaders, it is recognized for what it is. When a congregation is always invited to the judicatory only to deal with the judicatory's agenda, the frequency of attendance will drop off. When a congregation asks for help and is sent someone without skills the point is made (I mean, he is on the staff, and somebody has to keep him busy; or why weren't they secure enough to tell me they can't help and pass me the name of somebody who can!). People are forgiving and understanding, but a succession of such experiences makes a congregation ready to stop phoning.

A judicatory leader who identifies a critical community issue and speaks a word of genuine wisdom and leadership can become a "spiritual leader" for more denominations than his or her own, and can strengthen the roles of other judicatory executives.

A real shortcoming for all those in executive or staff roles in our denominations is their separation from those in judicatories of other denominations. Denominational walls remain high on most local scenes. Each operates as if executives in their judicatories are unique. In my experience about 90% of such talk is wrong. Strong judicatory training is needed in each denomination. What is available is spotty and leaves large gaps. The result has been hit or miss training for judicatory executives and bishops within their own denominational family. None of the denominations has the resource base to provide the depth and variety of kinds of training needed in these roles. What's needed is broad, deep training with colleagues from other denominations so that skills and insights can be wider and stronger. Denominations cannot do that by themselves.

D. The Character of the Pastor

The pastor (or pastoral team) in any congregation also is an influence on whether the congregation sees itself as autonomous or structured. Pastors within a denomination vary enormously in every way, and each also has individual baggage from their previous appointments. Pastors often receive and distribute communication from the judiciary - and they make selections when they do.

Many pastors try to be loyal to the polity/theology/ecclesiology they learned at seminary, but of course that is modified by their experiences in previous pastorates, by their friends in other pastorates, by the groups they are drawn to in their denomination, and by their own sense of what is best for them and for their congregation. All those factors interact within the pastor.

Pastors whose gifts are not accepted by the denomination (or by its system of pastoral placement) can become very negative toward the denomination and influence their congregation to an independent stance.

Some pastors have an axe to grind, needing recognition or power that makes them undercut the judiciary or denomination. I suspect that the individual pastor's feelings about autonomy or structured connections are as influential as any other one thing in whether the denomination or judiciary comes to see that congregation as "a team player," or "recalcitrant and obstructionist."

E. Orientation of the Leading Laity in the Congregation

This may not always be as important as the orientation of the pastor, but it comes a close second. At some times in the life of the congregation, this can be very influential. Very.

Every congregation has a handful (hopefully more) of lay people who are opinion-leaders in the community as well as the church. When those lay people have had good opportunities to know and participate in important work of the judiciary, they will move the climate of the congregation toward the judiciary. Note that I say "important work," not "busy work" or powerless and endless task forces.

Judiciary executives need to be recruiting such leaders, listening to them and engaging with them. Efforts to that end will bring life to the relationship between congregation and judiciary, and will be an asset when there is a change of pastorate or some other congregational crisis.

F. Relationship to the Denomination

Relationships between congregations and their denomination include much said above, but I want to point to a different dimension of it.

Sometimes a congregation will have a relatively healthy relationship to its regional judicatory, yet have very adversarial feelings about the national or international dimension of their denomination. It may be that some national committee or council has passed a resolution that is quite contrary to the feelings of many local residents (a national anti-smoking action in a community full of tobacco farmers; a statement about gun control in a community whose highest recreational value is deer hunting; a statement about the death penalty in a community still traumatized by the rape and killing of a young girl; or almost anything else). Sometimes such things are accompanied by what I call a "fire-storm" of anger and rage. These things happen, and they are honestly frightening to congregational leaders and pastors who are thrown on the defensive, often without any information.

Some years ago a wise friend who at the time was bishop of the Episcopal Diocese of Spokane described his theory of what happened in this homely way:

"I think what probably happens is something like this. A bunch of old cronies have coffee every morning downtown. They kid each other, taking pot shots at one another, mostly in fun. And they love to get 'one up' on one another. One day one of them who is a Lutheran layman who runs a filling station sees his friend, a Methodist who works in the feed store, and says, 'Hey Bill, what is this I hear about your church?' 'What? What do you mean,' Bill replies. 'Oh, I read in the state paper that you all are going to… (at that point the person says something "outrageous" he had heard or read that a Lutheran committee or commission had suggested…). Bill is embarrassed. He has no idea what his friend read or whether he's making up a practical joke. He can't connect what's been said to anything he knows anything about, but it DOES sound outrageous the way his friend said it. He gets defensive and angry at his church, assuming his friend is right. My bishop friend says that after that the layman will storm over to his parish office and confront his pastor with "What the Hell is the Church doing now!" and the pastor hasn't a clue of what's happened either. So- it all escalates into fury, into motions put before the board, phone calls to the bishop.

The scenario sounds like what might happen. Or it may be that an ecumenical agency related to the denomination has issued a statement that appears in the local paper and seems totally out of touch. In my time I have seen things like this begin, spread, and first thing you know there is a national firestorm. At the end most people have lost touch with what the original event really was. Hundreds of Presbyterians still fume when people bring up the name of Angela Williams. Lutherans and Methodist, particularly go bananas over "that meeting in Minneapolis." I'm aware that people do have justifiable concerns about positions taken publicly by their churches and leaders, but in this I'm pointing to the cases we've all experienced in which the fury feeds on itself and soon is out of all proportion to whatever it was that started it. Usually these feelings and this fire storm focuses on something far off in national structures.

Strong feelings like this will, however, have an influence on relationship to the nearby judicatory. This is particularly true where advocates of a position are organized and continue bombarding church members about issues long since forgotten by many. It is not anything most judicatories can do much about. Rejecting the unpopular position doesn't seem to help and often makes the judicatory look weak; efforts to "explain" the unpopular position never seem to catch up with the allegations.

Action in any one congregation in the community will affect congregations in that community. If one congregation in town is having a donnybrook about something, it is likely to affect others. Although in small towns, particularly, the congregations are very distinct from each other, we sometimes forget that people from different congregations work together, have coffee together, meet socially together. They play golf together and they go to the same high school football games. If a very strong passion develops in one congregation in town about something "bad" one denomination has said or done, it is very likely that other congregations will experience fall-out. Because judicatory executives do not communicate with judicatory executives of other denominations they may miss the signals of "hot spots" of anger or of need for pastoral care. I once ran into a group of judicatory executives who wanted to talk about the problems they were having with conflict between pastors and church boards. When I asked them where the trouble was worst -and four of the executives named the same small town. All of them had thought they simply had a "problem pastor or problem congregation." All of a sudden they saw that they really needed to be in touch with one another.

The character of the community churches will be an influence upon whether or not a congregation located in that community draws closer to or is pushed farther from its judicatory.

G. Flow of Money/Resources

Between congregations and the systems within which they exist there is a flow of money. People in churches do not talk about that very clearly, often because they would rather not get it very clear -if it remains foggy; nobody has to take responsibility for it.

How that money flows, and whom makes decisions about it has a lot to say about how autonomous or how structured a congregation feels. Many small congregations (well over 50% of the congregations in the country have a membership of 120 or fewer) are financially unable to "break even." In many denominations there are elaborate systems by which the congregations with more than enough finances participate in the financing of the others. In many of the denominations, the judicatory is the "middle person" -the one to whom funding assistance is directed, the one who has to make decisions based on availability of funds, and who is invited to the role of "lady bountiful." None of these roles are easy or clear. Each of them brings temptations to manipulation.

At the same time the judicatory has to manage a system of finance out of which the congregations generate the funding for the tasks of the judicatory. All kinds of subterfuges have developed--sending all the money to the national church and having it apportioned from there, or asking apportionments from small congregations, then returning as much or more as a "mission grant."

Suffice it to say that if a congregation receives funding from the judicatory, it feels dependent and is less likely to miss the next judicatory meeting or raise uncomfortable questions for the judicatory. The congregations at the other, more affluent end, sometimes use their funds to control what happens in the judicatory.

This whole area of ambiguity influences whether a congregation feels it is autonomous or structured, or if it is just a paid servant of the denomination.

Here, then, are eight dynamics that interact within all congregations I've experienced, and that influence whether they will understand themselves as being autonomous of one another or how deeply they will feel themselves in a tight structure.

I see every congregation as balanced somewhere on that continuum between totally independent of or totally absorbed into the other congregations and institutions of their denomination. Even those at the extremes (Independent Baptist on the end of independence; Roman Catholic at the end of integration into the larger church body) I believe these eight forces are operating on all those congregations. Those forces will significantly affect denominationalism in the future.

The question remains to be discussed in the next section: if those 8 dynamics influence where a particular congregation is in our mental map, at what points can people in the congregations, pastors, or judicatory people make an impact on the connection the congregation has with the judicatory. How and when can one change the connection?

III. Intervention Moments: Places and Times when there is Opportunity for Change

Judicatory and denominational officers and agencies can affect how a congregation understands its "connection," occasionally bringing it more in line with what the denomination's polity calls for, or at least making the connection more constructive and helpful to each. In terms of this paper, it is possible for a congregation to shift its location on the mental map noted above.

A Confessional Introduction to this Section

In my experience judicatory executives and staff sometimes have a problem respecting the integrity of the congregation in this area -feeling so strongly about what is "right" behavior for congregations of that denomination, they have a hard time listening to what congregation's actually value and are tempted to seek to control its behavior. Even saying this makes me uncomfortable, because some denominations and individuals feel so emphatically about what is right behavior for congregations that they cannot, in good conscience "permit" what they see as "deviant" behavior. Such rigidity on one side makes real conversation difficult if not impossible.

The same is true on the other side -that of the congregation that will not engage with its judicatory in genuine conversation, but demands unilateral control over the relationship.

I am writing to share what I have experienced in these transactions, but as I write this it is clear to me that I am no "tabula rasa." I have a set of values and concerns I think I had better share. I am not only a witness. I am a biased witness.

The first two paragraphs of this section illustrate one of my biases. I believe judicatories and congregations have more creative relationships when there is constructive give and take, when each side is willing to hear the other, when neither seeks to impose its will on the other.

My bias is not the only legitimate one. If one believes theologically or philosophically in the absolute extremes of the continuum I described in part 1, then it genuinely is not necessary for there to be a conversation.

Another part of my bias is spread through part 1 and will probably affect what I say in this part -my personal experience of Church is as an Episcopalian. That is the air I breathed as I went to Sunday school and grew up. We always had a special chair in our parish church that was reserved for the bishop when he visited, about once a year. The bishops I knew for many years were splendid persons -not overwhelming minds, but solid, authentic human beings who loved God and led people. My congregation didn't have much to do with the bishop, but we tried to do what he asked us to do. I grew up understanding "connections" that way, and I think it has made me biased about judicatories in two ways: 1) On the 1 to 10 continuum from autonomous to subsidiary, I suspect I am personally about a 6 or 7, with a gut feeling that's toward being connected and being loyal to that connection while yet wanting some independence. 2) I find that my personal experience with judicatory leadership through a bishop, has given me a bias toward that form of governance in a person rather than a board or committee. It just comes more comfortably to me that way.

I make no case here that my position is right -indeed I would be the first to point to other experiences I have in which other systems have been spectacularly better and "my" systems have been spectacularly poor. For now, I just want to warn you of my biases as well as I can so you can adjust your reading of my material to take it into account. As I re-read part 1 of this paper, I think I smell my biases every now and then. I don't want to trick you with my biases, but I cannot erase them from what I know without erasing myself. You are warned, then.

A final point, since I am going to be talking about "interventions for change" in this section. For years I have worked as a consultant. That has been my bread and butter over the better part of my career an ordained Episcopal priest. I have worked to help people and congregations change. I have often been called into situations in which congregations and judicatories had found themselves angry at one another, suspicious of one another, or bearing strong grudges. When that happened, I had a rule of thumb I followed -if either the congregation or the judicatory was only interested in making the other fall into line, I would not accept the contract. If both were genuinely interested in trying to work something out and listening to the other side, I tended to be willing to take the contract. Also, if the congregation was a "known trouble- maker," and I determined that they were truly loyal to their system but fiercely opposed to some parts of what their denomination/judicatory was up to -again, I tended to take the contract. My value depended upon the loyalty of their opposition.

Now let me name the points in the life of the congregation at which some kind of intervention by the judicatory can result in significantly different relations between the congregation and the judicatory. I list six such and add a note about the use of consultants:

Change of pastor	Conflict	Financial Relations
Activities of the Judiciary	Congregational trauma	Pastor's trauma
A note on use of consultants		

IV. Specific Intervention Points for Changing Relationships

A. Change of Pastors

Anyone who knows my work would expect this to by my first point. Since 1973 when we first completed research on "the calling process," "the search process," "the appointment process," I have been clear in teaching and writing that this is the one point in the life of a congregation at which the most growth is possible.

What is true in the life of the congregation is also true in terms of the relationship between the congregation and the judicatory.

It is possible, during this period, for dramatic changes to occur in how a congregation views its judicatory. This is a time at which many members of the congregation, for many of whom the judicatory was a myth about something far away, may have their first direct experience with the judicatory -its executive, its staff. A personal face is put on what had been a far-off bureaucratic idea. Congregational members on the search team discover what resources the judicatory can provide or cannot provide. They find out if the people at "conference" answer their phones or not, treat people decently or not, know what they are talking about or not, are dependable or not.

At another level the congregation learns whether the judicatory really is interested in them, or is simply trying to use them to solve a judicatory problem -place an unemployed clergyperson, get a loyal "party man" into that pulpit, or something like that.

Down the line as the new pastor takes his or her place, the judicatory that has begun to build better relations with congregational leaders has a chance to help the congregation's leaders connect with the new pastor in the "start-up" period. Again, the opportunity to build better relations with the judicatory happens, even if it is subsidiary to the main task -getting the congregational leadership team and the new pastor to work together effectively.

A judicatory that works hard on this area will, over time, have opportunity to refresh relations with every congregation in the judicatory .Not only that, the opportunity recurs from time to time -there will be another opportunity in 5 or 10 years when this pastor leaves. A judicatory that is wise will develop resources that will assist in the pastoral change process.

Once when a bishop asked me what was most important for him to remember, I said, "Put all your energy into the congregations involved in pastoral change. Forget about the others!" Of course I was exaggerating, but not much. If you look at the calls on a judicatory as overwhelming, and if you fall back on a strategy of triage -those congregations experiencing pastoral change are the ones who need help NOW.

B. Conflict

Every congregation I've ever known gets into fights from time to time. Most of the fights are pretty modest disagreements, but often enough they escalate into real donnybrooks. I still remember when I was in high school reading in the morning newspaper of a fight in a congregation I knew where one elder (whose daughter I had dated) belted another and the two had to be held down from going at each other. I think it was about a church building project. I remember it because that really doesn't happen very often, but also because I remember a couple of situations in which I was tempted to similar behavior.

One of the problems is that church people tend to get surprised by conflict and overwhelmed by how it can escalate. Every institution has its disagreements and conflicts, but most have rules or processes people know about and can use to settle whatever is amiss. People in those institutions simply know that such disagreements go with being human.

In churches we have bought into the fiction that "nice people don't fight."

When a fight does break out, often the pastor and the leaders of the congregation flip from being defensive to angry to scared rapidly. Whatever they had learned earlier about dealing with disagreement evaporates from their memory and all they can focus on is either on "winning" or on "not letting those people win."

This is a time when a congregation needs help from outside -sometimes it needs someone who will give them some perspective, sometimes someone who can help them set procedures, sometimes someone who will be a referee so that they fight fair. The point is that this is an opportunity for the judicatory to be helpful to the congregation in a way that can improve the connection between the two.

Such perception of helpfulness depends on the judicatory really having help to give, real skills in conflict management.

My experience with judicatory staffs is that they are often splendid with some disagreements and conflicts, but they often underestimate the time it takes really to be of help. They often also underestimate the skills needed to bring resolution. Their own schedules require them to "handle" the conflict at one or two evening meetings, sometimes with another full day. There are conflicts, many of them, that require more time than the judicatory staff has available to it.

Poor or inadequate intervention in a conflict is probably much worse than no intervention at all. It can be like pouring kerosene on afire. A judicatory that does a poor job of its conflict interventions is likely to generate a lot of negative feelings in the congregation for anything the judicatory does. It harms the "connection."

A skill judicatories need badly is diagnostic skills. Speed Leas, my colleague at the Alban Institute for many years, developed a very helpful diagnostic tool when he described the five "levels" of conflict that he has encountered: 1) Solving Problems; 2) Disagreements; 3) Contest; 4) Fight/Flight; 5) Intractable. The higher the intensity of the conflict, the more skill and time is needed to work on it.

A judicatory with good diagnostic ability, trained in recognizing signs of different levels of conflict, is more likely to know when the difficulty is manageable by current staff members.

We also find that there is judicatory wisdom immediately to farm out some intense conflicts to outside consultants. Sometimes a "fight" is so hot by the time the judicatory is aware of it that the chances of a peaceful solution are near nil. It such situations, if it is likely that the fight will end with blood on the walls, it is better for the judicatory to stand back and let a hired gun (consultant) go in. That permits the judicatory to respond in a supportive, pastoral role to help people bind up the wounds.

Wise interventions by judicatories at times of congregational conflict can improve the "connection" between judicatory and congregation, wherever the two find themselves on what I have called the "continuum."

C. Financial Relations

Few areas have more potential for hurting the connection between congregation and judicatory than their financial relations.
I have been unable to find a logical explanation of this, perhaps because few of us relate to our finances in a logical manner. But I find that money talk between congregations and their judicatories almost always triggers irrational reactions -defensiveness, protectiveness, envy , outrage, suspicion, cupidity -you name it.

The facts are that judicatories exist largely because of the financial resources made available by contributions from congregations. This sets up a dynamic in the judicatory of aggressive search for funds for what are seen to be essential missional tasks. And a simultaneous dynamic of holding back, hiding, or seeking to reduce the contributions called for because of what are felt to be more pressing needs of the mission that is carried out by the congregation.

It is money that turns congregational/judicatory relationships into Us versus Them relationships.

By definition, this relationship demands open communication, direct talking, and sensitivity to one another's concerns. It demands negotiation and give and take.

Few judicatories, in the pressure of their work, can be anything but daunted and frustrated by the necessity to negotiate carefully with 40 to 90 individual congregations. The temptation to cookie cutter methods is overwhelming. The result is the search for a "formula" for judicatory asking, a formula that will be fair, yet will produce the necessary resources for judicatory program. And every time there is such a formula, it turns out not to fit some of the congregations while other congregations grow alarmed at the total size of the requests and ask for cutbacks in judicatory budgets.

What I am trying to say is that everywhere I look along the connectional continuum, 99% of the congregations and judicatories are in a system that will always put financial stress on them. The only people happy with it is the 1% at each end of the continuum -the ones who have nobody to tell them what to give and, on the other hand, ones who can take what they need by confiscation.

Bad news about connections? I don't see how congregations and judicatories will ever solve this.

Good news about connections? The relationships between congregations and judicatories will continually need to be in dialogue on this issue. It won't go away, and it won't let congregations and judicatories slam the door on each other.

Small solace, but it is some!

D. Regional Activities and Program

Most judicatories try to serve their congregations through a number of programs and activities.

Where these programs and activities result from careful judicatory/congregation interaction, there are two elements helping the connection. The first is the experience of dialogue in the planning can bring greater understanding of where each is coming from. The second is that good program and activity actually does sometimes bring positive interactive feelings and actual results that make a difference.

Some kinds of congregations' -very small, isolated ones, for example -can see a vision of church in a large denominational meeting that they never experience at home. Youth leaders can meet youth leaders of other congregations, forming important personal links as well as church links. Information about things such as new educational curriculum can be shared with other congregations. My own bias (as an Episcopalian) creeps in on me in that I see worship at such events as perhaps as important as the "program." (So correct for my bias, but check it out first!)

Judicatories can -in regional events -touch morale of congregations across the church the way few other media can. The ability to marshal resources of music and preaching for challenging and/or inspiration can be done in a kind of scope that makes a difference.

Judicatories need, in my estimation, to be cautious about this. Generating program and activity is a special need and it needs to be used strategically. I do occasionally get the picture that congregations are tired of feeling that the judiciary staff is just thinking up things to keep the congregations busy.

If you go that far, you've stopped helping the connection and started blocking it.

E. Congregational Trauma

Just as congregations can expect fights to pop up every now and then, so it is that trauma of one kind or another is just bound to happen.

I want to suggest that a judicatory that is aware of such trauma and responds to it has a chance to improve the connection. I do not have a formula for what that response should be.

Instead, let me name a few of the congregational traumas I have seen that were open

An airplane crash on the outskirts of a city
A church or one of its buildings burns down. Drug activity overwhelms a public school
A leading lay family is killed in a car crash
Somebody embezzles one of the congregation's funds
Somebody in the congregation is accused of a terrible crime. A leader of the congregation is in court in a big trial. Some scandal breaks out about a church member

That is just a sampler. How should one respond? You need to respond in a way that is genuine to you. I know of a judicatory executive who -with a raincoat pulled over pajamas joined a pastor out front of the church as it burned and simply said, "I came to help you watch your church burn down!" That was real, and that pastor and that congregation tell about it now, 30 years later. I know a bishop who went to a public school where the faculty was demoralized by drug raids on the students -and he just went and had coffee in the faculty lounge for several days.

The point is for a judicatory to have its feelers out to pick up signals like that, and not to be embarrassed because it does not have the "right" answer.

You will note that the trauma I listed is not always a specifically congregational trauma. My point here is that when a community hurts, the congregations hurt. A judicatory that acts on that will find it builds better connections.

The other side of this is true, also. When great, exciting things happen, judicatory attention pays off, too.

I return to the confessional once more for a moment. This week as I have been working on these notes is the week after the terrorist attacks in New York and at the Pentagon. Mayor Giuliani, to my mind, has been the image of what I'd hope a judicatory executive should be - present in the middle of the muck and mess, not giving out placebos, but encouraging those who are tired. When distress hits a community, I think it is important for the religious system to be aware and be present -in and through the pastor and lay people, primarily, but also in the symbolic presence from the larger church where possible

F. Pastoral Trauma

Here I speak more directly of the trauma that may affect the pastor of any congregation.

When a pastor or his/her family get into trouble, most judicatory executives know they have work to do, and most of them do it well. There are resources they know to call on - psychiatric resources, family counseling resources, often financial and legal resources. Most judicatories have provided financial resources for this help for years. My cautions here are that I suspect that those resources are getting strapped by higher and higher medical insurance and legal bills. Our judicatories may need to review their future needs in this area.

The list of traumas I am talking about here includes all the personal and family traumas clergy deal with daily among the people of the congregation. In most cases the "answers" are no different from the things good pastors already do with people in the congregation.

What I want to note is that what the judicatory does when a pastor gets into trouble is not always visible to the congregation as it is to the pastor. It may not have much impact upon how the congregation feels about the judicatory, but it will have direct impact upon that pastor, probably for the rest of his or her life. That can, indeed, have an impact upon the connection between congregations and judicatories.

One area of trauma in a pastor's life is also an area in which the whole congregation gets involved. If the trauma comes from actions in which the pastor proves him or herself to have violated people with whom he/she is in relationship -the trauma of the pastor immediately becomes a trauma of the congregation. In recent years the plethora of cases of sexual misbehavior of a pastor with a parishioner, staff member, or counselee give us examples of what I am talking about. In a few cases I have found that other moral issues sometimes touch a nerve in some communities that makes the case explode into a congregational trauma in almost a similar way (stealing or embezzling money, plagiarism -and I suspect that in other situations there may be other such emotional responses to the breaking of trust).

The judicatory will be drawn into such trauma with deep difficulties and split responsibilities -to the law, to the pastor, to the congregation, to the injured parties. In these traumatic areas a judicatory executive who operates without a lot of advice and training on top of uncommon wisdom will find him or herself in very deep water quickly.

Congregational-judicatory relations are strengthened where congregations are convinced that their judicatory has clear policies and good advisors and consultants for dealing with such eventualities. Congregations throughout a judicatory quickly get such information on denominational grape vines.

G. A Miscellaneous Note on the Use of Consultants

I am adding this note simply because I cannot find the right place to bring it up, yet I have found this issue complicating relationships between congregations and their judicatories. The issue has to do with the nature and deployment of consultants.

More times than I like to remember, I have discovered a real dilemma judicatories have in using consultants to work with congregations.

The difference, as I understand it, is this: a staff person carries out the policies of the judicatory and is responsible to the judicatory structure or executive. He or she is paid by the judicatory.

A consultant is hired and paid by the congregation and is responsible to the congregation.

Judicatories often want consultants to operate as staff, carrying out the intentions of the judicatory. Such an understanding assumes that the judicatory controls what will happen. This may be in the best interests of the judicatory, but it violates the integrity of the congregation. In the long run, I think this is very bad for the connection between congregations and judicatories. It is not honest.

In a true consulting relationship, the consultant works for and is paid by the congregation, which gives the congregation the power to terminate the relationship and maintain control of its own decisions. Such use of consultants strengthens the congregation's ability to be clear about what it needs and wants and help it enter genuine negotiations and communications with others. I think that is one of the most important ingredients in building a strong connection between congregations and judicatories -which is one reason I see that any genuine consulting process is a very important learning opportunity in the churches both for congregations and for judicatories.

I am not romantic about this. I know it is important that the consultant and the judicatory be trusting of one another. But if a judicatory asks me to be consultant to one of its congregations I have to say, "I'll be glad to talk to them, but they have to agree on a contract with me." And one thing is that I will not report to the judicatory unless the congregation permits me to do so. Indeed, if the congregation says, "We cannot pay your fee," I am willing to work with them to figure how to put the funds together -which may mean asking the executive for help on the bill.

Working that way, a consultant can help the congregation stand on its own feet and enter into adult relationship with its judicatory. In the long run, I think that makes for a stronger church, no matter what end of the continuum of connection you inhabit.

Loren B. Mead

9/16/01

*Hartford Theological Seminary, Hartford, CT

BIBLIOGRAPHY

PROLOGUE
-ECUMENICAL SHARED MINISTRY: Bringing Congregations Together from Several Denominations. An Alban Institute, On-Demand Publication by Roy M. Oswald and Arland D. Jacobson. Based on research conducted in 1992 and funded by the Lilly Endowment, Inc and the Otto Bremer Foundation.

Chapter 1
-POLARITY MANAGEMENT: Identifying and Managing Unsolvable Problems, by Barry Johnson Ph.D. HRD Press, Inc. 22 Amherst Road, Amherst, MA -01002
             800 822-2801. Copyright 1992, 1996

-RECLAIMING THE GREAT COMMISSION, by Bishop Claude E. Payne and Hamilton Beazley. Published by Jossey-Bass. A Wiley Company, San Francisco, CA
Copyright 2000   888 378-2537.

Chapter 2
-THE SEVEN HABITS OF HIGHLY EFFECTIVE PEOPLE, by Steven Covey Fireside Books, Simon & Schuster, 1230 Avenue of the Americas, NY, NY
Copyright, 1989.   800 223-2336

-COMPETENT MINISTRY, by Mark Rough, Abington Press, 1976

Chapter 3
-BEYOND THE BOUNDARY, by Gary Harbaugh, Jill Hudson, Bill Behrens, and Roy Oswald. An Alban Institute Publication.

-BEGINNING MINISTRY TOGETHER ... .A Resource for Congregations Experiencing a Pastoral Transition, by Roy M. Oswald, Alban Institute (available in 2002).

-WHEN PASTORS ARE FORCED OUT, by Alan C. Klaas, PhD. Research conducted for the Divinity School, Duke University. Funded by the Lilly Endowment. Copies may be obtained from Mission Growth Ministries, 14624 Shamrock Way, Suite 100, Smithville, MO 64089.   816 873-3401
Related Reading Suggestions
-NEW BEGINNINGS, A PASTORATE START UP WORKBOOK, by Roy M. Oswald. An Alban Institute Publication. Copyright 1989. Reprinted 1990, 1992, 1993, 1997 and 2000. 800 486-1318 ext. 244.
-RUNNING THROUGH THE THISTLES, How to terminate a Pastoral relationship. By Roy M. Oswald, An Alban Institute Publication. 800 486-1318 ext. 244
-SAYING GOODBYE, by Edward A. White, An Alban Institute Publication Copyright 1990. Reprinted 1991, 1994, 1996, 1998, and 2000.

-TEMPORARY SHEPHERDS, by Roger Nicholson, An Alban Institute Publication. Copyright 1999.
-MOVING YOUR CHURCH THROUGH CONFLICT, by Speed Leas, An Alban Institute Publication, 1984

-NATURAL CHURCH DEVELOPMENT, by Christian Schwartz, Church Smarts, 3830 Ohio Ave. St. Charles, Illinois, 60174   800 253 4276

-PERCEPT, Demographic Analysis for Congregations, 151 Kalmas Dr. Ste A104, Costa Mesa, CA. 92626.   800 442-6277

-VISIONS/DECISIONS, Demographic Analysis for Congregations, 800 524 1445

-DISCERNING YOUR CONGREGATION'S FUTURE, by Roy M. Oswald and Robert E. Friedrich, Jr. A Strategic and Spiritual Approach. An Alban Institute Publication. Copyright 1996. Reprints in 1997, 1998, and 2000

Chapter 6
-NEW THINKING ABOUT NEW CONGREGATIONS. Unpublished notes of a research conference on Dec. 8 & 9, 1998, taken by Ian Evison, Director of Research, The Alban Institute, Indianapolis Center for Congregations, 950 N. Meridan St. Suite 950, Indianapolis, Indiana 46204   317 237-7799

Chapter 7
-SIZING UP YOUR CONGREGATION for New Member Ministry, by Arlin J. Rothauge, PhD
Domestic & Foreign Missionary Society, 1995. Revised 1996.
Episcopal Church Center, 815 Second Avenue, New York, NY 10017

-THE IN-BETWEEN CHURCH, Navigating Size Transitions in Congregations, by Alice Mann, An Alban Publication, 1998

-RAISING SMALL CHURCH ESTEEM, by Steven E. Burt and Hazel A. Roper, An Alban Publication, 1992

-TOTAL MINISTRY, by Stewart C. Zabriskie, Reclaiming the Ministry of All God's People, An Alban Publication, 1995

Chapter 8
-IS THERE A PROBLEM? Research by Dr. Barbara G. Wheeler, Auburn Theological Seminary, Center for the Study of Theological Education, 3041 Broadway at 121st St., New York, NY 10027   212 662-4315

Chapter 9
-THE IN-BETWEEN CHURCH, ibid.

-THE VISIONARY LEADER SURVEY, by Marshall Sashkin.
 HRD Press, 22 Amherst Rd. Amherst, MA. 01003   800 822-2801

Chapter 10
-RECLAIMING THE GREAT COMMISSION, ibid.

-OPEN SPACE TECHNOLOGY, by Harrison Owen.
 Abbot Publications, 7808 River Falls Dr., Potomac, MD 20845   301 469-9269

Chapter 11
-LEADING CHANGE, by John P Kotter, Harvard Business School Press, Boston,
Massachusetts. 1996